"Dolphins entrance us. But, the real nature of these beguiling creatures has been largely hidden under the waves. Richard Connor, with 30 years of extraordinary insight, reaches deep into the minds of the dolphins, and their ever-shifting societies. They are individuals with strong and contrasting personalities. He shows us their world, and their nature"

—Hal Whitehead, Professor of Biology, Dalhousie University and author of *The Cultural Lives of Whales and Dolphins* (with Luke Rendell)

"If you've ever watched dolphins riding a ship's bow wave or frolicking at sea, you've probably wondered: "What is it like to be a dolphin?" Connor's engaging and insightful book answers this question--and more. His heartfelt account of the more than 30 years he's spent watching and studying the dolphins who live in the crystal clear waters of Shark Bay, Western Australia, tells the tales of the individual dolphins he came to know as his friends. By watching them daily, Connor has unraveled their societies and discovered they are as complicated--and politically driven--as our own. He argues that, as in humans, the need for demanding social skills drove the evolution of dolphins' large brains and intelligence. In his book, he describes the surprise of discovering that dolphins live in groups similar to the gangs of "West Side Story," with complex friendships, consortships, alliances and betrayals. And it is those social skills that have led them to be the brainiacs of the sea. An entertaining, moving and compelling read."

—Virginia Morell, author of the New York Times' Bestseller, *Animal Wise: How We Know Animals Think and Feel*

About the Author

Richard C. Connor, Ph.D., co-founded the dolphin research in Shark Bay in 1982, and more recently, a non-profit 501c3 foundation, *The Dolphin Alliance Project, Inc.,* to support the research. After receiving his Ph.D. from the University of Michigan in 1990, Dr. Connor held post-doctoral positions at Harvard, The Woods Hole Oceanographic Institute, The Michigan Society of Fellows and The Center for Advanced Study in the Behavioral Sciences at Stanford University. Dr. Connor has taught for 22 years at The University of Massachusetts at Dartmouth where he is a Professor of Biology. Beginning with his first scientific paper on dolphin altruism, co-authored with Professor Kenneth S. Norris in 1982, Dr. Connor has published 80 articles on the Shark Bay dolphins, general aspects of dolphin behavior and evolution, and on the evolution of cooperation and mutualism. His research has been featured numerous times in the media, including *National Geographic* and *NOVA* documentaries and *The New York Times.*

DOLPHIN POLITICS
in
SHARK BAY

A JOURNEY of DISCOVERY

Leaving Monkey Mia for a day of dolphin research on Shark Bay. © Simon Allen

Richard C. Connor

All profits from the sale of this book will support our research through The Dolphin Alliance Project, Inc., a non-profit 501(c)3 foundation. Visit the book website at **www.dapinc.org** for information on how you can support this important research.

Starring

Real Notch &
The Wow Crowd

Contents

New Insights 1988-1989

Part II

Beyond Red Cliff Bay: 1990s

Interlude: Nortrek & Nova 1991

The Wow Crowd 1994-1997

Preface

It has been 36 years since I first visited Shark Bay to see what the dolphins there had to offer an aspiring young biologist. In my wildest dreams, I could not have imagined the astounding discoveries that lay ahead.

When you take body size into account, dolphin brains are larger than all but our own. Why dolphins have such massive brains was the question that first ignited my fascination with dolphins and drove me to the other side of the planet in search of an answer.

As you will discover in the pages of this book, I certainly found what I was looking for, as Shark Bay is the best place to learn about dolphin intelligence in the wild. I have no special talent; Shark Bay was simply waiting to reveal the secrets of dolphin intelligence to whomever came to watch and listen.

For over three decades I have focused my studies on the alliances formed by male dolphins in Shark Bay. These alliances are a dramatic manifestation of the dolphins' social intelligence. How so? Because they are *nested* alliances; the male dolphins in Shark Bay form alliances of alliances of alliances! Only one other species does that: *Homo sapiens*. That fact, that convergence in alliance behavior between the two largest-brained species, one living on land and the other in the water, is extraordinary. In this book, I hope to convince you of something that I have believed since that remarkable day in 1987 when we discovered the nested alliances: the Shark Bay dolphins live in the most complex non-human society on the planet. Both dolphins and humans need their big brains to negotiate their astonishingly complex social lives.

The title of my book is a nod to the classic by Frans de Waal, *Chimpanzee Politics: Power and Sex among Apes*, which mesmerized and inspired me during my first year as a graduate student at the University of Michigan. As you read about the interactions of individual dolphins and alliances, and their alliance careers, you will also be convinced that the word "politics" is not only appropriate, but necessary.

My time in Shark Bay has been a wonderful adventure and in relating the stories that follow, I was fortunate that I did not have to rely on my faulty memory. Thanks to some sage advice from my undergraduate mentor, Professor Kenneth S. Norris, I kept a journal in the field since day one, first in notebooks in my nearly indecipherable scribble, then later, on laptop computers. This invaluable resource provided the backbone of this book, from those long-forgotten details about what happened on any given day to what I was thinking, at the time, about what I observed and heard. Everything in this book is described as I saw it; nothing is "made up." A description such as "I saw Real Notch petting someone" means I could not determine who "someone" was.

The Shark Bay dolphin society is huge, so there are necessarily a lot of characters in this book. I removed the names of many individuals that did not play a key role; such individuals are referred to simply as "a female" or "a juvenile." To further assist the reader, each of the four sections begins with *The Cast*, a list of characters mentioned in that section. The reader may also consult the glossary at the end of the book for definitions of unfamiliar terms.

Over half of the stories in this book are supplemented by video,[*] so you can be "on board" during many of our discoveries, see and hear what we saw and heard, see our reactions in real time and experience what it was like to be part of our team. Many of the dolphin behaviors and vocalizations on the videos have never been seen or heard by the public or other scientists!

So come along and experience the wonder of watching the Shark Bay dolphins, the chaos and confusion as I tried to make sense of what I was seeing, and the extraordinary thrill of discovery!

[*] *Visit the book website at www.dapinc.org to view the videos.*

Before Shark Bay

The obvious place to begin a book like this is to answer a question I hear often: "how did you become interested in dolphins?" I can tell you that dolphins have fascinated me since I was very young, but that is typical of a professional biologist who studies the behavior of animals. Animal behaviorists are simply people that never grew out of the "shark," "lizard" or "butterfly" stage of their childhood. Some might feed you a line about their fascination with this or that burning scientific question, but dig a little deeper and you will find that whatever species they study now they loved when they were children. Even the venerable British biologist Geoff Parker, who made significant contributions to game theory and conducted groundbreaking research on the behavior of dung flies, remembered with great fondness being a small boy lying in a field on a warm summer day watching dung flies on a cow pie. Well, I never saw dolphins during my childhood in central North Carolina, nor do I recall seeing them during our annual beach vacation. I can neither trace the origin of my passion nor pin down the moment when my childhood fascination matured into real scientific interest. Most likely, reading books that were anything but scientific, like "Mind of the Dolphin," by John Lilly, inspired that maturation. Most dolphin scientists from my generation will confess only with great reluctance to having been inspired by Lilly, primarily because he abandoned science for new age psycho-babble, possibly setting the field back 20 years by scaring away serious scientists. But for one young teenager, Lilly was just about all I could find on dolphins and anyway, he did focus on the one issue that inspired me, and still does: why do dolphins have those big brains? Now I had the perfect combination: an interesting and important question about an animal I really liked.

I was not doing well in high school, first in a football-crazed mountain town in southwestern Virginia, and then in a frozen midwestern industrial city. My dream of a life on the ocean studying dolphins seemed very far away. A summer with my cousins in San Diego and a marine biology course at the Scripps Institute of Oceanography Aquarium were game-changers; I realized that people really did this stuff for a living.

Back for my senior year, I embraced my course work, improved my grades and managed to get accepted to the University of California at Santa Cruz. I had done my own research on schools, limiting myself to Florida and the West Coast as this southern boy had enough of the snot-freezing Wisconsin winter. The UCSC catalog described a 2000-acre campus of rolling meadows grading into a redwood forest overlooking Monterey Bay and closer interactions with professors than one usually finds; they even offered a course on marine mammals! The school seemed like an educational Nirvana, and it was. UCSC was *laissez faire*; you could sit around all day smoking pot and grooming your rainbow aura or you could, as they say in California, "go for it." And many students did go for it; I remember my fellow students as an amazing collection of independent thinkers and doers. I counted myself among the committed groupies of Professor Kenneth S. Norris, a world-renowned dolphin expert and an extraordinarily charismatic pied piper of the natural world. Ken had a really nice, avuncular way with undergraduates. I am sure that he could not understand any of the incoherent blather that I nervously spewed during our first meeting, but he still responded with great enthusiasm. I left that meeting elated; I was special. Only later did I learn that he responded that way to everyone. Ken figured that he would just encourage everybody and we would sort ourselves out. Some students would make a career working on whales and dolphins but most would not. He was right.

My first experience with wild cetaceans could easily have been my last. Several of us decided to take a between-semester jaunt down to Baja to swim among gray whales in Scammon's Lagoon. We were full of anticipation as we rolled down the road through a desert in full bloom from a good soaking that winter, eventually pulling off road to a nice camping spot beside a narrow finger of water that branched off from the main lagoon. Female gray whales would swim slowly up and back with the tide, their calves in tow, and with young, eager would-be naturalists paddling out in their midst to experience the thrill of being up close and personal to so large a mammal.

Well, perhaps a little too up close and a bit too personal. A mother and calf swam by, closer than usual, and gee, if I just swam a little closer

I could touch that baby whale's flukes and mum would never be the wiser since the water was kind of murky and I was on the other side of the infant; so, why not? As soon as I stroked those "little" flukes a good "why not" suggested itself in the form of a 45-foot mother whale sinking down, angling over, then rising up right at me. I quickly did my best imitation of a floating log hoping she would think I was just a bit of harmless flotsam rather than a threat to her infant. Perhaps my effort to appear inert worked, because instead of being on the receiving end of a lethal swipe I was gently lifted out of the water on her flukes and just rolled off. Whew! Disaster averted, but lesson learned? Hardly. Not long after, I found myself mesmerized by a spy-hopping whale with its head up over 10 feet out of the water and only 15 feet away from me! "What a sight!" I thought, for the briefest of moments, until I saw that the whale's head was angled slightly away and, remembering that they were over 40 feet long and doing a quick bit of arithmetic, I planted my mask in the water only to see the whale's huge tail not far below. And just like a bad dream, before I could move quietly and sensibly away, I looked up again to see the head going down and oh boy, here comes that tail again! But this time "first contact" was made with the knobby aft part of the whale's back. The whale panicked and bolted, full throttle from a stand-still, and in that moment of chaos, in a cloud of bubbles, I struggled to backpedal against the slowing of time, now barely moving, as those massive flukes pumped up and down violently right in front of me.

I survived both of my close encounters, of course, but could easily have been killed. I had the immature sense of my own mortality typical of someone yet to emerge from their reckless teens. My behavior was not just dumb, it was selfish and hardly that of the environmentalist I fancied myself to be at the time. That is why we need laws to protect whales from harassment; there are too many idiots around, like my younger self.

I knew I wanted to have an academic career doing research on wild dolphins but I had to find a place where I could watch dolphins and a willing graduate program. The University of Michigan was the place to be for animal behavior, but they turned me down. I heard later that my application was a source of great amusement because I made the error of mentioning that I wanted to study dolphins. Had I not been so specific, and instead expressed only a desire to study "evolutionary biology" or "animal behavior," I would have been accepted straight away. Thankfully, when I visited Michigan I was able to gain the support of several open-minded professors who convinced the chairman to let me into those hallowed halls. But I will never forget walking into the office of the normally placid mammalogist* who pounded on his desk shouting, "You cannot study dolphins at the University of Michigan!" Then, having calmed down a bit, he revealed that he had also wanted to study dolphins until he interned with a well-known whale biologist at the Smithsonian who convinced him otherwise. I later found the phenomenon was not uncommon; people who had been dissuaded from attempting to study dolphins were often the most vociferous in discouraging others.

I have learned that there are two critical ingredients for success in this arena: perseverance, or "stick-to-it-iveness," as one of my advisors used to say, and luck. For me, luck was a delightful lady named Elizabeth Gawain, a retired city planner turned dolphin watcher who flirted with new-age circles. Elizabeth showed up at Santa Cruz my senior year to give a talk to the Ken Norris crowd about a remarkable place that she had been visiting for several years where one could interact with wild dolphins in the shallows by a beach. It was half a world away, on Australia's west coast at a campsite called Monkey Mia in Shark Bay. I had seen a small picture of the place in a National Geographic article on dolphins, but hearing about it first-hand from Elizabeth and seeing her pictures was inspiring. Between five and ten dolphins had been visiting the beach daily for years, where they accepted fish handouts from recreational fishers and tourists. Monkey Mia was just what I had been looking for, a place to watch wild dolphins at close range. The graduate students in the audience were all busy with their research projects and there were just two undergraduate Norris groupies in the room that day, Rachel Smolker and me. Rachel had recently spent a year watching spinner dolphins in Hawaii as a volunteer on a big research project led by Ken Norris. When Rachel

---

* *Technically, a mammalogist is someone who studies mammals. However, most biologists who use this term to describe themselves study only one kind of mammal, rodents, as this individual did.*

returned from her time in the sun, her skin was nearly as dark as her long wavy hair, setting off her ultra-bright smile, which came easily and often. Rachel is one of the most charismatic people I have ever met; people wanted to be around her, and over the years she broke her share of hearts. After meeting Elizabeth, we were both determined to go to Shark Bay, so we joined forces in the effort. It took over a year to raise enough money to make that first trip to Shark Bay—I even sold my cherished coin collection—but off we went at the end of July 1982.

Part I

Dolphin Politics in Red Cliff Bay

1980s

The Cast

Males of Red Cliff Bay:

The Beach Boys, Snubby, Sickle & Bibi (SSB), three males who accepted fish handouts from people at Monkey Mia.

Wave & Shave (WS), later joined by **Spud** to form a trio **(WSS)**, friends of SSB.

Real Notch's Crew was the pair **Real Notch & Hi (RH)** after their friends **Hack** and **Patches** disappeared in 1986.

Trips, Bite & Cetus (TBC) and **Chop, Bottomhook & Lambda (CBL)**. Associates of each other and RH.

The Gerries were a trio of old males, **Slash, Crinkles & Chunk (SCC)** and their old male associates, including the pair, **Steps & Kodoff**, as well as a pair from east of Red Cliff Bay, **George & Elroy**. One lone male **(Spike)** often associated with the other Gerries in Red Cliff Bay.

Lucky, Lodent & Pointer (LLP) were a trio that included one mature runt (Lucky) and two juvenile males.

Natural Tag, Prima, Fred, Barney & Crossfingers. Red Cliff Bay juveniles.

The B-boys, two impressive trios of adult males that visited from the north.

Sharkies, a male group that visited from the north.

Crunch Bunch, a loose group of 10 maturing males that visited from the northeast.

Codon, Chewy & Judas, a trio that visited from the northeast.

Females of Red Cliff Bay:

Holey-fin and her daughters **Nicky & Holly** accepted fish from people at Monkey Mia, **Crooked-fin** and her daughter **Puck** also accepted fish at Monkey Mia. **Crooked-fin** had a male calf, **Fudge,** in 1987 and another, **Cookie,** in October 1988.

Other Red Cliff Bay females (infants in parentheses): **Blip (Flip), Dent, E.D. (Ceebie), Fatfin, Munch (Lunch), Poindexter & Pseudopee, Square (Squarelet), Two-scoops, Tongue-fin (Lick), UHF (Muff), Yan (Yin) & Yogi (Boo).** Joy (Holey-fin's middle daughter,) **Joy's Friend, Scratches, Surprise & Tipless** were juvenile and maturing females.

Female visitors to Red Cliff Bay:

Chicklet, Couch, Fickle, Flo-Jo, Goblin, Gumby, Holey-hole, Jagged, Kubwa (Kidogo), Nip (Tuck), Nook (Cranny), Spongemom (Spongebabe) and **Waverly.** There were many more who are not mentioned by name.

N

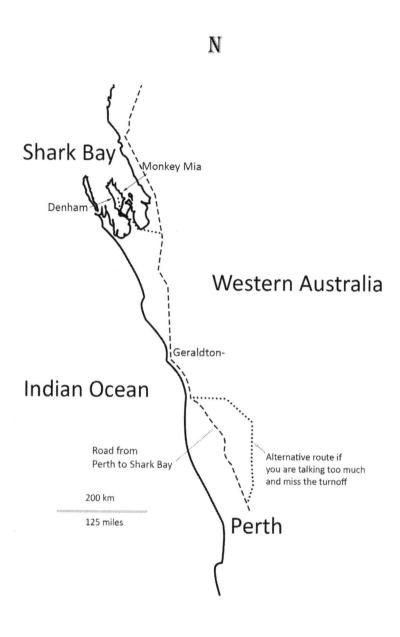

Shark Bay

Monkey Mia

Denham

Western Australia

Indian Ocean

Geraldton-

Road from
Perth to Shark Bay

Alternative route if
you are talking too much
and miss the turnoff

200 km

125 miles

Perth

BEGINNINGS

1982 & 1986

First Visit: Visions of a Dolphin Gombe

Shark Bay is an exceptional place; a marine habitat with no peer, bursting with a phenomenal mélange of fish, sharks, turtles, sea-snakes, dugongs (like manatees) and dolphins and even a few humpback and right whales. An extraordinary stew of tropical and temperate animals and plants reflect Shark Bay's position on the border of the temperate and tropical zones, some 500 miles north of Perth. It's a large bay, roughly 50 miles across, 100 miles long and bisected by the Peron Peninsula. The semi-arid bushland, pocked with salt pans, yields to striking red-orange and sulphur-yellow bluffs that look out over an abstract canvas of blue and green created by shallow seagrass beds and deeper channels and embayments. Those seagrass beds are the key to everything; they are the foundation that supports the abundance of life in the bay and, as we will see later, the reason the Shark Bay dolphin society is so exquisitely complex compared to other shore-hugging populations of bottlenose dolphins around the globe.

In 1982 Shark Bay was still a very isolated place; the 150 km road into the bay from the Northern Highway was yet to be paved. The "International Airport," as the sign jokingly said, was a mere strip in a salt pan. The Monkey Mia campground was on the southern end of Red Cliff Bay, a small embayment on the other side of the peninsula from the little one-pub town of Denham.

We were tired but excited when we arrived at Monkey Mia in the late afternoon on the first day of August. Rachel and I had spent a cold night on the side of the road 130 kilometers short of our destination after hitchhiking up from Perth but not quite making it to the finish line. There were almost no cars traveling into Shark Bay, so we thought we were going to be stranded a second night when, finally, a man from Denham gave us a lift to town, fed us steak and beans and then took us out to Monkey Mia. The proprietor of the campground, Wilf Mason, gave us a spot off the end of the park in the dunes where we pitched our little dome tents. We were operating on the proverbial shoestring; besides our tents, we had two cameras, hand-rolled black-and-white film, an underwater microphone called a hydrophone, a tape recorder and no boat. But at least we were there. Monkey Mia was pretty basic in those days, with a small shop and "ablution blocks" with toilets and slightly salty showers that gave you a nice little tingle from the stray electricity flowing through the place. Everything ran on a generator that was turned off at 11 pm, exposing a Milky Way that blazed brighter than in any place I had ever been. Our first attempt at dinner, boiling the small clams we dug up, was a gritty disaster, as we were unaware of the need to soak the clams to remove the sand that they had ingested. Fortunately, two genial hippies, Bruce and John, came to our rescue. They had traveled from the East Coast with a new-age group to commune with the dolphins, and remained behind after the others left. Bruce and John alternated days helping Wilf with work on the campground and looking after the Monkey Mia dolphins as unofficial "rangers." They had a large store of dried food and Coopers Stout, which helped get us through the next three months. We had many lively conversations over dinner.

Over the next few days we met the "regular" beach dolphins that Elizabeth had told us about. There was Holey-fin, her rambunctious daughter Nicky, who was nearly 7, and her younger daughter Joy who was still nursing as she approached her 3rd birthday. A little playmate of Joy who came in with them sometimes became forever known as "Joy's Friend." The other "old girl" that visited the beach, Crooked-fin, was timid, with a sweet disposition like her daughter Puck. During her visits in the late 1970s, Elizabeth Gawain had named the two romping infants, not yet known to be girls, "Nick" and "Puck," from the central characters in "A Midsummer Night's Dream." Snubby and Bibi were the most frequent male visitors, but Sickle, Wave and old Spike came into the beach often as well. Several years down the road, Sickle, Snubby and Bibi would teach us a lot about male alliance behavior and why people had to stop feeding male dolphins at Monkey Mia. I share a bit of guilt here. Snubby had evidently taken fish in the past but, for whatever reason, was too timid to approach people now. With some effort, over several days, I coaxed him in to take a dolphin favorite, bony herring, from my hand. At the time, I was simply thinking in terms of habituating another dolphin that we could study. From that moment on he was a "regular" at the beach.

Why were we so excited by the prospect of watching a few hand-fed dolphins by a beach? To answer this, we need a little context. Much of what we knew about dolphin behavior in 1982 came from captive

The dolphin Nicky investigates a tourist at Monkey Mia.

© Dolphin Alliance Project

observations and some of those stories suggested that dolphins were pretty clever, like chimpanzees. My favorite story involved two dolphins pulling around and generally tormenting a moray eel that escaped by swimming into a crevice in the rocks. After failing to dislodge the eel, one of the dolphins fetched a spiny scorpion fish and used it as a tool to poke the eel, which immediately fled the crevice, allowing the dolphins to resume their game.

Wild dolphin groups had also been compared to chimpanzees. In the late 1970s Bernd & Melany Würsig had learned to photographically identify individual bottlenose dolphins off the Patagonian coast of

Argentina using individually distinctive patterns of nicks and scars on the dolphins' dorsal fins. A dolphin extends what is essentially an individual identification flag above the surface every time it takes a breath. The Würsigs found the dolphins in small groups, but when they compared their photographs from different days they found that the composition of the groups was very fluid. Their dolphins had a chimpanzee-like "fission-fusion" grouping system where individuals and small groups often joined with others or split into smaller groups. Similar findings came in from a bottlenose dolphin study in Sarasota, Florida and even from a study of humpback dolphins (a different genus) off the coast of South Africa. As tantalizing as these findings were, the early studies were unable to penetrate deeper into the mysteries of dolphin society.

After learning to recognize individuals, the next order of business is to learn if you are looking at a male or a female. That's not so easy with dolphins, as males and females look very much alike and they usually keep their naughty bits hidden underneath away from the prying eyes of researchers. Once you know the gender of individuals, you need to be able to watch their social behavior; who does what, with, and to whom. Watch those social interactions, friendly and not so friendly ones, day after day for long periods, and you start to build up a picture of the pattern of social relationships among individuals. Individuals that spend a lot of time together and gently touch each other can be said to have a friendly relationship; those that mostly squabble and fight over food or dominance rank are considered rivals. But of course, even friends can have spats.

Friendly touches among primates involve stroking or grooming with hands and fingers. Dolphins don't have hands but they touch, pet and stroke each other with their pectoral fins or "flippers." They may also rub their bodies against each other's fins or bodies. Dolphin aggression often includes raking and biting with their teeth, or hitting with their flukes or peduncle (the area just before the flukes, sometimes called the tailstock).

We needed to find a place where we could really watch dolphins and observe their behavior. Watching monkeys and apes in the forest isn't easy either. At Gombe National Park in Tanzania, Jane Goodall famously offered chimpanzees bananas to acclimate them to her presence so she could watch their social behavior at close range. At Monkey Mia we had a ready-made Gombe; the dolphins were there each day interacting with each other in shallow water by the beach. This was our entry into dolphin society, our window into their world.

For the next 2.5 months we watched the dolphins and Rachel recorded their sounds with her hydrophone. We recorded who came and went with whom, and what they did together. We became terribly excited when an unfamiliar dolphin ventured close enough for us to snap a picture of its dorsal fin, and I wrote enthusiastically in my journal that we now had 20 identifiable fins in our dolphin catalogue, a number that pales in comparison to the well over 1000 fins in our current catalog!

We saw some fascinating dolphin behavior in the shallows at Monkey Mia. One of the oddest, in early October, was a funny "head-bobbing" behavior by Snubby. He would swim around with his head out of the water, bobbing his snout up and down in the air. After one head-bobbing episode, Snubby rolled belly-up, showing a puffy-pink genital area, and started arching his head and tail into the air! Then he rolled right side up and raced offshore about 25m. I wondered if Snubby was, like a deer, in a kind of male mating season "rut." Holey-fin was nearby during the episode so I thought maybe the bobbing behavior was directed at her.

Also in early October, the dolphins started chasing and catching meter long fish, "Long Toms," that would skitter along the surface just at the edge of the channel, with a dolphin in hot pursuit. When someone caught a Long Tom, they would lie at the surface for long periods, holding the fish near the head, diving with it occasionally. Nicky would swim right beside them and one time her head seemed pressed against the head of the dolphin with the fish. Once when Nicky left the dolphin's side we saw that part of the fish was missing. Food sharing in dolphins!

We described the possible food sharing cautiously, since we hadn't seen it directly, in our first scientific paper in 1985. The paper was mostly advertising the promise of Shark Bay, how wonderful it was to have a research site with "habituated" dolphins that could be observed at close range. Our caution was merited because in the decades since, we have never observed food sharing in our population! We have learned the dolphins often break off the heads of larger fish before swallowing them. Maybe young Nicky did get a piece of someone's Long Tom in 1982, but from what we have seen since, our dolphins are not terribly generous when it comes to their fish!

Over the years, we would learn a lot from the "beach dolphins" at Monkey Mia, and there are still studies being done on the "Beachies" today. But the real magic of Shark Bay was revealed to us on two October days, when Wilf gave us permission to use his little dinghy to see what the dolphins were up to offshore. Those two days were a complete revelation. We roamed around little Red Cliff Bay from one group to another; the place was teeming with dolphins! And they all seemed completely comfortable around our boat, sometimes riding our bow or socializing with each other. To continue the metaphor, if the beach dolphins gave us a window to look through, the boat allowed us to ride right through that window into the dolphins' world where we could really learn about their society.

Among the many dolphins we photographed that day were Real Notch and Wow, two of the key dolphins in my study and in this book (although Wow would not feature in our studies until the 1990s). It amazes me that 30 years later, Real Notch and Wow were still plying the waters of Shark Bay. By 2012 they were at least 40, well past their prime, and I cannot help feeling a twinge of nostalgia every time I see them and think back on all that they have taught us over the past three decades.

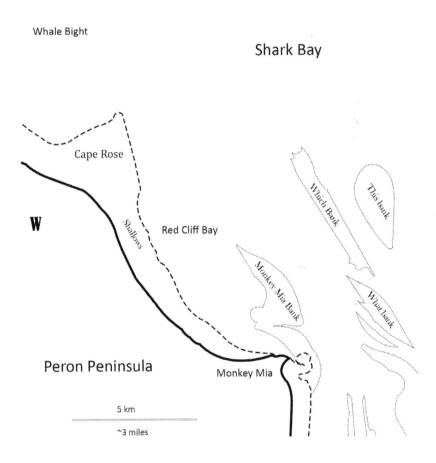

N

Whale Bight

Shark Bay

Cape Rose

W

Shallows

Red Cliff Bay

Which Bank

This bank

Monkey Mia Bank

What bank

Peron Peninsula

Monkey Mia

5 km

~3 miles

§

The University of Michigan: Getting Back to Shark Bay

The 1982 season was wonderful, but now I had to go off to the University of Michigan to start my graduate course work. I would not get back to Shark Bay until 1986 and before I could do that I had to convince my graduate committee and a funding agency that it was worthwhile. Fortunately, Rachel returned to Monkey Mia in 1984 and 1985 with the help of Bernd Würsig and a grant from the National Geographic Society. Rachel bought a small 12' aluminum dinghy (a "tinny") and set to watching the dolphins in Red Cliff Bay and recording their sounds. She made an important discovery; if you gave the dolphins a bow-ride, they would often roll upside down displaying their genitals and you could see if the dolphin was a male or a female. Rachel determined the sex of over 40 dolphins this way: a real breakthrough.

One of my two advisors, Richard Wrangham, was a prominent primatologist who had studied chimpanzees at Gombe for his doctoral dissertation. The method he and other primatologists had used successfully for years was called "focal follows." During a follow, you focus your attention on one individual and systematically record its behavior and interactions with others. Nobody had tried following dolphins before, but I knew that was what I wanted to do. The other method that had been used, and that is still widely popular today, is the "survey" method, where you spend a brief amount of time with each group you encounter, recording who is there, where they are and what they are doing. The survey method has taught us a lot, not only about bottlenose dolphin societies, but also about other cetaceans such as sperm whales and killer whales. However, surveys yield only a static picture of a dolphin society and I wanted to learn about their social relationships. Following individuals was the key, I figured, because I would be able to record the critical information that was missing from surveys: what happens when individuals join and split from those small groups. To convince my thesis committee, the National Science Foundation and the National Geographic Society, I needed more than simply a plan to follow dolphins, which is where Rachel's success determining the sex of the dolphins came in. I wrote a proposal to compare the activity budgets of male and female dolphins; that is, how much time they spend feeding, resting and socializing. Exciting stuff? Hardly, but my only concern was to get approval and money and I thought that would do it. I just knew that if I started following dolphins I would see them doing new and unexpected things and more interesting questions would emerge. I made sure that I had my grant proposals on the table for that critical thesis committee meeting; I figured they wouldn't knock me back right away if I had submitted grants that were pending. My other graduate advisor, Richard D. Alexander, saw right though my little charade and remarked, "I've got nothing against a natural history thesis; I just hope you find something interesting." Those were fantastic words to hear; we were on the same page. Alexander, it turned out, preferred that his students take on a risky project in hopes of discovering something important rather than following the conservative, safe route to obscurity. With the support of Richard Wrangham, I was awarded both a National Science Foundation predoctoral grant and a National Geographic Society grant, which was enough for my boat and two field seasons. I was on my way.

§

Back to Oz: Stumbling to a Start

I returned to Australia on 25 April 1986, ANZAC day, when Australia commemorates their soldiers who fought and died at Gallipoli. I spent the first 12 days in Perth shopping for a new boat and camping supplies before taking that long bus ride up to Shark Bay. I was joined at Monkey Mia by my first field assistant,* Denise Myers, a University of Michigan undergraduate. Wilf greeted us warmly and then directed me to pitch our tent on the hard pan behind the generator house; easily the worst site in the place. I'm sure he got a good chuckle out of that one. But I was anxious to see the dolphins, so I hurried down to become reacquainted with the cast of characters that were now visiting Monkey Mia.

A list of assistants and other team members, by decade, is included as an appendix.

Holey-fin had a new infant, a beautiful 2.5-year-old girl named "Holly." Holey-fin's oldest, Nicky, had grown up and would become pregnant for the first time later that year. She now had some speckles on her belly; these dolphins develop speckles on their underside as they approach maturity and become more speckled as they age. Holey-fin had lots of speckles.

There are always a few noticeably undersized runts among the dolphins in Shark Bay. Holey-fin's daughter Joy, now a juvenile, was clearly tiny. As we came to realize just how aggressive her older sister Nicky was, we blamed Nicky, only partly in jest, for being the reason why Joy was a runt and why she had never joined the beach dolphins to take fish from people. Woe be unto Joy who, by being born, made the mistake of taking mom's attention away from Nicky. We knew Joy for decades in Red Cliff Bay and her daughters were also runts. Crooked-fin was still visiting in 1986, as was her daughter Puck, who was as sweet as Nicky was obnoxious.

The three "Beach Boys" who were to play such an important role in my research, Snubby, Sickle and Bibi, were visiting Monkey Mia on a regular basis. Sickle, who had formed a bond with Snubby and Bibi, had just started taking fish from people in the last year. Lifting their heads out of the water to take fish from people is a learned behavior, and I heard that before he took fish from people, Sickle was seen "practicing" by swimming into the shallows and lifting his open mouth out of the water when no people were around. Snubby was an older, well-speckled male, but Bibi and Sickle were just maturing in 1986. Their younger buddies, Wave and Shave, also visited the beach, as did old Spike, but they never took fish.

The Beachies were being fed on a regular basis now, unlike the situation in 1982 when they depended on handouts from recreational fishers and decaying baitfish sold by the campground shop to tourists, ostensibly for fishing. The West Australian Department of Tourism had recently put up a small building by the feeding beach that was mostly staffed by "rangers" from Denham who were led by a prickly older Brit who did not shy from dressing down tourists who did not interact with "his" dolphins in the proper manner. He meant well and did help us change things when we discovered that the fish being fed to the dolphins were not fresh, but he was soon replaced by a local, Tony, a 20-something blue-collar guy of Italian descent who had no real background for the job but muddled along pretty well. We became good friends.

The Beachies were interesting, but I was anxious to get out in the bay to watch dolphins. I dressed out my 13-foot tinny boat with the new 18 hp motor, echosounder and safety gear and was ready to take her for a spin. Now, my knowledge and experience with motor boats and dolphins was limited to those two days in 1982, so I was in for a rude surprise when I found a group of dolphins and tried to follow them. The dolphins were traveling slowly but I could not. The motor was great when I wanted to zip around the place, but the word "idle" was clearly not in its vocabulary. If I tried to slow down to even twice the dolphins' normal slow cruising speed, it would cough and hack and sputter like an old smoker. Attempts to adjust the motor (by people at camp who knew a thing or two about such things) were futile. I had to come up with a "Plan B;" so it was back to Perth to get a smaller second motor and a bracket on which to mount it. We would look for dolphins with the cantankerous 18 hp motor and follow them with a 5 hp motor. Not the most efficient way to do things, but I convinced myself that having a back-up motor was a good idea for safety anyway.

Upon returning to Monkey Mia, I learned that Nicky had left the same day I did, with some "strangers" that had come into the shallows. She came back after a week's absence. Knowing how addicted Nicky was to free fish from humans, that seemed quite odd.

With my new auxiliary motor I was ready to go again but then I made another heart-sinking discovery; the bracket for the 5 hp wouldn't work. I could not position the bracket to both tilt the motor up high enough when we were not using it and have it low enough in the water when we were. On to Plan C: I needed an adjustable bracket. I ordered the new bracket from Perth and it came up a few days later. We put that on and I was finally ready to follow wild dolphins. Well, almost. Once offshore we realized that in the "down" position the auxiliary motor was precariously close to the water. That would not do. On to Plan D: we had to drill a new hole in the bracket so the motor would sit at the correct height when in use. With help from the usual "handy" folks at camp, we put a new hole through the stainless-steel bracket. Now at last, I was good to go, fully five weeks after arriving in Australia.

I could tell a similar story of equipment woes we experienced during the beginning of every new project that we have started in Shark Bay. Of course, if I had known more about boats and motors going into it maybe I could have saved myself some time and aggravation, but that's the way it goes when you do field work and the way it often went when we started new projects with new, unfamiliar "toys." I often tell students who want to study dolphins and whales that they should expect to spend fair bit of time dealing with such problems.

In the big picture, the problems we have doing our research are a minor nuisance. We are very fortunate to be working on dolphins in a place like Australia, where nothing is going to eat you if stay out of the water and with a little care you can avoid the poisonous creatures on land. I think of my friends who study monkeys and apes in Africa and who must deal with what I call the "Three Ps:" Predators, Parasites and Politics, any of which can kill you.

§

Following Wild Dolphins

Rachel had arrived while I was sorting out my boat problems. She was with Andrew Richards, a quiet, slight, bearded man from Michigan, who had joined Rachel in 1984 after traveling to Shark Bay to see the dolphins. Rachel and Andrew had quickly fallen for each other, so he helped with her research for several years before starting his own dolphin project.

We spent our time at Rachel and Andrew's much nicer campsite, or that of friends, instead of my campsite in the hinterlands behind the generator house. Rachel and Andrew accelerated my learning curve enormously that season. They already knew the cast of characters in Red Cliff Bay from their previous two seasons and I was able to study their catalog of dorsal fin photographs. When we were on the water they often buzzed over in their boat to help me identify dolphins I had encountered. They had also discovered that in the crazy quilt of the dolphin society there were quite stable bonds among some adult males.

Trips was nearly always seen with Bite and Cetus. Chop was usually with Lambda and Bottomhook. In fact, they were together so much, and acted so much like a single unit at times, that we started calling them TBC and CBL. What were these relationships about?

The author trying to determine the sex of a bow-riding dolphin.
© Dolphin Alliance Project

On 5 June I tried my first "focal follow" on a wild dolphin. In fact, I tried twice, and lost both dolphins in short order. But I realized it was possible; I would just have to get a lot better at recognizing individuals and keeping track of them. I was encouraged when we found the first dolphin we lost later in the day with a different group! The dynamics were there, so if we could just stay with them we would see a lot. What I also learned during those first few weeks was that we would only be going out about half the days. Western Australia is a windy place, and once it gets choppy dolphins are hard to find and even harder to follow; never mind recording their behavior. The wind could also end a follow and send us home at any time.

Two days later I successfully followed my first dolphin, a full 1.5 hours with Lucky, a runty adult male whose main friends were the juveniles Pointer and Lodent. On this day, we found him with Pointer and Sickle, just moseying along doing nothing in particular. That wouldn't last long. Holey-fin and Holly soon joined, followed by Crooked-fin and Puck, and as the younger ones started romping, the mothers left to fish. The action quickly escalated as other dolphins came on the scene, including Trips, Bite & Cetus, the female Square with her calf Squarelet, and the male trio Chop, Bottomhook & Lambda. Everybody was flying around feeding, then there was a small group raising hell socializing, then more porpoising and feeding and then most were spread out milling around in the area before yet another intense social group formed. Trying to keep up with these guys was both exhausting and exhilarating! Toward the end of the follow, Lucky was with Sickle, Nicky and Puck, and the beach males Snubby and Bibi. A large group appeared nearby so we popped over for a look. There with some other dolphins were Real Notch and his mates Hack, Hi and Patches. The two groups did not join.

It is remarkable to me now, that on my first dolphin follow, I encountered the key figures in a fantastic drama that was to play out over the next three years. And we would learn why a group with the Beach Boys might hesitate to join with Real Notch and his friends.

For the next few months I followed as many different male and female dolphins as I could; I needed to get a sense of how I should focus my project in the next few years. The follows were incredibly revealing. I quickly began to learn about the lives of female and male dolphins, and their interactions with each other. But most of the observations I made that first season raised more questions than they answered.

§

Female Dolphins: Different Personalities and Lifestyles

A few days after my first successful follow, we chaperoned Square and her infant Squarelet around the bay for a few hours. Square was kind of a central figure in Red Cliff Bay, fairly sociable with a solid cohort of female friends, several of whom she was with that day. At one point, she found herself without her female friends in a rowdy group of males that included Snubby, Bibi and about seven members of the "Crunch Bunch," a loose assemblage of ten maturing males that mostly roamed an area just northeast of Red Cliff Bay. She swam casually over beside our boat, then ducked under it, came up on the other side and floored it. A streaking trail of fluke-prints revealed the speed of her flight and we last saw her at 500 meters and going fast. I guess she wasn't in the mood for male company today and used our boat to conceal her exit. We did relocate Square, 50 minutes and 3 miles later, back in her central area hanging out with several female friends.

The next day I followed Real Notch for four hours. He was with his boys, Hack, Hi and Patches, but also the female Two-scoops, a well-speckled adult female. Two-scoops, as we would come to learn, was practically "one of the boys." She was frequently with Real Notch & Co. and often swam right alongside them, as a typical male would, instead of in front like other females. Two-scoops reminded us of one of Jane Goodall's oddball chimps, a masculine, aggressive and sterile female named "Gigi" who also spent a lot of time in the company of males as she had fairly constant estrus cycles. We came to think of Two-scoops as a dolphin Gigi and thus were greatly surprised when she finally produced a calf in 1999. It didn't survive and Two-scoops died two years later.

The next morning, I was on the beach taking note of which dolphins were in. Snubby was just hanging at the surface in two feet of water as he often did, lazily waiting for the fish buckets to arrive. Nicky came slowly cruising by just inshore of Snubby, when she suddenly turned and lunged at him, biting at his face; he bit back and they exploded with tails flailing and water flying. In the churning water I saw a pair of flukes lift up and pound down on the adversary. The other dolphins came flying into the melee and the fight stopped immediately; over just as fast as it started. Did the others break up the fight? I could not really say, neither could I tell what precipitated Nicky's attack. She had probably been stewing over some perceived slight; perhaps Snubby had snatched a fish that she thought had her name on it. That is the way it usually goes; we see the altercation but not what started it.

I could not begin to imagine a sweet dolphin like Puck starting a fight like that. The difference between their personalities was like night and day. Nicky could be a real curmudgeon; she was aggressive with people as well as other dolphins, and she once even beat up her own mother, Holey-fin. That dolphins have distinct personalities was already known from captivity, but we could also see that clearly in the beach dolphins and even among many of the dolphins in the bay.

If a follow can be fascinating, exasperating and excruciatingly boring at the same time, it was the one I did on Spongemom. Here I must digress. Back in 1982, an elderly recreational fisherman told Rachel and me that if we drove a tinny "seven minutes straight out" we would find a dolphin with a "strange growth" on its nose. We were intrigued, so when we had the boat for those two days we went out there for a look but saw nothing. However, two years later Rachel and Andrew found the dolphin with the funny growth. They watched the dolphin, surprised and stunned, wondering out loud about how the poor dolphin was surviving with this horrible looking tumor on its face, when the dolphin popped up without the "tumor." On closer inspection, they realized that it was not a tumor but a sponge, a filter feeding marine animal that grows up from the seafloor like a plant. The dolphin was wearing the cone-shaped sponge over its closed mouth like a glove, water pressure holding it firmly in place. Now what on earth was this about? Our speculation ran the gamut, from self-medication with compounds found in sponges to using the sponge as a tool to protect their snouts as they probed the seafloor for fish hiding in the sand.

By the time I arrived in 1986, Rachel and Andrew had identified a number of sponge-carriers, including Spongemom. I was anxious to follow a sponge-carrier so I jumped at the chance to follow her; maybe

Spongemom with a sponge in 2010, 24 years after the author first followed her in 1986. © Dolphin Alliance Project

I could see what Spongemom was doing with her sponge! She was with her calf, appropriately named "Spongebabe," and they were fishing in the 20-foot deep channel southeast of the park. Now, if I could just get close enough perhaps I could see what she was doing with the sponge on her dives. I had already learned that if I drove at a certain speed, I could anticipate where dolphins would come up after a dive. But she wasn't having it; I would travel in the direction she went down, but she came up over there, I would go there, she would come up over here. Sometimes she would come up without the sponge. On it went for six hours as she fished alone coming up hither and yon, as I tried in vain to get a good look at what she was doing. At the end of the follow, as the sun was setting, she was joined by another sponge-carrier and they traveled side-by-side, each holding their sponge.

I learned two things from that follow. First, "sponging" simply had to be a fishing tactic. They have to eat sometime and her behavior was otherwise typical of deeper-water fishing, with tail-out dives and frequent direction changes. Second, fishing with a sponge did not leave her much time for a social life.

We now know many sponge-carriers; most are females but a few are males. Dolphins learn how to sponge from their mothers and they do it in the deeper channels, seeking out fish hiding in or on the bottom. Spongemom's lack of a vigorous social life is the norm; spongers have to work long hours alone to fill their bellies, but they seem to be as adept at producing and raising babies as other females. Incredibly, in 2011, 25 years after I followed her, Spongemom was still sponging in the same channel. Later in 1986 I conducted a seven-hour follow on Blip and her calf Flip that could not have been more different than my experience with Spongemom. Blip and Flip were blasting all over the bay leaping and porpoising after schooling fish with gobs of other dolphins. Between feeding bouts they mixed and matched in a dizzying array of resting and socializing groups that at one point included well over 30 dolphins.

If there is a single word to describe female dolphins in Shark Bay, it is *variable*. Females vary enormously in how sociable they are and the size of their living area. Blip's home range exceeded 100 km^2 whereas Joy's Friend remained in a little 7 km^2 area of Red Cliff Bay. We think this huge variation is linked to the different fishing specializations of females.

Some females, like Spongemom, practice a solitary feeding strategy that is locale specific and demanding, leaving little time for a social life. Others, like Blip, may feed more on schooling fish, which requires them to range widely but also allows for more time socializing. Then there are females like Square, who have a modest home range and a rather steady cohort of female associates.

The discovery that dolphins use tools and feed in different ways in the same population is remarkable, but I don't think it is the reason they have big brains. For one thing, such individual feeding tactics are common in marine mammals, and are especially striking in the California sea otter, whose brain is not unusually large. But once you have a big brain, it can be used for many things, and it may well be that being smart has made figuring out new ways to get food a lot easier for dolphins.

§

Male Dolphins: The Politics Emerge

In mid-June, during our longest follow yet (nine hours!), Real Notch and his crew, traveling with Trips, Bit and Cetus, began porpoising rapidly. Then they stopped abruptly and started again and stopped again. They seemed indecisive about something. We looked ahead and saw another group only 100 meters away. Our focal group started porpoising towards the other group again, this time in side-by-side synchrony; an impressive sight. The other group porpoised away from ours, then everybody slowed down, now only 20 meters apart. We got a fix on the other group; it was the Beach Boys, Snubby, Sickle, Bibi, Wave and Shave! A stranger, probably a female, was also with them. Our group then moved towards the Beach Boys, who initially oriented away but then turned suddenly back around toward ours and then away again. It was a face-off! Real Notch and Hack raised the stakes, moving out from their group and advancing towards the Beach Boys to within 10 meters before turning back. The groups were now only 15 meters apart. Neither side would retreat or engage. The dance continued. Real Notch & Co. turned away and the Beach Boys turned towards them. Then the Real Notch group turned back and began approaching the Beach Boys, who then turned away. Then the Real Notch group began slowly moving away, for good this time. It was over. I did not get the sense that either side had "won," but it was becoming clear that these two groups were not the best of friends.

Unfortunately, Hack was last seen on 23 June 1986. We have no idea what happened to him. We rarely find a body; usually we just don't see them anymore. Although it is possible he moved to a new location, I suspected the worst.

Later that same day I followed the trio Slash, Crinkles & Chunk. They were old guys with heavily speckled bellies and wrinkled faces so we started calling them "Gerries." The Gerries traveled slowly, and when that became too much of an effort they would just sit at the surface resting, their flukes drooping down so low their dorsal fins vanished below the surface, like three sausages lined up side by side. Sausages are "snags" in Australia so such surface resting behavior became known as "snagging." The Gerries did have to fish of course, but they also did that slowly, spreading out from each other, lifting their flukes up and diving toward the bottom to search for fish, slow ones I'm sure. The Gerries obviously didn't have a lot of spare energy for dolphin politics, but over the next few years they would occasionally surprise us.

The next day we were feeling adventurous so we went way out northeast of Monkey Mia. We found Crunch and four of his mates from the Crunch Bunch. But who was that familiar looking dolphin with them? It was the Beach Boy, Bibi! What was he doing way out here "alone" with these guys? We were with the Crunch Bunch for four and a half hours and so was Bibi. Was he auditioning with a new group, perhaps looking for greener pastures, or just spending a day with friends?

On 22 July, we had another fascinating interaction, or non-interaction I should say, between the Beach Boys and Real Notch & Co. It was a "bony-bashing" day, with tons of dolphins in the area chasing schools of bony herring in the shallows and smacking them up to three meters in the air. The Beach Boys were in on the feeding frenzy, as were CBL, TBC and Real Notch & Co., and even the Crunch Bunch arrived on the scene. There were tons of females of all ages all over the place and there was the usual chaotic oscillation between chasing fish and socializing in large groups, but as the feeding settled down we again saw that the

Beach Boys were in a group separated from, but close to Real Notch & Co. There was a large group of romping young females between them; we watched with amusement as either group of males would join but not at the same time. It was also clear that Lucky and Pointer could move more freely between the rival male groups; they evidently managed to stay on the good side of both.

A week later we had a replay with massive schools of bony herring in Red Cliff Bay. Several large groups of dolphins and our two research boats congregated in one small area. Rachel was filming and recording underwater sounds. The Beach Boys, Snubby, Bibi, Sickle, Wave and Shave were near a large group of females that were socializing over a big school of bony herring. The Beach Boys were not oriented to the females, but in the opposite direction toward CBL and TBC. The two male groups approached each other head to head and then joined. All sat snagging at the surface and then a head-to-head "tiff" broke out between Chop and another male. Bibi immediately swam between them

Two male dolphins line up head to head, having a "tiff," while a third contributes his opinion to the dispute. © Dolphin Alliance Project

and broke it up. There was a lot of petting and socializing between the two camps; amazingly, in the absence of Real Notch's crew, they seemed to be getting along. Then another tiff broke out, this time between Snubby and Bibi! Facing each other, heads shaking up and down, they were really telling each other off, with intense long whistles. In air, the noise they made sounded like a bad Donald Duck imitation. Neither would back down; they erupted into a fight, thrashing the water and whirling to deliver blows that were clearly audible in Rachel's hydrophone. A minute later Bibi and Snubby were furiously petting each other, as quick to make up as they were to fight. To me, the context was even more interesting than the fight itself; something about joining with TBC and CBL caused Bibi and Snubby to get angry with each other. Clearly these dolphins had complex relationships!

A few minutes later everybody was in one huge mob of over 30 dolphins. Even the old guys, the trio of Slash, Crinkles & Chunk and also Spike, were here. Such large groups never last long, and this one began to split up into smaller groups. We joined CBL and watched as others came in from the north; it was Real Notch, Hi and Patches! They had not been here for any of the excitement so far, but they didn't waste time creating their own. As soon as they joined, five dolphins lined up against one. It was an extraordinary and even creepy sight, as the five formed a near semi-circle all pointing head-to-head against the one. I was so startled by this coordinated aggression and it ended so quickly that I didn't see who was being ganged up on, but I thought it was Patches. Rachel filmed a nearly identical case another day and it was clearly poor Patches being targeted by his "buddies" Real Notch and Hi, and CBL. In that case the other males didn't just threaten Patches, they attacked him. Patches avoided the first rush with a nifty somersault, and quickly turned to flee, but not before one bit him in front of his flukes. They then chased him off into the distance. After another round of abuse, Patches was left cowering at the surface with the other males milling around him.

Patches was named for all his scratches, so he may have been on the receiving end of aggression from the other males for some time. Yet seeing his own allies turn on Patches with CBL was astonishing. Patches was losing his place in the group and when we returned in March of 1987 he was gone. Did it have something to do with Hack's disappearance? Was Patches killed by a shark, driven from the area by his own allies, or worse? The five-on-one line-ups looked downright ritualistic and I have never heard of anything similar in other mammals—except in our own species. One has to wonder if such ritualistic aggression is sometimes taken to a lethal end.

To this day we have never seen the males kill each other, but I also realize that we might witness lethal aggression and never know it if the victim did not succumb immediately. Dolphins cannot do much damage by biting, unless an eye is hit. Serious aggression by dolphins is delivered through blows, which can cause massive internal damage that is not externally visible. A mortally wounded dolphin could swim away from the scene of the crime, quietly bleeding internally, and die sometime later. We would only note it as another disappearance.

On the morning of 1 August, we found TBC with their buddies CBL. A few minutes later Real Notch, Hi & Patches came zooming in; the socializing was intense but it was hard to tell what was going on. They settled down and TBC drifted away, just watching other dolphin groups from a distance, orienting to this one and then that one. One of the groups they seemed to check out repeatedly was CBL and Real Notch & Co., who were entertaining Rachel & Andrew. TBC finally joined up with a group of three females and Snubby, Bibi and Pointer! Hmm, more evidence that TBC and the Beach Boys could get along when Real Notch and his mates were not present. All six males lined up snagging side by side as the females moved away and then the males split up as well. TBC went back to doing nothing until they got wind of a feeding frenzy ahead and off they went, ditching us to join the riot of cormorants, pelicans and leaping dolphins. When we found them again they were with Real Notch, Hi and Patches but CBL were nowhere to be seen. So, we initially had TBC and CBL together, then Real Notch and his pals joined, and TBC left; later TBC was back with the Real Notch crew. This was our first hint of the remarkable dynamics between these three groups that was to unfold over the next three years.

Through the rest of August there were more days with large feeding frenzies in Red Cliff Bay. It was difficult following dolphins during the bony herring feeding melees. The large feeding groups would quickly turn into social parties and back again. Several times we saw Real Notch's crew in the same area and, if only for brief periods, in the same group with some of the Beach Boys. For example, one morning when lots of feeding and social groups were quickly forming and disbanding we found Real Notch, Hi and Patches in a group with Sickle, Shave, Pointer and Puck. This limited ability to tolerate each other would not last.

Occasionally we saw interesting interactions between the Red Cliff Bay males and others from surrounding areas. Real Notch, Hi and Patches had a strange interaction with a fearsome looking group of six males that we had christened the "B-boys." The B-boys were two very stable trios that were almost always together. Their ragged fins, tight military swimming formation and precision synchrony impressed us that these were tough guys that had been through some wars. They formed a tight group with our three, snagging at the surface, then dove for a long time, emerging at the surface like a blossoming flower, unfolding in all directions. Then they repeated the act. To this day I have no idea what was going on during those long dives. Rachel heard sounds through her hydrophone that seemed aggressive but there was nothing overt; none of the usual chasing and fighting—we would come to see plenty of that, and it was quite obvious!

§

Males and Females: Consortships and Questions

Although males spent most of their time with males, and females spent most of their time with females, we encountered mixed groups often, especially during and after the feeding frenzies that were so common in 1986. We saw different kinds of interactions between males and females.

One day we were with CBL and TBC when they swam up to a group of Crooked-fin, Puck, Joy's Friend and Nicky, and no sooner had they joined then they started chasing Nicky; on and on for nearly a mile, all the way into Monkey Mia. Later, the ranger said Nicky had come sauntering into the beach with Snubby and Bibi. Why did the males chase her? Were they upset with her about something? We didn't know, but we found it interesting that she had found refuge in the shallows at Monkey Mia.

On 11 July I followed Bibi for two hours. His buddies were not with him that day. Bibi was fishing in an area with other dolphins, then moved toward one that was fishing in the shallows. He approached and popped up beside the other dolphin; it was Two-scoops! They surfaced like that several times and Two-scoops resumed fishing, poking around in a patch of seagrass for fish hiding there. Not having any luck, she began moving slowly toward another area of seagrass. Bibi swam a circle around her. She ignored him. He porpoised beside her and rolled belly-up. She ignored him. He swam several more rapid circles around her, again rolling belly-up. She ignored him. He porpoised alongside of her. She chased a fish. He circled her again, swam over her rostrum, porpoised beside her, and then jerked his head toward her—a clear threat. She ignored him. Incredible! I knew about the "head-jerk" threat behavior from reading the old papers on the behavior of captive dolphins from the 1950s and 1960s. Bibi lifted his head out of the water and head-jerked at her again, then he swam in front of her and over her rostrum again. She ignored him. Finally, he gave up and started looking for fish.

Through July we had seen males with certain females for brief intervals but in August we noticed that the males were favoring particular females for extended periods.

CBL were with the female Dent for 12 days in August. Their association was striking; CBL would join and split from other groups, including groups of females, in and out of feeding melees and socializing groups, but Dent would always stay with them. As they traveled along, the three males would swim in a line abreast right behind her. The female Pseudopee was also popular that month, trading off between TBC and Real Notch's crew. These striking patterns were exciting. Nothing was known about the bottlenose dolphin mating system and it seemed as if we were getting a glimpse of something important. Rachel said she had seen similar extended associations between male groups and single females the previous year. Maybe we were seeing consortships, a kind of association where a male and a female stay together for a while and mate, but in this case it was three males and one female! If they were consortships, we wondered how they formed. Did the female come into estrus and join the males, or did the males court the female?

One of Rachel's main interests was communication; she spent a lot of time listening to the dolphins' impressive range of sounds with her hydrophone. We didn't have a hydrophone but we could sometimes hear dolphin whistles through the hull of our boat. But on 7 August, when Real Notch, Hi & Patches were with TBC and Pseudopee, with lots of petting and rubbing going on, one of the dolphins, who was resting at the surface, favored us with a loud vocalization in air: "pop-pop-pop-pop-pop." We couldn't tell who was making the sound. Later that same day, when Real Notch's crew was with CBL and Dent for a while, we heard the same popping sound, sort of like someone knocking on a hollow block of wood. Why were they making that sound?

Two days later we got another interesting glimpse of the nature of the consortship between CBL and Dent. The males were lined up behind Dent in what I was starting to call "formation," when all three simultaneously arched up out of the water and began bobbing their heads up and down while keeping their chins above the surface. This was the same bobbing behavior that I had seen by Snubby at Monkey Mia in 1982.[*] Then Dent dove and CBL followed, but Chop was not done. Over the next several minutes he performed what we would later come to call the "rooster strut" display a few more times. The rooster strut looked downright comical to us but I'm sure it was a serious audition by the males hoping to impress Dent. Displays by courting males are common in the animal world, but observing three males perform a synchronous display was anything but.

On my last day of dolphin watching in 1986 we had a nice several-hour follow with TBC, who were, at times, with their buddies CBL and their female companion Dent. TBC and CBL were clearly the best of mates. But why did TBC and CBL enjoy each other's company so much? Their friendship was as amazing as it was puzzling; I had never heard of anything like this in other animals. Normally, males simply compete for opportunities to mate with females. In a few species two males might form a coalition to defend a female or vie with another male for dominance in a group, but a friendship between two male groups?

And what were these trios about? Why were Trips, Bite and Cetus together so much? It probably had something to do with these single female companions like Dent and Pseudopee, but what? Why three males with one female? I knew that sometimes, in other mammals, an estrus female might be guarded by a single male, but not three! After all,

---

[*] See: *"First Visit: Visions of Dolphin Gombe"*

only one male can sire an infant.

And then there was that strange behavior by Snubby inshore at Monkey Mia. We were having so much success following dolphins offshore that we quit taking data on the dolphins that visited the beach; they were usually just lolling around in the shallows waiting for the fish buckets to arrive and it didn't seem like a productive way to spend our time. But I would often look to see what was going on with the Beach Boys when we were loading up the boat, moored just down the beach from the feeding area. In August we noticed that the boys would sometimes come into the beach with another dolphin, usually one we didn't know but sometimes one we did, like the female Yogi. Were these female consorts like Dent and Pseudopee? One morning, as we were prepping the boat, the fish buckets arrived brimming with the dolphins' favorite, bony herring! The dolphins ploughed into the shallows, practically crawling up on the beach to get at the fish, craning their necks as high as possible so the tourists might target their gaping mouth with a fishy reward. All except for Snubby. He was in an absolute tizzy, stationed halfway between the fish buckets and the strange dolphin that had come in with them that morning, whirling back and forth between the fish buckets and the stranger but not approaching either. I watched the whirling dervish for several minutes with amusement and fascination; was he afraid the stranger would leave if he went in for the fish? What was that about? Then it was all over and the dolphins left the beach. I replayed that scene in my mind for months afterwards back at the University of Michigan. What was going on with Snubby and that stranger? I had missed something important. Damn. I should have been taking more data on the beach males. I could not wait to get back to sort it out.

A Year of Discovery

1987

Breakthrough!

When I returned to Monkey Mia in early March 1987 I found that I had moved up in the world, from behind the generator house to a spot right on the beach just up from where the dolphins came in to be fed. I had a front row seat for the beach dolphin show and it was a show I was anxious to watch. Back in Michigan I had picked up a copy of Jane Goodall's just-published *The Chimpanzees of Gombe*, and there on page 465 I read an account that stopped me in my tracks: "Once, in 1963, Goliath appeared leading an unhabituated female, in estrus, toward camp. She was understandably terrified and hastily retreated when she saw me and my tent. Goliath rushed after her and attacked her, trying in vain to lead her toward the bananas he knew were waiting; but she refused to follow. Goliath was torn between conflicting desires: for five minutes he alternately ran down the slope toward camp, then turned and rushed back up to make sure his female was still there."

Substitute Snubby for Goliath and bony herring for bananas and Jane Goodall was describing exactly what I had seen at Monkey Mia! I could not wait to see if the beach males would come in with more females.

I would not have to wait long. Early on 6 March the boys came in with a female that had a tiny new baby. We ran down to the edge of the water for a look. The female was completely unfamiliar to us and yet, there she was, with a brand-new baby in less than a meter of water with people wading nearby! Before we could say anything, she turned and rocketed offshore; the males chased; there was intense splashing and back in they came with the female in tow. We fetched the camera and started snapping pictures of her fin and she bolted again. Sickle was right behind her and the others quickly followed. When they caught up to her there was intense splashing again, and again they escorted her back into the shallows. This poor female clearly did not want to be there and was being kept against her will. She must have been scared to death and worried for her new baby, being forced to swim in the shallows near these strange and scary land creatures.

It all fell immediately into place: last year's observation of Square bolting from the Crunch Bunch, using our boat to conceal her escape, Nicky being chased over a mile by CBL and using Monkey Mia as a refuge, as well as her strange week-long absence from Monkey Mia in May. The episode with Snubby and the stranger was indeed just like the Goliath affair. The male dolphins were using aggression to keep the females with them! This was astonishing. How common was this behavior? Were the consortships, like the one between CBL and Dent, coerced? Maybe that was why the males were in pairs and trios. I recalled how Bibi had attempted to entice and threaten Two-scoops and how she had simply ignored him. These males are not that much bigger than the females, so maybe they had to cooperate to keep a female with them. My mind was in flight, and the questions and ideas came fast and furiously. This was an incredibly exciting and totally unexpected discovery; nothing like it had ever been reported from other dolphin studies. I would have to start taking careful data on the boys and the females they brought into Monkey Mia, and keep a close eye during follows offshore for evidence that the consortships were coerced.

Between the discovery of the aggressive male herding of females and the interesting tangled relationships we were seeing within and between the male groups, I knew what my thesis was going to be on. Although I could jettison the boring "compare the activity budgets of males and females" idea, I decided I shouldn't abandon the females just yet. I could, for instance, do most of my follows on males and perhaps a third of them on females. That would work.

Rachel had come up from where she was living in Perth to help me get started this year. After some initial motor problems, we finally went offshore on 8 March and started following a variety of male and female dolphins. It was great fun seeing the Red Cliff Bay dolphins for the first time since last year and there were some delightful surprises, such as finding Crooked-fin with a new 5-month-old calf on only our second day out. She would shortly start bringing "Fudge," a male and a delightful little scamp, with her on visits to the beach.

§

A Day With the Gerries

Rachel and I spent 20 March hanging out with the old guys; Spike was with Steps and Kodoff, and Slash and Crinkles were there, sans Chunk. Steps and Kodoff had a third partner in 1984-1985 but he was gone by the time I came on the scene in 1986. We always supposed that Spike, a loner, was the last surviving member of an alliance. Sometimes when I saw old Spike I wondered what war stories he could tell; maybe in his heyday he was a tough guy and part of a strong alliance that ruled Red Cliff Bay. Those old friends were gone now; he was mostly alone but sometimes Spike would hang out with the other old codgers that frequented Red Cliff Bay. As I looked at Spike I saw that the wrinkles on his face extended down to his throat area. Just how old was he? I didn't know, but a lucky few males make it into their 40s. Old age had not been kind to Steps. I saw that he had a short, pale erection that would not go away. A better look revealed that Step's penis was pushed out by a cauliflower-shaped, tumor-like growth that protruded from his genital slit. Not a good idea to leave anything so resembling bait exposed in this dangerous habitat. The poor guy.

The old female Tongue-fin and her calf Lick were with the Gerries for a while, drifting in and out of the group, clearly not being herded but just there for the company. Lick stayed with her mom, even trying to nurse, for 7-8 years, about twice as long as normal. It perhaps made sense for a female like Tongue-fin, near the end of her life, to spend her remaining energy on her current calf rather than trying to bring up a new infant. She died a few years after Lick was weaned.

The day was calm; the bay was glass and we could see everything. Soon after we started the follow we saw Spike petting Crinkles, and it was on. The day became a virtual petting party as the males traded off in pairs, sometimes one was petted by two on either side of him. No part of the body seemed off limits as we saw flippers petting blowholes,

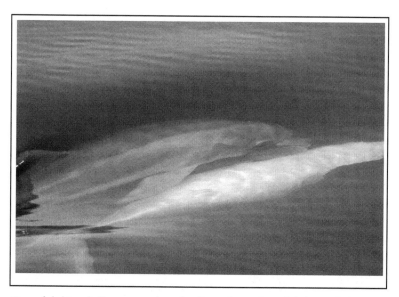

One dolphin, belly-up, strokes the face of another dolphin while being petted in the genital area. © Dolphin Alliance Project

eyes and genitals. Commonly one male would stroke the genitals of another male while being petted on the face. We even saw flipper-to-flipper touching that looked like a handshake. The males would approach each other and tilt, receiving and giving strokes; off and on it went for hours. Days like this taught us that when one male surfaces right alongside another and tilts to the side they are petting. That insight allows us to record petting behavior in choppy water when we can't see well under the surface.

It must feel good to have another dolphin stroke you. Dolphin petting is like grooming between monkeys. A monkey being groomed not only enjoys having parasites removed; they find it relaxing and their blood pressure drops. Social bonds, including alliances and coalitions, are formed, cemented and, after an altercation, repaired by grooming. Dolphin petting probably isn't as much about parasite removal but it may help remove dead skin as dolphins shed their skin cells 200 times faster than we do. With their stubby little flippers, dolphins can't groom themselves like primates. They can give themselves a scratch, using objects like clumps of seagrass or mooring lines, but mostly they seek stroking from each other. Today the Gerries were reinforcing their friendships and Spike, the loner, was the most active of all.

I was struck by how the dolphins were slapping each other in sensitive areas; while it probably felt good to have your genitals stroked I doubt the same could be said for eyes and blowholes. Certainly, anyone who ventured to pet the beach dolphins near their eyes and blowholes was asking for a smack or a bite, but these dolphin friends didn't object to such touching from each other. An Israeli zoologist, Amotz Zahavi, came up with an ingenious idea to explain such touching. He suggested that by grooming and stroking sensitive areas, animals (including humans) are "testing the bonds" they have with each other. Touching that would be aversive from strangers is at least tolerated and perhaps even pleasant among friends, so if you are able to stroke the blowhole or eye of another dolphin you can be confident that your friendship is secure (at least for the moment!). People don't have such friendships with dolphins so the beach dolphins enforced strict rules about touching by people; a gentle stroke down the side was ok, but do not touch or grab fins or flukes and don't put your hand anywhere near their eye or blowhole. Of course, people were uneducated in dolphin etiquette and would often go to "pat" a dolphin's head like they would a dog, right on the blowhole! More than once I asked an offending person, who had expressed surprise at a dolphin's hostile reaction to their overture of friendship, how they would like to have a stranger stick a finger up their nose.

The Gerries' mutual admiration society was interrupted only once, when TBC approached, then bolted away as the Gerries gave a short chase. At least when they had the numbers on their side, the old guys could still hold their own against younger males.

§

"Pop" Goes the Dolphin

Snubby, Sickle and Bibi came in with another strange female and her 2-3-year-old infant on 22 March. We would later learn that she lived in the deeper channel to the southeast of Monkey Mia. Just as we started watching them Bibi charged at her, then a few minutes later he charged again. He prodded at her genitals but she quickly evaded him by rolling over. Then Bibi started making that funny popping sound we had heard offshore last year, "pop-pop-pop-pop-pop;" he was much more focused on the female than were Snubby and Sickle. He made the popping sound several more times over the next 20 minutes. He popped loudly and she approached him. When the fish buckets arrived and the males were thrashing around in mere inches of water, each vying to get more than their share, she bolted, but only Sickle and Bibi chased, while Snubby continued to stuff his face. Bibi and Sickle came back in with the female and Wave & Shave. Maybe Wave and Shave had blocked her escape. Bibi kept making the popping sound, then turned and head-jerked at the female. Bibi popped at her yet again and then chased her in a small circle. He would not let up as he continued popping and rushing at her. A few minutes later he charged again, chasing her in circles, and Sickle and Snubby jumped into the fray as the group moved just offshore, water spraying and flukes flying. We heard the unmistakable sound, "whack," of one dolphin hitting another. They moved back inshore and Bibi popped a couple more times; the female approached him in both cases.

It was on this day that we really started to understand what the popping sound was about. We were learning that this strange sound was associated with herding behavior and was a threat directed at the female to keep her close. The female would often approach in response to pops, and if she didn't, she risked being attacked. What we observed on this day in March was typical of what we would observe for the next two years, on an almost daily basis.

Our discovery of the function of pops was exciting because people knew next to nothing about dolphin communication. We knew from captive studies that there were two broad classes of dolphin sounds, whistles and clicks. Each dolphin had its own distinctive "signature" whistle, and by 1987, evidence was emerging that these phenomenal mimics could imitate each other's signature whistles. The other category was derived from the echolocation clicks dolphins use to "see" in their watery world; their remarkable sonar ability is a skill that dolphins share with bats. Dolphins repackage these clicks into a variety of social sounds, frequently called "burst-pulsed" sounds, that they use in all manner of interactions. The aggressive sounds are obvious, like growling and screaming, but Rachel had been recording more subtle ones as well, that she suspected were of a friendlier nature.

Sonar clicks occur in very rapid succession, several hundred per second, and each click has a huge range of frequencies that extends far above the top range of human hearing (20,000 sound waves per second or 20 "kilohertz," kHz). Pops are just a slowed-down train of clicks, at only 6-12 pops/second, with most of the energy in each click under a few kHz. Such low-frequency sounds travel in all directions so the male doesn't need to be oriented towards the female to pop "at" her.

Over the next two years we demonstrated that popping induced the female to approach the male. Pops are a "come-hither" signal, backed up by stronger threats (the head-jerk) and more overt kinds of aggression (hitting). I remember well the day in 1988 that Peter Tyack, a well-known cetacean biologist from Woods Hole Oceanographic Institution, came for a visit with his graduate student Laela Sayigh. Peter was an expert on dolphin vocalizations so I was anxious to share with him our discovery of the pop vocalization. I led him down to the beach where Snubby was attending to the female of the day. We did not have to wait long. Snubby began popping at the female, but she ignored him. More popping and she ignored him still. "Ha," said Peter, happily starting to voice his objection to my claim about the function of pops, when Snubby, as if on cue, turned and head-jerked at the female and then charged and smacked her with his tail right in front of us. I felt like I owed Snubby a bucket of bony herring.

Pops are really remarkable. The reason that we knew little about dolphin vocalizations was that we could not tell which dolphin was making which sound. Humans can't localize sounds underwater and dolphins don't help matters since they do not make facial movements like we do when talking. But in the shallows at Monkey Mia, the males made the pop sound in air so we could identify the culprit. A study of dolphin vocalizations in air! The very thought is absurd. And as we saw in 1986, males offshore often make pops in air (of course, we learned from listening to them through underwater microphones that they make many more pops underwater than we hear in air). Males often snag at the surface before changing direction, a good time to remind the female to stay with them.

§

A Mother's Grief

6 April was one of those beautiful, calm glassy days that we live for. Rachel had her boat running now and had launched a few minutes before us. So when I was scanning for dolphins and saw that her boat was stationary, I headed her way to see who she was with. Rachel was leaning over the edge of the boat just staring down into the water. Something was clearly amiss. As we drew close we saw it; a small dolphin, not moving, listing on its side at the surface. Crooked-fin was hovering nearby. The dead dolphin was her infant, Fudge, only 6 months old. It was very sad as Fudge had been so playful and full of joy and we thought that he would, like his mother, grow up to become a regular visitor to the beach at Monkey Mia. Dolphins sink when they die and refloat once decomposition gasses accumulate inside, so Fudge had probably been dead for a day or so. I stayed with Fudge for the next seven hours to watch his mother's behavior. Early on Crooked-fin spent a lot of time just snagging at the surface by her infant or slowly circling him. Twice she made an eerie, high-pitched and drawn-out sound from her blowhole that, throwing the usual cautions about attributing human emotions to animal behavior aside, sounded to me like wailing. I never heard that sound again.

Eventually, Crooked-fin began to make fishing excursions, but always returning to Fudge, like clockwork, every 8-12 minutes. The only time she snagged by her infant's body again was during the only visit by other dolphins: Slash, Crinkles and young Pointer. They milled around Fudge's body for a few minutes and left. Eventually, Crooked-fin stopped coming back and, as a storm was brewing, we retrieved Fudge's body, took measurements and sent him to Perth for a necropsy. Of course, we can't know if Crooked-fin would have returned later to visit her calf, but most likely it would have been scavenged by a shark before long.

We never found out why Fudge died. The necropsy was inconclusive and the only external wound was a deep dolphin bite, which could have been inflicted by his mother in her panic when he died and sank. Just over half the infants in Shark Bay don't make it to weaning and they die for all kinds of reasons, including sharks, disease and starvation. Contrary to popular belief, dolphins do not have an easy time of it living in the sea.*

There are many reports of dolphins remaining with their dead offspring, sometimes even carrying them around in an advanced state of decay. Dolphins have strong emotions and social bonds so it is easy to imagine that their grief at the loss of an infant would be not unlike our own. Crooked-fin would not, however, have much time to grieve. Only three days after we found Fudge dead, the boys herded Crooked-fin into Monkey Mia. The poor dolphin had almost no respite between losing her infant and being harassed by obnoxious males. Bibi was popping and getting after her constantly. Well, being a beach dolphin herself, at least she could get a few free fish during the ordeal.

§

The Great Escape

The Beach Boys faced a dilemma when they herded females into the shallows at Monkey Mia. The fish buckets and females were in opposite directions. Focus too much on the female and the other dolphins get the fish; focus too much on fish and the female might get away. On the 16th the boys came in with another female we had never seen before (they were increasing our catalog size nicely!) and again Bibi was focused more on her than the others, but Sickle was also interested. I watched Bibi closely. As he frantically maneuvered around people to locate the fish buckets, every few seconds he would whip around and orient to the female, but just for an instant, and then he was back pursuing fish again. These "quick looks" allowed him to keep tabs on her while "hunting" for fish handouts. But it was a balancing act. When the three males all crowded in to get fish handouts, the female bolted. I didn't see her go; Bibi did a "quick look" and blasted offshore. The female's path was revealed by a trail of "fluke-prints" at the surface where water had welled up from her vigorous stroking. Incredibly, Bibi didn't chase in the same direction; he headed off at an angle to

* See "Starving Dolphins" and "Jaws"

the right of her path, and Sickle took off at an angle to the left; they were cutting off her escape routes! The tactic worked and they bought her back to the beach. Snubby had not bothered to chase, and I wondered if he was involved at all.

The next day they were back with the same female. Sickle and Bibi were both very excited about her, but again, Snubby ignored her. There were lots of quick looks and popping by both males and Sickle did a rooster strut, placing his bobbing head slightly over the female's side. They charged at her more than once, chased and hit her. After this abuse, she was so intimidated and cowed into submission that she stayed right by Bibi, hanging on his every move, glued to him like an obedient dog. Or so it seemed. The fish buckets came down and all three males plowed in toward the beach, thrashing around with heads out of the water and mouths agape. There were no "quick looks." I looked up at the female; she began slowly moving offshore and then accelerated and tore away from the beach. The males were oblivious. A full 12 seconds ticked off before one finally turned around from the pile-up to check on her. Sickle and Bibi, panic stricken, blasted wildly offshore but it was too late; she was long gone.

Sickle and Bibi came back inshore, empty handed and in a bad mood. Side by side, they got into a tiff with Puck, with Bibi doing most of the bitching. Puck had the audacity to bitch back. Bad idea. They chased her offshore and Puck came back in with a bloody gash over her eye.

That night we were in hysterics joking about the female's apparent tactic that facilitated her escape: "I love you Bibi; you are the only one for me; you are so strong Bibi, I want to have your baby," then sneaking off when an overconfident Bibi didn't check on her soon enough. Such anthropomorphizing provided us with an endless source of laughter over the years and we engaged in it often and everywhere; over dinner, on the beach and in the boat.

Of course, we had no idea if the solicitous behavior the female exhibited just prior to escaping was a deliberate tactic, or if she was simply intimidated but still able to take advantage of an opportunity to escape. Whatever the motivation for her obsequious behavior, it likely did render the males overconfident. We would later learn that a female had a chance to get away if she had a four- to five-second head start;

anything less than that, forget it. But 12 seconds was an eternity, and we never saw anything like that again.

§

All for One and One for All?

Sickle didn't show up right away when the boys came in a few days later with a female named "Waverly" for her funny quavering whistle. Snubby and Bibi were with Waverly, as well as their buddies Wave and Shave. Sickle came in 15 minutes later but showed no interest in the female. Now this was an interesting development. Sickle and Bibi had been very attentive to the females and Snubby had seemed disinterested, but now Snubby and Bibi were herding Waverly, and Sickle was out of it. Why weren't all three working together to herd the female? After all, they were a trio, like CBL and TBC, right? I was beginning to wonder. Then on the 22nd and 23rd, Sickle and Bibi were paired up again, with "Gumby" this time, and Snubby was back on the outs. On the 24th the boys came in with two females, Gumby and a new one, Jagged! Everybody was excited about Jagged. Snubby and Sickle were probing their rostra into her genital area, a behavior we call "goosing," and chasing her in circles. However, when Jagged started bolting, one time after another, Bibi and Sickle chased but Snubby stayed back to guard Gumby. Snubby was not herding Gumby alone; young Shave was his partner! This was the first day we had two females herded by two male pairs at Monkey Mia, something that would be repeated many times over the next two years. Our first "double herding" was short-lived. Evidently, the presence of Jagged was just too exciting, so Snubby and Shave let Gumby go and got into formation behind Jagged with Sickle and Bibi. Jagged wasn't the brightest bulb. She didn't clue into the opportunity the fish buckets provided so she would just start bolting when she was with the males, and of course that didn't work out well for her.

As we were learning that Snubby, Sickle and Bibi paired off to herd females, we were also marveling at their capacity to multi-task: herding a female while having sex with others. When they came inshore with Jagged on 27 April, they got after Puck immediately and then turned

Snubby, on guard duty, watches as the other dolphins are fed, but he remains near the female (farthest out) in case she tries to escape.
© Dolphin Alliance Project

their attention to Shave, goosing and mounting him. Wave was mounting and goosing his buddy as much as the others. Then Nicky became the target of the boys' "affection." All this activity directed at other dolphins did not stop Sickle and Bibi from guarding and threatening Jagged to keep her close.

By the next day Sickle and Bibi were bored with Jagged. They were inattentive and I didn't hear any pops. Shave was a no-show and I wondered if it was because of the attention he had received the day before. Snubby, who seemed to be picking up Sickle and Bibi's "leftovers," was herding Jagged with Wave on the 29th. Shave was back, but he may have regretted that decision. Sickle and Bibi were all over poor Shave, goosing and mounting him, sometimes synchronously. The partnerships had changed again by 1 May, as Sickle came in with Wave and Shave and later Snubby and Bibi showed up with Jagged. Snubby and Bibi still had Jagged early on 5 May, but by that afternoon she was gone and Sickle and Bibi were back together herding Crooked Fin, popping and guarding her while Snubby left with Wave and Shave. Snubby and Bibi came in briefly with Jagged, but no Sickle, on 7 May.

These April observations made two things clear. Snubby, Sickle and Bibi may have looked like a trio traveling around together, but they did not act like one when it came to herding females. Instead, they herded females in pairs, and which two were paired could change on short notice. And the third male, who we started calling the "odd-male-out," might get together with one of their younger friends, Wave and Shave. It was also evident that herding a female didn't keep Snubby, Sickle and Bibi from causing trouble with others.

§

Aquatic Chimpanzees?

In May we had important visitors to Shark Bay. The first to arrive was one of my Ph.D. co-advisors, Richard Wrangham.* A Brit who was educated at Oxford and then Cambridge for his doctoral degree, Richard was a chimpanzee expert who had worked at Gombe with Jane Goodall. Richard was fascinated by the natural history of the animals he studied and passionate about achieving a broad theoretical understanding of animal social evolution. I thought the dolphin behavior we were seeing was astonishing, but would someone with Richard's experience watching chimpanzees and other primate species think so as well?

We already knew that our dolphins had some chimpanzee-like attributes. The way they changed groups so often during the course of a day was one such feature; this "fission-fusion"† business, with dolphins coming and going during follows, had kept us and our cameras busy!

The Shark Bay dolphins' "life history," or age at which individuals are weaned, mature and die, is similar to chimpanzees. Dolphins and chimpanzees are typically weaned by age 3, but nursing can last longer in some cases. Most of our female dolphins give birth when they are 12 (a few at 11) while first-birth in chimpanzees occurs at age 13-15. Lucky dolphins and chimpanzees can live to be well over 40 and some chimpanzees live into their 50s.

Like our dolphins, the chimpanzees that Richard knew also had quite complex male relationships. Male chimpanzees compete to be the top-

---

* In later years, all three of Richard's sons, Ross, David and Ian, would spend part of their "Gap Year," between high school and university, as assistants on our project.
† See "First Visit: Visions of a Dolphin Gombe"

ranking "alpha" male, a position rewarded with priority access to estrus females. However, the male chimp who wins that prize often isn't simply the biggest and strongest male, as is typically the case in other mammals. Male chimpanzees form coalitions to compete for rank, so a successful male chimpanzee is one who is good at cultivating a strong ally. Since other males are competing with you for those preferred allies, the ascent to the alpha male position is negotiated along a tricky and even dangerous social terrain. The complex social gamesmanship of high-ranking male chimpanzees was described beautifully in Frans de Waal's book, *Chimpanzee Politics*, and by Toshisada Nishida, who founded a chimpanzee study in the Mahale Mountains of Tanzania around the same time Goodall initiated the Gombe study. de Waal described shifting alliance relationships among three males in the Arnhem Zoo in the Netherlands; something Nishida called "allegiance fickleness." Although the shifts we were observing among Snubby, Sickle and Bibi were about who was going to herd the next female rather than who was going to be the alpha male, their behavior could certainly be described as "fickle!"

The Snubby, Sickle & Bibi trio was one of several that we knew. The complex jockeying in chimpanzees is usually restricted to one such group: the three or four males at the top of the community hierarchy. Our dolphin pairs and trios often moved around the bay as a unit, surfacing side by side synchronously (which we abbreviate as "synchs") and often interacting amicably with other pairs and trios. It seemed like the dolphin pairs and trios had relationships with each other that were like the relationships between individual chimpanzees, as though the dolphins had added a social layer to a primate society. I knew of nothing else like it.

So I was really hoping that Richard would see at least some of the amazing behavior that we were seeing inshore at Monkey Mia and out in the bay. I had written to him about it of course, but there is nothing like seeing things with your own eyes.

I was not disappointed. On 9 May, Sickle and Bibi had a new female, Chicklet, and they put on a show for Richard. Chicklet bolted several times and both males were popping constantly and even simultaneously. Richard was thrilled. The next day the boys were back with Chicklet, and Richard got to work testing out new and better ways to record the herding behavior.

Unfortunately, the weather was not cooperating for the offshore work. Ken and Ruth Musgave, whose daughter, another Ruth, had been helping me out for the past two months, also joined us during this time. Ken was a federal judge and the executor of an estate that donated money for animal causes. We were anxious for them to enjoy the experience, but the gray, windy, chilly weather was not helpful. So we decided to make a quick run a few hundred kilometers up to Coral Bay for spectacular snorkeling on the reef. The weather had improved when we returned to Monkey Mia, and the morning of the 15th revealed another switch; the boys still had Chicklet but she was now with Snubby and Bibi. We didn't know if that switch had happened while they had her or if she had escaped and been recaptured.

That afternoon we went offshore and didn't have to venture far before running into tons of dolphins. At one point, we had three alliances in view: Real Notch and Hi (with the macho Two-scoops); TBC; and Sickle, Wave, Shave, Lucky and Pointer. Richard's eyes lit up; "You mean these are three different alliances, all here in the same area?" I could almost see the lights, bells and whistles going off in his mind as they had in mine. This was one complex society!

Yes, in some ways our dolphins were aquatic chimpanzees. But the way the dolphin alliances moved around and interacted was decidedly unlike chimpanzees or any other animal for that matter. Richard Wrangham, one of the top experts on non-human primates in the world, confirmed this after spending just one afternoon on the boat!

There was something else going on with our dolphin alliances and I had to find out what it was. We talked it over and Richard gave me the green light to focus my research on the males. From now on I would follow only males offshore to learn about their fascinating alliance relationships.

§

Wave and Shave Get "Owned"

On 17 May we were offshore watching a group of socializing dolphins including Nicky, Two-scoops and Joy's Friend. To our astonishment, Nicky and Two-scoops started getting after Joy's Friend just like males would. They lined up side by side in formation behind her and began surfacing in precise synchrony. They started goosing her and pushing her up from below as she lay on her side at the surface, in what we were coming to realize was a submissive posture. From their position on either side just behind her they moved in closer and synchronously turned their bellies in toward her, a behavior that when performed by males includes erections. I found it fascinating that the two most "masculine" females that we knew had taken on "male" roles.

We didn't know if Joy's Friend was Nicky and Two-scoops' "captive," but there was no doubt about the herding case we observed the next day. We* found Wave and Shave traveling together. They spread out to fish, moving steadily toward a large social group. At first Shave joined a small group that had splintered off the larger one: Trips, Cetus, and a couple of young ones. But when they started to move back toward the larger group, Shave left to join Wave and they hung back from the group. We saw the reason for their hesitation: Real Notch & Hi were there, along with Bite, Two-scoops, Puck, Joy's Friend and some younger dolphins. The large group split into two groups and Wave and Shave joined the group that did not contain Real Notch & Hi, but then the two groups fused again. Now this was interesting; what would happen? Maybe Wave and Shave's presence would be "buffered" by the large number of other dolphins in the group. Then we saw someone get goosed, and again, and the other dolphins quickly left. Wave & Shave were alone with Real Notch and Hi.

Shave was their first target. Real Notch and Hi lined up in formation behind Shave and started goosing him. There was some head-to-head and Hi goosed Shave again and then charged him. Wave just sat at the

---

* *Richard Wrangham was in Rachel's boat today and missed this incredible observation.*

surface, facing away from the assault. Hi goosed Shave again and was biting at his peduncle. Shave lay on his side and Hi moved, open mouthed into Shave's side, biting at him, and Shave slapped his flukes mildly in protest. Shave rolled belly-up with Hi holding Shave's flipper in his mouth. We saw that Hi had an erection as he continued to goose and bite at Shave. Real Notch then joined in as Wave continued to snag nearby. Real Notch and Hi became synchronous in their pursuit of Shave and we saw Real Notch with an erection. They turned their attention briefly to Wave and then back to Shave. Real Notch and Hi, in formation, turned away in opposite directions, allowing Wave and Shave to reunite, and they began petting each other. Real Notch and Hi came back and Wave lay on his side; then both he and Shave turned around and approached Real Notch and Hi. I had the distinct impression that they had been ordered to approach. Had Real Notch or Hi made pops underwater? Now it was Wave's turn; they goosed him twice before going after Shave again and then alternated between Shave and Wave, goosing, charging, chasing and biting at them, often with erections. We heard loud popping in air and then Real Notch charged at Shave and goosed him. At one point, Real Notch and Hi came in under Shave with their bellies up, erections visible, and pushed him up out of the water. Then Hi and Real Notch separated about 20-40 meters, Hi with Shave and Real Notch with Wave. Each spent the next 10 minutes repeatedly goosing and mounting his captive. During this period, Hi made pops in air and Shave approached him. Things gradually died down as some females entered the area and everyone started feeding, but when we ended the follow, Real Notch, Hi, Wave and Shave were still together.

We had just witnessed an astonishing display of dominance: one male alliance herding another! Wave and Shave, just now maturing, were no match for the powerful Real Notch and Hi. While they did not try to really hurt Wave and Shave, Real Notch and Hi were making a clear statement, and I suspect it was mostly about the company that Wave and Shave chose to keep.

§

More Fun Than Baboons!

Richard Wrangham had invited Irven DeVore along for his visit to Shark Bay. Irv was a famous professor of Biological Anthropology at Harvard who had been one of the first people to study wild primates in Africa, baboons especially, and who had mentored many a budding primatologist over the decades. Irv arrived on the 18th and from that point, Richard and Irv alternated between my boat and Rachel's.

On the 19th Richard came on my boat. I started a follow on Spike, who was with a group of females. There was a chase; suddenly Real Notch and Hi were there but Spike was gone. That kind of interaction, where one or two individuals chase another away, was familiar to Richard from his chimpanzee watching days, but not so the interactions we saw between alliances later that day. We found CBL and settled in for a nice follow. They joined up with TBC and RH but after a time RH peeled off and TBC and CBL spent the next couple hours traveling and fishing together.

On the 20th, with Irv on board, we found CBL again, but incredibly, they were with Snubby, Sickle and Bibi as well as some of the younger males, Pointer, Lucky, Lodent and Fred! Irv had his video camera and he would get a lens full today. For the next two hours these 10 males treated us to a real show. There was some intense aggression but it was not simply CBL against SSB. Rather, at times it seemed to be SSB and CBL against one of their own. At one juncture Bibi was clearly "it;" he was being chased and goosed. During one chase he flipped around to face the aggressor and they fought briefly. Later Bottomhook was "it," as the other five lined up, then charged and goosed him. He rolled belly-up to avoid their charge and then lay on his side at the surface. A minute later Bottomhook again rolled belly-up as he was rushed by two others who were biting and chasing him around, and then rubbing against him.

All of this looked aggressive; the movements, charging and goosing were intense and performed with great energy; even the surfacing was vigorous as if the males were all hyper-charged. I can only say that if the males were playing, it was like an intense game of rugby with tempers sometimes flaring. Trying to get a handle on what I was seeing, I recalled the episode from last year when Snubby and Bibi got into a fight after joining CBL.* Again, it seemed that CBL and SSB could be together when Real Notch and Hi were not present, but it was tense.

Then SSB turned their attention to Pointer and CBL got after Fred! Snubby and Sickle mounted Pointer at the same time from either side; both had erections. The behavior was just like Real Notch and Hi herding Wave and Shave, but now we had two trios with two younger males. As before, each group separated with their younger target. About 10 minutes later the two groups settled down and came back together with all six adult males bunched up behind the juveniles. Suddenly there was an explosive chase; fluke prints revealed the path of dolphins streaking away from the group. Six dolphins surfaced abreast in a broad line, with 2 to 3 meters between each dolphin. This "military" lineup presented a beautiful and striking scene with their blows glowing in the late afternoon sun. I looked at the fins; it was Chop, Bottomhook, Lambda, Real Notch, Hi and Two-scoops! Real Notch and Hi had suddenly appeared out of nowhere and, with CBL, chased away the Beach Boys. Wow.

Irv was elated, remarking that it was the longest sustained social interaction he had ever seen in any mammal. He added that it was more fun than watching baboons, and that was his highest compliment.

We caught up to Snubby, Sickle and Bibi. Sickle and Snubby were surfacing in synchrony; Bibi was clearly the odd-male-out. Did that relate to the earlier aggression against Bibi?

Irv came out with us again on the 24th for a five-hour Shave follow. Wave and Shave were with Lucky, Lodent and Pointer as well as SSB off and on as they alternated between fishing and socializing. Wave, Shave, Lucky, Lodent and Pointer rested at the surface oriented towards another intense social group for several minutes. We popped over for a look; it was Real Notch and Hi, TBC and at least eight females. We saw Nicky goose Hi before returning to our group of Wave and Shave and their buddies, who got busy mounting each other. Sickle joined and he was "it" for a bit, then evidently somebody got upset as Pointer sat at the surface squealing and shaking his head up and down and the other

---

* See "Male Dolphins: The Politics Emerge"

five all lined up against him head-to-head. It didn't escalate any further.

A bit later we lost our focal dolphins and went from group to group looking for them. We found an intense social group that included Real Notch, Hi and Two-scoops, TBC and some other females. Spying another group 100 meters from those, we went over and found our focal group: LLP, Wave, Shave and Sickle. They were snagging at the surface, orienting to where the Real Notch group had been. I looked that way but saw nothing. Sickle started squealing and then they all dove, turning away as they vanished underwater. Then they surfaced in the same place; only it wasn't our dolphins; it was TBC, Real Notch, Hi and Two-scoops! In primates, a subordinate individual will sometimes move away from and thus be "displaced" by an approaching dominant individual. We had just observed one dolphin group, Real Notch and his friends, displace Wave, Shave, Sickle and LLP: an expression of dominance, albeit a bit less dramatic than the day Real Notch and Hi herded Wave and Shave.

On the 25th Richard Wrangham was back in my boat for our last trip out before he and Irv left. We had CBL in view for several hours. Bottomhook went off to fish while Chop and Lambda were socializing with the younger males Fred, Barney and Crossfingers. Crossfingers was kind of a loner and was "it" so much during juvenile sex play that we thought "he" was a "she" until finally someone else was "it" and we saw his erection.

Bottomhook returned with Sickle, Lucky and Pointer, and Sickle became "it." CBL were trailing behind as Sickle was pushed up, goosed and mounted by the younger males. Were the juvenile males dominating Sickle? Perhaps he had to put up with such treatment from the juvies because CBL were there. But I don't think that was the case; the interaction seemed much friendlier and more relaxed compared to the intense thrashing and bashing we saw when SSB, Chop and Lambda were getting after Bottomhook the other day. I was beginning to understand that dolphin sexual behavior could be employed as a social tool in many contexts, from dominance interactions with other kinds of aggressive behaviors, to more playful, friendly encounters. A goose or a mount could be performed violently or in a gentle, playful way. Sex among these dolphins was as complex as their relationships.

§

An Alliance Triangle

I traveled with Richard and Irv to Perth and then hitchhiked back up to Shark Bay a few days later. We found Real Notch and Hi consorting a female and hanging out with TBC on 2 June. While we were with that group Rachel found CBL with some of the younger males. She had seen the female with RH on the 28 May so they had been with her a few days. RH and TBC were still together the next day but now each alliance had a female consort; TBC had Yogi and her calf Boo. Real Notch and Hi were surfacing synchronously and got into formation behind TBC's female Yogi! Then Real Notch paired off with Trips for several synchronous surfacings, and Hi and Bite did the same: a little male bonding between the groups. I wondered if Real Notch and Hi getting in formation behind TBC's female necessitated that inter-alliance bonding.

On the 4th Rachel found RH and their female, and CBL joined them for a time. We had TBC for over three hours on the 7th and they were back with RH who now had the female Blip. Trips and Cetus synched a lot, which was unusual as Trips and Bite were the stronger pair in that trio. There were also some inter-alliance synchs again. We followed Real Notch & Hi for six hours on the 8th, still with Blip, but now with CBL instead of TBC. There were a few inter-alliance synchs but mostly they paired off with their own.

In the space of a week we had Real Notch and Hi traveling with TBC, then CBL, then TBC and then CBL. Hmmm, this had a familiar ring to it. It was the same kind of partner switching behavior we had been watching between the Beach Boys as they switched between Sickle and Bibi and Snubby and Bibi, but in this case it was between alliances!

What was most striking to me was that we were seeing RH with TBC or CBL instead of TBC and CBL together. However, the next time we found these guys, on 22 June, CBL and TBC were together but RH was absent. At one point Chop and Trips paired off away from the rest and petted each other, then they became synchronous and did a beautiful Tango display, turning sharply left, then right, then left and right again.

Then on the 25th we found them all together, TBC, CBL and RH with Two-scoops. It would not last. Real Notch and Hi dropped back behind the group, became synchronous, then rushed back into the group. Several were after one dolphin, who lay on his side at the surface. Suddenly the group exploded into a chase with RH and CBL after TBC. CBL and RH continued to travel together. Twenty minutes later CBL raced ahead, leaping, and caught Yogi and Boo. RH came plowing into the group and Real Notch and Chop were head to head underwater. There was more intense chasing around as all were terribly excited around Yogi. Lambda and Real Notch paired off, petting, then they surfaced synchronously and performed tail-slaps as they dove. Everybody began to settle down, with members of CBL petting each other. RH left with Two-scoops a few minutes later. Then CBL picked up the action again, chasing and goosing Yogi and performing displays around her. Chop and Lambda broke out in a nearly synchronous rooster strut.

While Chop and Lambda were carrying on, we saw dolphins leaping around Rachel's boat, several hundred meters away in the direction Real Notch and Hi had traveled. Rachel had been watching Snubby, Sickle and Bibi, who had just chased and caught Crooked-fin, only to have Real Notch and Hi blast into their group. There was intense splashing, and Crooked-fin was gone. Rachel thought that Real Notch and Hi had thwarted the Beach Boys' effort to herd Crooked-fin!

After their displays, CBL settled down and were just slowly meandering about for the next half-hour when we noticed that Yogi and Boo were gone. We watched as TBC slowly approached CBL from 100 meters, finally pulling up in front of CBL just as females often do when joining males. Cetus and Bottomhook synched and there was petting between Trips and Bite. After another 15 minutes CBL changed direction but TBC did not, continuing on their way. The reason TBC kept moving became apparent five minutes later when Real Notch and Hi joined CBL. There was petting between Real Notch and Bottomhook and then the two groups settled into slow traveling mode for the rest of the follow.

It was an astonishing and revealing day. Seeing Real Notch and Hi clearly initiate the aggression with CBL against TBC showed who was pulling the strings in this alliance triangle. Since losing Hack and Patches last year, Real Notch and Hi had been moving in on the relationship between TBC and CBL. Only I still didn't really know what these relationships between alliances were all about.

§

Those Bizarre Boys

The relationship competition among Snubby, Sickle and Bibi continued to play out at a dizzying pace. On 4 June, the Beach Boys came in with a new female who lived southeast of Monkey Mia. There had been a partner change as two days before Sickle and Bibi had Crooked-fin, but now Bibi and Snubby were herding the new female. We followed them when they left Monkey Mia. As they traveled east away from the park, Snubby and Bibi executed a beautiful series of seven synchronous "double roll-outs" in which they would approach the female from behind on either side, tilt their bellies in toward her as they angled their snouts into her underside and then turn up and out so that their genital areas brushed past her tailstock. The way they peeled away from her on either side reminded me of the petals of a flower opening.

After traveling a while, they sped up, moving fast until they met up with Lucky, Lodent and Pointer. Sickle engaged the youngsters in some intense social behavior, with goosing and chasing, while Snubby and Bibi hung back with the female. Nicky showed up and jumped right into the socializing, petting with Lucky. Sickle and Lucky got in formation behind the new female, then there was a fast 30-meter chase and Lodent was gone. Lucky and Pointer goosed Snubby, and Snubby lightly slapped Pointer in the face. Except for Lodent being chased away, none of it appeared aggressive as the dolphins were also petting a lot. The petting continued after the more intense activity died down: Lucky with Nicky, Sickle with Pointer, then with Lucky. Once Pointer and Sickle came up on either side of Lucky, flukes undulating in perfect synchrony as they stroked him. The action then escalated again, but this time everybody was after Nicky. Bibi guarded the female while Snubby joined in on the chasing and goosing of Nicky, then they switched places and Snubby guarded while Bibi jumped into the fray. Later, as they were traveling we saw another group 200 meters ahead, snagging in our direction. We went up for a look; it was the Gerries: Slash, Crinkles, Chunk and Spike, with Lodent! The little squirt was right there with the old guys. That was kind of nice, I thought; maybe Lodent had sought solace with these mellow old males after being chased away from his mates.

Sickle and Bibi flanking a herded female in "formation."
© Dolphin Alliance Project

On the afternoon of 14 June, we searched fruitlessly for someone interesting to follow before finally giving up and heading back to Monkey Mia. There we found the Beach Boys very tight abreast, almost touching, with Snubby in the center. Suspecting mischief, we followed them when they moved offshore. Sickle and Snubby were tight, petting and synching a lot. Bibi managed a few synchs with Snubby. Less than a half-hour had elapsed and we saw Gumby with her infant some 30 meters in front of us; the boys rushed up and porpoised all around her. Loud whistles and screams were audible through the hull as the males popped at Gumby, head-jerked and performed synchronous double roll-outs with erections at full mast. When they finally settled down they traveled abreast behind her with Sickle in the center. They were not done. Twenty minutes after capturing Gumby they ditched her as they blasted into a group of feeding cormorants after Jagged. When they settled down again Sickle and Snubby synched repeatedly; they were still tight, but only for now. The next morning Sickle and Bibi came in with yet another female, Waverly.

Snubby and Sickle had a great run through mid-July, herding Surprise, a maturing female that loved to catch a ride on our bow as we left Monkey Mia going west, as well as Crooked-fin and Chicklet. On the 17th they came in with Poindexter. Poor Bibi must have been getting frustrated; he had not been excluded for so long all year. But the next morning Bibi was a player, herding Poindexter with Sickle. We didn't know how the change occurred but it seems likely, given the brief nature of most consortships during the winter months, that she escaped and was recaptured. SSB left later that day and when they returned, Snubby and Bibi were herding Crooked-fin! Early the next morning, 19 July, Snubby and Bibi swam into Monkey Mia in formation behind Crooked-fin. When the fish buckets arrived half an hour later she bolted and escaped. Five hours later all three males got very tight, packed together like sardines, with Bibi in the center. There was some petting and then Sickle was in the center. While they were glued together like that, two of the males started rooster strutting, with no female present! I could see the male on the right listing on his side and then all three started rooster strutting in an exaggerated manner, accompanied by intense whistles in air by one or more of the males. They remained plastered to each other like that for 15 minutes and then blasted off to the west. We hopped into the boat and followed. When we caught up, Sickle and Bibi were racing side by side, with Snubby trailing, as they chased and caught Crooked-fin again. They were excited around her and turned back to Monkey Mia. Snubby leapt in ahead since he was now the odd-male-out. That strange "sardine" formation had signaled a partner switch. When the fish buckets arrived 20 minutes later, Crooked-fin was clearly raring to go, edging out, looking for that moment to make her escape, but Bibi turned and rushed out at her. Twenty minutes later she found her chance and bolted; the males' fluke prints traced 10° angles on either side of hers. As we had seen before, they were cutting off her escape routes. She didn't make it, and after they returned with her, Bibi was very attentive and popping a lot.

Over the course of the three days, we had seen Poindexter and Crooked-fin herded twice each with three partner changes among the males: Snubby and Sickle with Poindexter, then Sickle and Bibi with

Poindexter, then Snubby and Bibi with Crooked-fin, and then Sickle and Bibi with Crooked-fin!

Sickle and Bibi remained paired through the 30th, herding Crooked-fin and two other females, one for eight days. Snubby would not be idle the whole time. On the 26th he paired up with Shave again to herd Poindexter for the day.

We were roaming offshore looking for dolphins on the 30th when we spied a rowdy social group; it was Snubby, Sickle and Bibi with Surprise, whom they had evidently just captured. They were all very excited, chasing along and surfacing with great enthusiasm around their new prize as a unified trio. Or so it seemed, until Snubby suddenly stopped and just sat there at the surface, whistling, while the others carried merrily along. I kept looking back; he just sat there, for two full minutes. As we moved steadily away, Snubby went down briefly and then came back to the surface, oriented our way, but not moving. I don't know if dolphins pout, but if they do it would explain Snubby just sitting there, having been excluded from all the fun, watching his "friends" carry on without him. And fun they did have with a series of double mounts on Surprise from either side. But Snubby wouldn't have long to feel sorry for himself. The next afternoon we watched Snubby and Sickle capture Surprise again.

The relationships among Snubby, Sickle and Bibi were a continuing soap opera and, I must say, a very entertaining one! But why did they travel around as a trio if only two worked together to herd a female while excluding the third? And what about the other trios we knew, like CBL and TBC; did they also have an alternating odd-male-out?

§

Told Off by Slash

I knew I was in for an exciting follow on 24 June when I found the old male Slash alone. But you never know what interesting things might happen once you start a follow. Slash was obviously a male, based on his behavior, but I wanted to "officially" sex him by getting a good look at his genitals. Females have mammary slits and no space between their genital and anal slits, and males have a nice gap between slits. Of course, we can sex a female when they have an infant and sometimes males are more obvious. As Slash started chasing a fish belly-up, I saw an opportunity so we moved in closer for a better view. I sexed him as male, but I also disrupted his chase as the fish escaped under our boat. Slash swam over to the boat, tilted to his side and looked right up at me for about five seconds and then head-jerked sideways at me with an open mouth! He moved off and I stood there dumb-founded. I never had any inkling that the dolphins distinguished us from the boat we were in; in fact, I had never given it much thought at all. But Slash had threatened me! I felt guilty and gave him all the bow-rides he wanted for the rest of the follow. We are only with particular dolphins a tiny fraction of their lives, and I'm sure our presence is often mildly irritating, but they do enjoy the bow-rides; dolphins often like to lounge on the bow at very slow speeds.

The other startling observation of the day happened when Slash and Crinkles started blasting toward a group of leap-feeding dolphins over 500 meters ahead. By the time they arrived things had died down, but then the group ahead was herding a school of fish into the shallows and back out, leap-feeding again. Slash and Crinkles just sat there and watched. Why didn't they join in? Were they not allowed? A bit later they moved away and started leap-feeding on their own, so they were clearly hungry. Occasional observations such as this indicate that the dolphins may, sometimes, exclude others from feeding with them.

§

Starving Dolphins

The soap opera of relationships among the Beach Boys and their buddies Wave & Shave was going full tilt as July ended and we moved into August. After capturing Surprise the day before, Snubby and Sickle came in with her on the morning of 1 August. Snubby was the main guard; he got only a few fish, until Surprise escaped, then he plowed into the beach and got more fish than anybody. On the 3rd, Sickle and Bibi came in together with no female, and a bit later Snubby and Wave came in with Munch. When they all left together, we decided to follow them. As we went in the direction they had traveled, we saw an intense social group blasting along, including a huge synchronous leap by two dolphins. When we finally caught up we saw Munch, but now she was with TBC and RH, who had the female Nip. Incredible; what had happened? Had Munch escaped from the Beach Boys and been recaptured or did the other males steal her? I wished that we had been a little quicker getting offshore.

Trips was popping a lot. Munch responded immediately each time and in an incredibly stereotyped fashion; she would approach Trips from the right, swim under him mid-flank and rub her right side along his left flipper. This sequence was repeated numerous times. Then Munch's 2-year-old infant Lunch showed up and Munch started ignoring Trips' commands to approach, but went unpunished. I glanced at Lunch and did a double-take. The sight of him was shocking; Lunch was emaciated, sunken in behind the head and under the dorsal fin. He kept trying to

Lunch was visibly emaciated (note how large his head appears relative to his body) as he surfaced in "infant position" beside his mother, Munch, on the last day we saw him in 1987. © Dolphin Alliance Project

nurse from his mother but was clearly not going to survive. After a while they let Munch escape; she bolted, but TBC just sat there snagging at the surface, watching her go.

That was the last time we saw Lunch. In fact, Munch never had an infant survive to independence. We used to joke that we had jinxed Munch by our choice of names for her infants, "Lunch," "Slurp," "Mayhem" etc., but Munch was not unique; some females just have a hard time in Shark Bay.

Back inshore at Monkey Mia the next morning, there was another partner switch as Snubby and Sickle came in with Crooked-fin, but she bolted and escaped the moment the fish buckets came down. Later offshore we found Snubby and Bibi herding Yan. Sickle was there but now he was paired up with Pointer, and Wave was with Lucky. They let Yan go after a short while and everybody turned their attention to Pointer, with up to three males trying to mount him at once. I got a great look at Sickle mounting Pointer, and could clearly see his penis pushing into Pointer's genital area. On the morning of the 5th it was back to Snubby and Sickle who came in with Crooked-fin; she was clearly an easy mark given that she spent most of her time just west of the park. She bolted again and Snubby chased her almost immediately this time and Sickle followed a few seconds later. But then the fish buckets came down, and after Bibi got a few fish, Sickle and Snubby came zipping back in without Crooked-fin. Clearly fish was their priority this morning. Sickle and Snubby did return in the early afternoon with Joy's Friend, but Bibi wasn't with them.

Later, out in the boat, we saw some dolphins porpoising so we went over for a look. Snubby, Sickle and Bibi were there, with nobody else around. Their behavior was just bizarre. All three were side by side, touching. They were sardines again, but this time they were turning in tight little circles. Bibi was on the outside, with his flipper, unmoving, seemingly glued to Sickle's right side, below and behind Sickle's flipper. Around and around they went, one, two, then three times. They went down, with Bibi's flipper still plastered against Sickle's side, but two minutes later Snubby and Sickle were petting furiously. Wave, Lucky and Pointer were just ahead, and as SSB approached, they were again very tight side by side with Sickle in the center. Then, in perfect synchrony, they turned left, then right, then left; I was reminded of a Tango. Another tight circle followed, with Snubby in the middle this time, his face was pressed against Bibi's. Snubby then got "squeezed" out and fell behind as Bibi's flipper was plastered against Sickle's side. Then

Sickle and Snubby were again petting. Suddenly it clicked, what all this weird behavior was about. These three males were competing to be part of the pair; the outcome of this circling, touching and petting would determine who would catch and herd the next female together. Amazing.

Now, as they moved along, with Wave, Lucky and Pointer, the outcome was clear: Snubby and Sickle were still a pair, traveling side-by-side and surfacing synchronously and petting a lot. Bibi was tight with Wave. Lucky was with his pal Pointer, but they left shortly. It was fascinating to consider why Bibi was on the outside of the circle touching Sickle; was he trying to partner with Sickle, who was turning away from him and staying next to Snubby?

Over two hours later, a rapid succession of chases signaled that Snubby and Sickle had found their female. It was Chicklet, and she was clearly in no mood to be herded. Equally clear was the importance that Snubby and Sickle placed on maintaining their fragile partnership by herding her. The result of that conflict was a sequence of bolting, chasing, charging, hitting, mounting and displays that covered 5 miles during the next hour and a half. The aggression was intense and the displays were spectacular. They leapt out, over 2 meters high, in opposite directions, then again at a 70° angle. Ten minutes later another leap-out in opposite directions, then they porpoised out and synchronously slapped their snouts on the water on the way down. More synchronous "roll-outs" and "porp-outs" followed. There was a beautiful leap going in opposite directions, crossing side by side at the apex of their leaps. Throughout all of this, Bibi and Wave just followed and watched.

The photographs I took of the synchronous displays were absolutely amazing. I had two synchronously leaping dolphins expertly framed and in perfect focus. These astounding pictures would appear in *National Geographic*, I was sure of that. I was positively giddy as I continued clicking away, capturing one great display after another. Picture number 35, click, number 36, click, number 37… number 38… uh oh. There were only 36 pictures in a roll. My "high" was replaced instantly with dread as the film kept "winding" forward. I realized the film had never even caught when I loaded it – I had been too hasty in my excitement. I had no pictures. Damn.

Snubby and Sickle brought Chicklet in on 6 August but she was not with them on the 7th or 8th. On the 9th the boys had her again, but this time she was with Sickle and Bibi. She was in very close to the beach and people standing in the shallows. It seemed odd that she would be so "tame." Then I saw why: Chicklet was starving. Like Lunch, Chicklet had a distinctive "neck" and her flanks were hollowed out under her dorsal fin. That also explained her stubborn resistance to the males the other day. She knew that she could not afford to be herded, especially by these guys. I'm sure she remembered her earlier experiences of being herded into Monkey Mia, forced to sit in the shallows and watch, hungry, while the males were stuffed with fish by tourists.

It was completely unnatural for a female to be trapped inshore like this, unable to hunt. During consortships offshore, the female may be led away from her typical feeding areas but she can still fish. A common male behavior during consortships is simply "follow the fishing female;" she hunts while they follow along. In Chicklet's condition, being herded by the Beach Boys into Monkey Mia could be fatal. We decided to intervene.

I waded out with a bucket to see if she would take some fish. I offered the first one to her underwater; she took it eagerly. She would take a fish, turn away to swallow it, circle back around and nudge me insistently with her snout. Hunger had quickly cured her of any fear of people. I had given her eight fish, and was about to hand her another one, when the tourists came traipsing down with fish buckets, and the boys rushed into the beach. Chicklet took advantage of the moment and shot offshore. Bibi was after her in a second but she got away. We were thrilled for her. On 18 August Bibi and Wave herded Chicklet into Monkey Mia (Snubby and Sickle had a different female). I fed her over 30 fish; she was more than eager to take them: she was downright frantic. Chicklet survived her ordeal. When we saw Chicklet again in 1988 her flanks and neck had filled back in. She was back to normal.

§

"This is Like Science Fiction!"

The TBC-RH-CBL triangle had continued to surprise. We found Real

Notch and Hi herding Nip on 26 July in the company of a remarkable "mixed" pair, Trips and Bottomhook, who were herding a female. That was a first! Then, after being with TBC on 3 August they were back with CBL, who had another female, on the 7th. On the 11th we were treated to spectacular inter-alliance displays, likely because Real Notch and Hi, now with Nip for a record 17 days, were with CBL, who did not have a female of their own. It started with a pair synchronously slapping their "chins," then their flukes, on the water in rapid succession. Then two inter-alliance pairs executed two splendid synchronous double roll-outs on either side of Nip; Chop with Hi on one side and Real Notch with Bottomhook on the other. Such synchrony between alliances was extremely rare; we were blown away!

Another member of my Ph.D. committee, Barb Smuts, arrived on the 17th. Barb had done an important study on baboons, showing that females had male "friends" that would help protect them and their infants. Barb decided to visit after hearing rave reviews from Richard Wrangham and Irv DeVore, that the Shark Bay dolphins were a "must see." She came with considerable insights into data collection methods and a wonderful dose of good luck.

On the morning of the 18th Sickle and Snubby were in with Waverly for the third day and Bibi and Wave showed up with Chicklet. Waverly bolted, and only Sickle and Snubby pursued her; when Chicklet bolted, only Bibi and Wave chased her. On the water with Barb in the late morning, we found CBL with Holey-fin and Holly, and Real Notch and Hi with Munch. They did a lot of nothing for the first four hours, but my, how things can liven up in a heartbeat! The group was lazing along, petting each other; Real Notch with Hi, Chop with Holey-fin. We spotted a leaping group of dolphins over a kilometer ahead. Munch was petting Chop. Huge side-slapping breaches erupted in the group ahead; our group launched toward them, full-speed, leaping and porpoising. I spotted Holey-fin at a distance, calmly traveling away from us toward Monkey Mia. Our group caught up to the other group; there was TBC! Intense aggression erupted; they were whirling around underwater; someone was after Chop, biting him on the side. Bottomhook and Chop pursued another. Nip and Tuck were here! Suddenly TBC were gone. Two were biting the tail of another; Lambda and Real Notch were biting Munch. Chop and Lambda did a tango, then Bottomhook went nuts; he started a rooster strut then rolled over slapping his tail, his head arching wildly up and down.* There were a few more displays; we saw a mount attempt and the intense social activity gradually abated. CBL had Nip. This was incredible! CBL had apparently stolen Nip from TBC! The great leaping we had seen was probably TBC capturing Nip, then our guys raced up there to take her. Had Real Notch and Hi helped? Could they have helped while they were herding Munch? Regardless, it was an exceptional day. I could not have imagined that the next day would be even better.

The next morning, 19 August, Holey-fin came inshore. The Beach Boys were extremely excited, swimming around her, doing chin-slap displays. Snubby and Sickle were clearly still paired. Suddenly Trips and Bite, of TBC fame, appeared in the shallows. This was extraordinary; they had never come into Monkey Mia. We readied ourselves to document a fight. Trips and Bite sat at the surface oriented toward the Beach Boys with Holey-fin. Sickle and Snubby were in formation behind Holey-fin and did a synchronous turn-out right behind her. Trips and Bite moved in closer, now to within a mere four meters. Nothing happened. Trips and Bite turned offshore and left. Oh well, that was anti-climactic. My adrenalin fell back to baseline levels, but I decided that we should follow them offshore; maybe this show wasn't over. We got out quickly and found them over a kilometer north of Monkey Mia, with Cetus, Real Notch, Hi and Munch. TBC had not been wasting time as they already had Yogi and Boo! Yogi bolted. Only TBC chased and they caught her quickly amidst intense rowdy splashing. Real Notch and Hi then got in formation behind Yogi, followed by petting between Hi and Trips and then between Trips and Real Notch. We had seen that sequence of events before!† The males were excited around Yogi for a bit longer, then things settled down and she was gone. Then all five males and Munch turned south.

There were many synchs as they cruised steadily along, Trips and Cetus and Real Notch and Hi. Both pairs surfaced synchronously several times with Bite out of step between them. There were even several triple

---

We later named this the "apeshit" display.
† See "An Alliance Triangle"

synchs by TBC. Twenty minutes had elapsed since they let Yogi go. Some of the synchs were now between alliances, Cetus and Real Notch, Real Notch and Trips, Hi and Cetus, Trips and Hi, as they turned right toward Monkey Mia. Barb had the video camera going. We drew closer to shore. I motioned frantically with my walkie-talkie to Andrew who was standing on the beach. I told him who we were with and to get ready for all hell to break loose. Rachel was standing in the shallows recording with her hydrophone.

Trips and Cetus bolted forward from the group toward Monkey Mia but turned immediately back again. Snubby, Sickle and Bibi were about 8 meters from shore near the jetty. Suddenly our group charged into Monkey Mia and the shallows exploded with thrashing, fighting dolphins, moving rapidly down the park, veering wildly among the moored boats. We sped down the beach offshore of the dolphins, catching up just as they porpoised rapidly out from the shallows; Holey-fin was with TBC and RH! "Andrew!," I shouted into the walkie-talkie, "this is unreal, they got Holey-fin, they went in there and stole her, this is like science fiction!"

It wasn't over. The TBC-RH group was highly animated with Trips and Cetus pursuing Holey-fin. Snubby and Sickle surfaced right behind them, then fell back 10 meters. Snubby and Sickle turned away from the TBC group, then immediately back toward them. Trips and Cetus turned back toward Snubby, Sickle and Bibi, then back toward the rest. Then TBC and RH all turned back toward SSB. Cetus was incredibly excited, jumping around all over the place. They sped up, leaping north, away from SSB, who were racing up from behind. TBC and RH turned back toward SSB, who turned and fled a short distance before turning back and approaching again. Then TBC and RH turned and charged SSB, who fled immediately. The TBC group turned back north, and Bibi porpoised forward while Snubby was racing around our boat, clearly beside himself with excitement. As the TBC group porpoised away, there were huge side-slapping "victory" breaches like we had seen in the distance yesterday. SSB remained in hot pursuit at a comfortable distance. TBC and RH turned west, leaping along, leaving SSB further and further behind. SSB slowed down as we could see more huge leaps in the group ahead. As we went to catch up to the TBC group, we saw

SSB heading slowly back to Monkey Mia, engaged in that same sardine behavior with all three very tight together and one on his side flailing his tail. It looked like they were having another dispute over who would be paired with whom.

We stayed with TBC, RH and their females for the next six hours. There was a huge number of synchs, with quite a few inter-alliance synchs before settling into their normal pattern. Rachel kept tabs on SSB. When they returned to Monkey Mia the outcome of their pair dispute was clear: there had been a partner switch. Sickle and Bibi were now tight. SSB then left Monkey Mia and, perhaps feeling brave, came out looking for TBC and RH. They had clearly located us several hundred meters ahead as they excitedly porpoised our way, but they approached no closer than 200 meters. Snubby seemed to want to keep approaching, but Sickle and Bibi, side by side, kept turning back. Evidently, they gave up the idea of getting Holey-fin back, changed direction and went off to capture Poindexter, whom they brought into Monkey Mia the next morning.

Poindexter's escape three days later was fascinating. She bolted, the boys chased, but she was quickly back inshore while they were looking around for her in the channel. Nicky and Puck got on either side of her, and all three moved swiftly northeast away from the park. They lingered out in the channel until the boys came back in (prompted by fish buckets of course) and then swam slowly west into Red Cliff Bay. To my eyes it certainly looked like Nicky and Puck had aided and abetted Poindexter's escape. We have seen very few cases of females cooperating against males, so any hint of such behavior commands our attention!

The events of 19 August were repeated nine days later on 28 August, albeit with much less drama. Again, Holey-fin came in from her offshore consortship, and Sickle and Bibi immediately became very excited around her, popping and displaying. And again, Trips and Bite, with Cetus this time, came into the shallows, lingered a bit and left. After they left, all eyes were glued offshore and the video camera and boat were ready to go. We knew what was going to happen. An hour after TBC left, we spotted fins approaching from the northwest. SSB and Holey-fin oriented that way, and slowly moved offshore toward the approaching group. Rowdy porpoising, leaping and chasing erupted as we scrambled to my boat. When we caught up, we had TBC with Holey-fin, Real Notch and Hi with Munch, but no SSB. They had not put up nearly as much of a fuss this time. But TBC and RH were certainly excited to have Holey-fin back as the intense social activity continued for some time. As before, there were a lot of inter-alliance synchs in the period right after the theft.

September would offer more insight into the function of the "alliances of alliances." Real Notch and Hi were paired with TBC for most of the month and usually both had females. When they were not in the same group, they would shadow each other, often not right together but within shouting distance. They weren't together to help each other steal females; they already had consorts. It was now getting into the peak mating season and theirs was a defensive formation. We noticed also that some tough looking alliances had moved south into the northern reaches of Red Cliff Bay. We saw the B-boys and the rough looking Sharkies, who seemed friendly with the B-boys. Real Notch, Hi and TBC seemed to lurk for extended periods deep in Red Cliff Bay. I suspected that they weren't thrilled with the idea of running into those other alliances, as they laid low and kept their friends nearby. We finally found CBL with RH again in early October. TBC had been herding Goblin since 25 September. We saw them together with Real Notch and Hi, who had no female on 1 October. On 2 October, we found Real Notch and Hi possibly herding Two-scoops, but now with CBL, who had Goblin. Then the next day, we found CBL alone and Real Notch and Hi with TBC and, you guessed it, Goblin! Another indication, I thought, that Real Notch and Hi were playing TBC and CBL off against each other.

19 August 1987 stands forever as the most important and exciting day in the history of the dolphin research in Shark Bay. It could not have been a more perfect day. There was no wind, so the bay was like glass. Trips and Bite had come in early but had not engaged SSB. They clearly went out and recruited RH to help, and RH did help, even though they already had a female consort. Rachel recorded the aggressive sounds inshore during the fight and followed SSB afterwards to document the behavior of the vanquished.

The theft of Holey-fin revealed clearly for the first time that in our dolphin society there were not just alliances, but alliances of alliances.

We had discovered earlier that pairs and trios were about herding females, now we knew that the relationships between pairs and trios were about stealing females. We started calling the pairs and trios "first-order" alliances and first-order alliance friends like RH & TBC "second-order" alliances. The only other species with such nested male alliances is our own, an ability that we have extrapolated in modern society to alliances between nation states. Humans have the biggest brains, relative to body size, on the planet. Most primatologists and others were lining up behind the idea that complex social relationships, including alliances, were the driving force behind large brain evolution. Dolphins have the largest relative brain size after humans, and we had just documented that they had human-like nested male alliances. To me, what we witnessed on that day was absolutely mind-blowing, hence my "science-fiction" comment to Andrew that was later immortalized when Barb's video of the theft was spliced into a NOVA television documentary about our research.*

A second-order alliance, composed of a pair and a trio, resting ("snagging") at the surface. © Dolphin Alliance Project

*NOVA: *The Private Lives of Dolphins, *1992*

§

Dolphins Burning

Holey-fin was back "on" in a big way as September drew to a close. Sickle and Bibi had come in with Joy's Friend early. A bit later, Snubby came in alone and started following Holey-fin around. Bibi and Sickle left for a time and came back without Joy's Friend, and all three started following Holey-fin. Sickle and Bibi were clearly still "the pair" but Snubby was into it as well. A bit later, to our great surprise, Holey-fin turned toward Sickle from about 4 meters away and basically told him to get lost. She started head-jerking at him and making donkey-like "hee-haw" sounds that we knew well as an aggressive vocalization. Sickle had been underwater when she started bitching so we don't know what he said to set her off. I would not be surprised if he had just popped at her one time too many. Holey-fin was like that with people also; she was usually very gentle but she had a clear threshold. Unfortunately, when someone pushed her "last button" it was not the offender but the next innocent to extend a hand who got chomped. She moved toward Sickle; he had only bitched back a little, but nothing happened. And it certainly didn't settle him down. His excitement grew until he seemed to go berserk, performing what amounted to a rooster strut on steroids. Instead of simply arching and bobbing his head, Sickle was arching half his body out of the water while on his side or belly, whistling intensely and tail-flailing at the same time; back-slaps, side-slaps and tail-slaps punctuated his display, as he careened all over the place. We call this the "apeshit" display.* One definition of "apeshit" I found was, "an undignified loss of control," and that is certainly what an apeshit display looks like to human observers. Perhaps Holey-fin was impressed, but she didn't show it. A few minutes later Sickle and Bibi performed a "butterfly display." Quite unlike the apeshit display, a butterfly display is beautiful and seems exquisitely choreographed as the males perform synchronous figure eights (the wings) on either side of the female (the body of the butterfly).

---

* *The display by Bottomhook described in "This is Like Science Fiction" was also an apeshit display.*

Sickle and Bibi continued to consort Holey-fin for the next several days. Sickle would follow her around like a puppy. On 2 October we saw Puck just offshore with two eastern males that we didn't know well; so she was also being consorted. 6 October turned into a comic opera with the return of Puck from her dalliance. The boys immediately dumped Holey-fin for Puck and there was a partner change as well, as Snubby was now with Sickle. Puck bolted and was caught, but escaped later, and Sickle and Snubby turned right back to Holey-fin. Sickle then abandoned Snubby and left. Snubby popped at Holey-fin, but she left in the other direction. He followed a short distance but soon gave up. We saw why Sickle had left when we saw him following Bibi and Shave back in. They now had Puck! She managed to escape again, flying right past Snubby and Sickle as she went. Bibi and Shave gave chase but it was too late. The next day, Snubby and Sickle had Holey-fin, but Puck elicited no interest from the boys.

The tide was extremely low on the morning of 8 October. When the tide is that low the banks beyond the channel in front of Monkey Mia become connected to the shore by an exposed sandbar just east of the park. The Beach Boys and their females always swam over those shallows after leaving Monkey Mia as they headed southeast, their "hiding place," to avoid you-know-who in Red Cliff Bay. On this morning they had not dared to go around the banks, which would have brought them to Monkey Mia, right through Red Cliff Bay. They showed up later after the tide turned; Sickle and Snubby with Holey-fin, and Bibi and Wave now, instead of Shave, with a female. Bibi, the odd-male-out among the Beach Boys, was perhaps now playing Wave and Shave off each other.

9 October was a big day. Edwin Snider, with The Center for Research and Exploration at The National Geographic Society, was coming for a site visit! We had heard through Richard Wrangham that The National Geographic Society considered ours to be one of their top two projects! I really wanted to make a good impression and for everything to go well. I pulled the stick-on name, "Phucifino" off my boat. People would study the name quizzically, fumble with the pronunciation, and then ask what it meant. I responded with a different pronunciation and all enjoyed a hearty laugh. But I thought a bit more decorum was in order for a visit by the man that held the key to past and future funding for our project.

Ed was staying in town, so we drove in for a nice dinner with him at the pub.

The boys did not show up the next morning. By noon the tide had come in so I knew something had happened. Then Bibi wandered in, and a bit later Snubby and Sickle without Holey-fin. We took Ed Snider out and found Holey-fin, and as I expected, she was with Real Notch and Hi. They were with TBC who had Blip. We saw a big chase under a kilometer away so we blasted over, thinking the Beach Boys were causing trouble. To our surprise it was Lucky, Lodent, Pointer (LLP) and another juvenile male, Prima, and they "had" Crooked-fin and Two-scoops! What? These youngsters, and the runty Lucky, herding adult females? It wasn't clear if they were trying to herd one or both females. Pointer came to the surface, snagged and started popping. He got no reaction from either female. Shortly, Nicky, Puck and an unfamiliar mother/infant pair joined ours. The female and infant departed after a few minutes, but Nicky and Puck remained in a tight group with Crooked-fin and Two-scoops in front of the males. There was no further indication of the males trying to herd the females. Maybe that was their original idea, but they had given up on it quickly, perhaps because of the arrival of female reinforcements.*

The Beach Boys were in early on the morning of the 11th and Snubby and Sickle had a female in tow. While I was taking data, I noticed that Sickle and Snubby had some kind of skin problem along their sides, so the rangers asked the tourists to not touch them. The female bolted and escaped when fish buckets distracted the males. I left and was returning to the beach with Ed to introduce him to the dolphins when two rangers came running up and said that Holey-fin was "bubbling up all over." The sight of her was horrible and frightening. There were huge bubbles of skin on her head, and behind that a large area of skin had sloughed off and was hanging loose. Holey-fin had been burned by the sun. Holly had burns in a strip right along the top of her back. Bibi had some burns as well. All I could muster to say to Ed was that we wouldn't be going out today. I spent much of the rest of the day talking to marine mammal vets all over the place.

*We have not seen overt cooperative aggression by females against adult males, but females may cooperate to thwart harrassment by younger males as described here and in "A Female Coalition" and in more subtle ways --- See how Nicky and Puck helped Poindexter escape in "This is Like Science Fiction."

How and when had it happened? They must have become stranded on the banks during low tide the previous day; it takes a while for blisters to appear. These dolphins know these waters and tides too well, they would not have just cruised into shallow water and stranded. Something dramatic must have happened. I thought about the previous day, how nobody had shown up until well after noon and how we had found Holey-fin with Real Notch and Hi. The boys must have become impatient during the morning and tried to go around the banks via Red Cliff Bay, but then ran into their nemesis. Panicked, they probably tried to flee across the banks to Monkey Mia but didn't make it. Holey-fin, being herded and hence in front of the boys, would have been stuck in the shallowest water, explaining why her burns were so much worse than the others. Her daughter was beside her, but being smaller only the strip along her back was exposed. The males were likely flopped on their sides behind the females in slightly deeper water, thus the spotty burns on their sides. When the tide came back in, Real Notch and Hi were there with TBC to take Holey-fin. It all fit together. I looked at Snubby, Sickle and Bibi with more than a little disgust. You idiots!

A vet came down from Carnarvon, the town across the bay to the north. He said the burns were only second degree, which was some relief. The bubbles had peeled off. Holey-fin was missing the skin along one side from the middle of her melon back to her dorsal fin. The vet fed Holey-fin a fish with antibiotics that evening. Their behavior didn't seem too unusual but Holly lacked her usual pep. The next morning Sickle and Snubby were still herding Holey-fin! Snubby popped, head-jerked and charged her once. She looked hideous. I gave her a fish with antibiotics; the vet had left a "prescription" for a five-day course of pills. Ed Snider left that afternoon; for better or worse, he had certainly experienced some dolphin drama. On the 13th, Holey-fin did not come in with the boys so I went to look for her offshore but didn't find her. The next morning Holey-fin came in with Holly early, before the others, and then left after a few minutes. She did not return. Clearly, she did not want to be inshore with the boys, who continued to herd other females, and I suspect she didn't want to be around people either. We found her offshore and gave her the medicated fish, then as many fish as she would take, but she would only eat a few. With that Holey-fin and I fell into a pattern; I would meet her early with a bucket of fish, before the rangers showed up for work and before any other dolphins arrived. Then I would find her offshore a few hours later for another feed. She would only take five to six fish during each "session." As the vets had instructed, I had thawed the fish out in fresh water. They said with her skin barrier broken, Holey-fin would be vulnerable to dehydration. But I think Holey-fin was wearing an adaptation that addressed that problem. The red-raw exposed dermis was now covered with a layer of thick yellow mucous and that mucous layer may have acted as a temporary "skin" keeping the water in. There were red splotches in the yellow mucous, leading my assistant, Leslie Sharky, to comment that Holey-fin looked like "a tomato and cheese pizza with extra cheese." I split my sides on that one; I needed a good laugh.

On the 17th I got 24 fish into Holey-fin; in batches of six to seven. Holly's wound was healing fast but not Holey-fin's. In one extended morning session on the 20th Holey-fin ate 26 fish; she was coming around! On 24 October, two weeks after she was burned, Holey-fin ate 45 fish and I knew that she would be okay. From that point, I turned her care over to the rangers.

Eventually, new skin filled in about half of the burned area; the rest remained white scar tissue for the rest of her life. Upon her death in 1995*, we retrieved her body, and a model was created, replicating her scar. Visitors can see the model at Monkey Mia.

§

"You Killed Spike!"

Holey-fin wasn't the only dolphin medical crisis we were dealing with at the time. I had traveled to Perth in early September to buy the first in a series of "vintage" recreational vehicles, or "caravans," that would free us permanently from tent living. Shortly after I returned, on 11 September, a woman approached me with news of a dolphin that "didn't look good" and who was "acting strange." The dolphin had bumped into her boat - while the boat was moored. That did not sound good. I found the

* See "The Death of Holey-Fin"

dolphin in the shallows at the west end of the park. It was Spike and she was right, he looked terrible. Yet another starving dolphin, poor Spike was gaunt, with a visible neck, and his flanks were horribly sunken-in. Just sitting there with his eyes closed, surrounded and being touched by people in the shallows, he seemed very weak. Even though Spike had never been a "beach dolphin," he clearly wanted fish. The beach dolphins were often fed from boats and no doubt he had learned that trick. Now he had come into the shallows seeking more. I went back to get some fish for him as he meandered away from the park. He eagerly took the 20 fish we offered after catching up to him in my boat. But he seemed out of it, disoriented. He cut his dorsal fin on my 5 hp motor. It didn't seem to bother him. We fetched six more fish that Rachel had been carrying along the beach as she walked parallel to us in the boat. Again, Spike bumped into the bottom of my boat. What was wrong with him? Another trip and we fed Spike 15 more; but the last ones he ate much more slowly. Small wonder; we had fed him over 40 fish.

Spike was a very old dolphin who was clearly on his last "fins." Without our intervention, he would not last long. Spike seemed a sweet old guy, so I thought we could easily add him to the crew of beach dolphins and extend his life a bit. Clearly, it would be a win-win situation. The next day we found Spike near the park and gave him another 15 fish. Two days later we saw him again but this time we didn't have any fish. I reached into the water and he gummed my hand, his front teeth long ago worn to the nub. By the 16th, after stuffing him with 30 bony herring, the transition was complete. Spike was a beach dolphin now and stayed close to the park where he was fed. But when hand-feeding Spike, it was clear that something was still seriously amiss. I could see him orient to the fish and hear his sonar clicks, but he didn't seem to locate the fish in the water directly in front of his mouth; I had to practically stick it inside. And to make matters worse, he didn't seem to be getting better or gaining weight. One of the men who came up with his family every year for the school holidays said he had found Spike stranded at low tide on a sand bar west of the park. He had returned Spike to the water. Now, no two men could lift one of our adult male dolphins; they are solid, heavy animals. But Spike was emaciated.

So when the veterinarian from Carnarvon was down for the Holey-fin crisis, I spoke with him about Spike. Since we were slipping antibiotics into fish for Holey-fin we decided to do the same for Spike. Then the wheels started spinning and I had what I thought was a brilliant idea. Since we had been feeding Spike a lot of fish and he kept getting thinner, maybe he had worms! Maybe Spike's health was so compromised that he had lots of worms and was unable get enough nutrition from the fish we were feeding to him. Maybe we could "worm" Spike and give him a new lease on life. What did my new vet friend think of my clever idea? Well, in fact, he thought it was reasonable. However, all he had was some medication for horses(!) but we could give that a try. The stuff was like toothpaste so I squeezed out the amount he recommended into the gullet of a fish and fed it to Spike.

The next morning, 14 October, I was standing by the water with Tony, the head ranger. All the dolphins were in, but not Spike. We both looked around for a few minutes, then Tony turned to me, exclaiming, with a great big grin plastered across his face, "You killed Spike!" Tony was laughing; he thought it was hysterical. He knew that Spike was a goner anyway and that the whole exercise had been futile.

My heart sank. He was probably right. I suddenly imagined Spike having a horrible reaction to the horse medication; cramping terribly, in agony, shitting himself to death. I found myself hoping that he had been killed quickly by one of the large sharks that had been seen near the park that week. I felt awful.

§

Reliving Old Glories

We went offshore early on 29 October and found Snubby and Shave with Yogi and Boo. The boys entertained us with some of the most striking butterfly displays that I have ever seen. I should have just described the physical moves but I could not stop myself from spilling out superlatives: "beautiful synch by Snubby and Shave; they are in front of her and they turn around beautifully, then go behind her, then turn out in beautiful synchrony behind her, then go back forward again." And so on it went, like watching a ballet; I wanted to applaud and shout "bravo" after each perfectly executed maneuver. For two males that did not have a huge amount of experience "working together" they certainly knew what they were doing. Maybe they felt that they had to go the extra mile to impress Yogi, or perhaps they were testing each other.

The Gerries, Slash, Crinkles and Chunk, joined our group. There would be some mellow petting now I thought, but suddenly the group exploded in a chase, everybody was leaping along, intense splashing and bashing! We saw two other dolphins racing in to join from the side and all hell broke loose with splashing, synchronous porpoising and general chaos. Suddenly two were snagging away from the group; it was Snubby and Shave! We had just seen a theft! I predicted out loud that it was Steps and Kodoff who had come to help their elderly buddies take Yogi. The victors were still racing along, very excited, tail slapping and leaping. We caught up; it wasn't Steps and Kodoff, but two males we didn't know! One of the strangers was side by side with Slash and the other was with Crinkles. Yogi bolted; Slash, Crinkles and Chunk raced side by side after her with the two strangers behind. They easily caught Yogi and they traveled as a group for the next 25 minutes. Then the two strangers casually left in the same direction from which they had arrived. Slash, Crinkles and Chunk continued to get after Yogi for the better part of an hour and the level of violence took me completely by surprise. They went at Yogi with astonishing intensity, charging and hitting her. Then they stopped, snagged at the surface, popped for 10 seconds and turned away. Yogi moved away from them, slowly at first, then faster and she was gone. The old males sat there, breathing hard; they were completely winded! Then slowly they began traveling again.

The whole episode, which lasted only one hour from start to finish, was completely unexpected. I had come to think that the Gerries were incapable of such aggression. Clearly, I was wrong; but I never saw anything like it again. It was as if they mustered their reserves to engage in behavior that had once been routine for them. They could still do it, but not for long.

Later we learned more about the two males that had joined the theft. Also very old, they were eastern friends of Slash, Crinkles and Chunk, whom we would christen "George" and his boy "Elroy."

The next morning Snubby, Wave and Shave were very tight and clearly looking for trouble; Snubby even did a rooster strut, so we hopped in the boat to follow them. They didn't go far, just across the channel in front of Monkey Mia to the edge of the banks and back. I got it; they were hanging around until the fish buckets arrived. When they did, Snubby rushed in for a feed. We stayed in the channel waiting, then out came Sickle and Bibi and, in a bit, Snubby. Now they were ready for business. They traveled out to the northeast, in the general direction of yesterday's troubles. There were a huge number of synchs, Sickle with Bibi, and mostly Wave with Shave. On they went, as if on a mission. Suddenly they picked up speed; we saw a dolphin 100 meters ahead. Then they were leaping, right past Joy's Friend, whom they had herded twice in September. Intense splashing signaled the capture; it was Yogi! Once they had Yogi they turned back to Monkey Mia. One could not help thinking that she was the target from the beginning. Although Snubby was clearly eager early on, and involved in lots of synchrony with Wave and Shave, once they got underway it was just Wave and Shave synching together, so it wasn't surprising that Sickle and Bibi herded Yogi. They kept her for the next five days.

§

A Stranger in a Strange Land

I was alone the last week of the season. To go out, I'd just toss a cinderblock in the front of the boat to balance her out and I could tootle around and enjoy the solitude. It was very warm and calm on 10 November; the bay was a sheet of glass, so I invited one of the rangers, Christine Weir, a young woman who always seemed cheerful and upbeat, to come along for the ride. We found a couple of female groups; then were surprised by a turtle that approached our boat and started biting at our 18 hp motor (we were running the 6 hp). That was very strange; usually they just pop their heads up for a look and then dive in haste. It must have been turtle mating season as well.

We saw a dolphin in the shallows, arching its flukes up in the oddest manner. The first thought that popped into my head was that we might be about to witness a birth, something never before seen in the wild!

My heart was pounding, but slowly, slowly, I drove the boat into the shallows a good distance from the dolphin. We anchored and watched. No sign it was giving birth, so I got out of the boat and cautiously waded over; the dolphin was in very shallow water and as I got closer, I realized

The stranded "offshore" dolphin. © Dolphin Alliance Project

it was stuck there, sort of stranded with its back exposed. We were still quite far out from the beach, about 200 meters, as the shallows are wide in that area. As I approached I saw that it was…HUGE! This was not one of our dolphins! This beast was much larger than our dolphins; it was from the offshore bottlenose dolphin population. This was incredible; I had never seen one in our study area.

Now I was right beside the animal; what to do? As I started to reach down toward the dolphin's side I could see his eyes open wide in what I'm sure was fear, if not terror. I gently stroked him down the side; he visibly relaxed and closed his eye. Astonishing! Any other animal cornered like that, even Bambi, would have thrashed out savagely at me. The dolphin certainly could have lashed out; we had just been watching it arching that powerful tail into the air. Somehow that one stroke had communicated instantly that I intended no harm. I stroked him a few more times and sprinkled water on his back. I looked him over; the dolphin was dark and had no belly speckles like ours have. He had a blunt wide rostrum and was listing to one side.

Since stroking had been successful, I thought I would try placing my "flipper" against his side, unmoving, in the manner I had seen between Bibi and Sickle during the "sardine" display. We had been seeing that behavior more often this year, especially between females who were being harassed by males. It was visually striking, as one female would station herself next to and slightly behind the other female, with her flipper resting against the other females' side. The two females would swim around like that, often for several minutes. We had taken to calling the behavior "bonding," reflecting the fact that the two dolphins appeared to be "glued together" as much as the obvious role it played in social bonding.*

I gently rested my hand behind and above the dolphin's flipper in the "bonding" position. He put up with it for about 10 seconds, then slapped his tail on the surface, moving forward a bit. Again, that was fascinating. It was not at all an aggressive motion towards me (that would have been a lateral swipe); it was just a mild protest: "don't touch me like that!"

OK, now it was time to have a real close look at this guy and think about the problem at hand: why was he stranded here in the shallows so far from home? Christine and I got out the tape measure; we confirmed that it was a boy, and at 2.7 meters he was a half-meter longer than our largest guys. We talked about what to do next. The dolphin did not look emaciated as it was not sunken in under the dorsal fin. But that didn't mean that he wasn't hungry and thirsty, as they get their fresh water from the fish they eat. I saw nothing else wrong with him so I figured that we might as well try to give him some fish. I didn't think this wild dolphin from another population would eat dead, thawed fish from a human hand but what the hell. I zipped back for some fish. I put the first one in front of his mouth and after a moment's hesitation he took it! He ate the rest eagerly. This guy was hungry! This time Christine went back for more fish. The tide was coming in and the dolphin started to move around a bit. Since it had been stranded in a listing position for so long the muscles on one side weren't working well and it could only swim in little circles. We fed him the rest of the fish and I went back for a third bucket. Christine later revealed that, on my final fish run, she

* See "This Bonding Business"

became quite concerned about the water level rising around her, given that she was so far from shore in the aptly named Shark Bay. By the time I returned the dolphin's circulation was being restored and he was swimming in larger circles in the deeper water, so we fed the last few fish to him from the boat. We just slapped the surface with the fish and he came up and took them. Finally, after an unbelievable 50 fish, he was swimming in a straight line, traveling north up the coast in the direction of his home. Sometimes, to this day, I wonder about him.

Shortly after, I was on my way back to Michigan, but I would be back in eight months for the last big push prior to writing up my Ph.D. thesis. That fall, I prepared a poster, describing the herding behavior, thefts and two alliance levels, to present at the Biennial Marine Mammal Conference in Miami. I was anxious to see how the dolphin research community would react to our exciting new discoveries. Incredibly, for the most part, they did not react at all. Perhaps it was just too new and unfamiliar.

New Insights

1988-1989

Any Female Will Do

I arrived back in Monkey Mia on 6 July 1988 for my last field season before writing up my Ph.D. thesis, but it was going to be a long one, stretching to the end of July 1989 with a five-week break in New Zealand. Rachel had already been here for several months and was keeping tabs on the Beach Boys' misadventures. Mostly Sickle and Bibi had been paired, while Snubby herded females with Wave or Shave. Occasionally Snubby and Bibi had teamed up to herd a female.

On 11 July Snubby and Shave swam in with an unfamiliar female and a brand-new baby that looked to be only a few days old. The still sharp memory came flooding back of that first dramatic case of herding back in March of last year.* Everybody ran down to look at the tiny new baby in the shallows. Barb Smuts, back for a full field season, suggested the Swahili names, Kubwa and Kidogo, which mean nothing more than "big" and "little," but even mundane Swahili words sound very cute to the English-trained ear.

Now, females don't start cycling until their infants are over 2 years old, so it wasn't obvious why males would herd a female with a new infant. We certainly had noticed that the Beach Boys seemed quite forgiving with respect to the reproductive state of the females they herded. Later we demonstrated that females herded by the Beach Boys were less likely to have a calf the next year than females herded by other males. Why herd females that can't get pregnant? Like anything in biology, there is likely more than one correct answer. We can think about what stimulates the males to herd females and what the payoff might be for their own reproduction.

In mammals, females give off signals that they are in estrus. Such

* *See "Breakthrough"*

signals could be a visual cue such as the swollen red rump seen in many female primates or an odor. These cues are produced in response to rising estrogen levels in the bloodstream. We don't know what cues male dolphins look for but they often appear to angle in and inspect the genital area of females; sometimes two males will do so synchronously from either side. Rachel had recorded extremely intense echolocation sounds during genital inspections that sounded like a beehive. It seems possible that males might use echolocation to detect changes in female reproductive tissues associated with estrus or they might taste the water near a female's genitals for chemical cues, or both.

Like females in estrus, females that have just given birth have high estrogen levels. The levels of another hormone, progesterone, are also high during pregnancy, and likely prevent estrus signals from appearing. Progesterone levels crash after birth while estrogen remains high for a while. Perhaps Snubby, Sickle and Bibi were responding to that, but we still have to explain why the Beach Boys were so much less discriminating than other males in the bay, who didn't go around herding females with new babies. An obvious answer is that the Beach Boys' indiscriminate approach to herding was a maladaptive consequence of the free lunch they received at Monkey Mia. When I showed up in July 1988 they looked bloated from the stuffing they received from tourists. Now that type of overfeeding could not be a good thing for the dolphins, so we lobbied for and were able to get a dramatic reduction in the amount of food fed to the beach dolphins. But that did not stop the crazy boys from herding females at a ridiculous rate.

There was another possibility, more indirectly related to the feeding: the fish buckets and female were in opposite directions. The competition for fish required the boys to focus their attention on people entering the water from the beach while the female remained offshore of them, looking for chances to escape. The problem of who was going to guard the female and who was going to feed likely exacerbated conflict among the males, explaining the frequent partner changes and herding of females that were not in estrus. If dolphins could talk, the argument following a female's escape might go something like, "You should have been watching her;" "No jerk, it was your turn." Herding a female together may have been a way for two of the Beach Boys to reinforce their fragile bond, so it needn't always have mattered that the female was in heat. A friend of mine, Susan Perry, reports that the male capuchin monkeys she studies in Costa Rica will often reinforce coalition bonds by jointly threatening an inanimate object, such as a rock or a turd.

§

Role Reversal

We found Bottomhook lounging around with some females on 15 July. They were joined shortly by Wave and Shave with other females. There was intense social behavior and the group splintered in several directions, leaving Bottomhook with Shave. Bottomhook swam up rapidly behind Shave, rubbing along his side, then he mounted him, again and again, as Shave lay passively on his side. Wave was in the area but didn't approach them. It was clear who was dominant to whom! Or was it? Bottomhook left Shave to start fishing and soon we saw Lambda and Chop among the several other dolphins fishing in the area. About an hour later I saw Wave and Shave on an intersecting course with Bottomhook and they joined up again. To my surprise, Shave goosed Bottomhook, who rolled belly-up; then Shave also rolled belly-up and tail-slapped. Shave circled Bottomhook, who lay on his side at the surface. Bottomhook righted himself and Shave approached him with his Pink Floyd fully erect, trying to hook it into Bottomhook's genital slit. Shave approached and mounted Bottomhook a second time and then swam over his rostrum. I saw Shave with his belly against Bottomhook twice more and then Shave mounted Bottomhook a third time. As in the earlier interaction, Wave was off to the side. Probably attracted by the "goings on," Chop and Lambda approached and joined, but Shave and Bottomhook had regained their composure and were no longer misbehaving. Seriously, it was an amazing turn of events; big tough Bottomhook mounting little Shave and then only an hour later their roles were reversed! I recalled the day last year when Sickle was similarly "pursued" by Lucky and Pointer.* Then I had wondered if the presence of CBL had allowed Lucky and Pointer to dominate the older Sickle. But on this day it was

*See "More Fun than Baboons!"

just Bottomhook and Shave, with Wave nearby. A week later we saw little Ceebie, not even 2 years old yet, mounting practically everything in the group that moved, including Cetus and Bite.

It is well known from captivity that even tiny infants will sport erections and mount other dolphins, including their own mother. Little Ceebie was no threat to anyone, so the adult males allowed him to "play" with them as he wished. What was so intriguing about the Bottomhook-Shave affair was that it involved two adult males from different alliances. Still, Shave was much the smaller and younger of the two and not at all a threat to Bottomhook, so they could have a friendly interaction where Bottomhook allowed Shave to be the "mounter" instead of the "mounted."

§

Wave's Bud Spud

On 31 July, I followed Sickle for eight entertaining hours. Initially he was with Bibi and TBC and Pointer and other youngsters, who quickly left as Sickle and Bibi got after Pointer, chasing, goosing and mounting him. I reflected that Pointer seemed to be "it" quite often, but maybe that allowed him to hang out with the big boys; something that might yield payoffs down the road.

Incredibly, Sickle and Bibi started performing beautiful butterfly displays around Pointer, interrupting the choreography on one occasion to mount him synchronously from either side. There were numerous inter-alliance synchs and petting, Trips and Bite with Sickle or Bibi. TBC didn't join in getting after Pointer at first, but later did for a short time.

After an hour of fun with Pointer, they met up with another group, and Sickle and Bibi blasted off after the female Uhf and her infant Muff. Wave and Shave appeared and joined Sickle and Bibi after they captured Uhf while TBC and Pointer lagged behind. The boys turned back toward Monkey Mia and went into the shallows with Uhf, but as soon as the fish buckets arrived Uhf bolted. Sickle and Bibi simply turned and watched her go, but Wave and Shave shot out after her. We followed in the boat and found Wave and Shave alone, but 50 meters away TBC was with Uhf and Joy's Friend. They traveled together for 10 minutes and then Uhf and Joy's Friend slowly ambled away from the males. There was no indication that TBC were herding Uhf so we had to wonder if Uhf had sought refuge with TBC.*

When they left the beach, Sickle traveled with Snubby, Wave and Shave for a time, then just Snubby. Bibi joined and they immediately spread out to fish as they traveled southeast from Monkey Mia. Sickle was fishing alone for a while and then he joined up with an unfamiliar dolphin. They picked up speed and started surfacing synchronously. Five minutes later they blasted after another dolphin and caught her! What was this? Sickle had joined up with a dolphin that was unfamiliar to me to capture a female! All of them seemed afraid of our boat and were evasive, but we managed to get pictures of the two with Sickle. The female bolted three times over the next half-hour. They caught and mounted her and I heard Sickle pop in air once. An hour after they captured her she was gone and Sickle left his strange friend and began fishing again.

What was I to make of this new development? I had never seen a male we knew well pair up with a total stranger to capture a female like that. Maybe they sometimes reinforced bonds with less frequent associates that way.

But when I checked the photographs I realized that I had seen the stranger before. Late in August in 1987 we had found Wave, Shave and the same stranger on the Monkey Mia Banks. I had remarked at the time how interesting it was that Wave and Shave behaved evasively in the company of this strange dolphin. They were with the stranger, so when he moved away from us, they did as well. That is how we were introduced to Spud.

The crazy partner changes among Snubby, Sickle and Bibi that had been the norm for July and August of last year were fully manifest again this year. There were 17 partner changes among SSB during July and August, and we had six of the ten possible pairings among SSB and Wave & Shave.

---

* See "An Alliance Triangle" for another possible case of a female (Crooked-Fin) being protected by one alliance from another.

Perhaps the craziest day of all was 12 August. The day before Snubby and Shave had been herding a female and Sickle and Bibi were tight, but without a female. On the 12th, Snubby and Shave came in with Joy's Friend. She bolted but was recaptured, but by whom? We noted four head-jerks at her by Sickle, but once the fish buckets arrived, she was gone. After the boys were fed, we were treated to another "circle-swim" partner dispute. As in previous cases, the males appeared stuck together, with Sickle on the inside, Bibi in the middle and Snubby on the outside frantically tail-flailing with his chin arched up out of the water. Thus, Sickle and Bibi were effectively turning away from Snubby as they swam in 4- to 5-meter-diameter circles. They moved offshore and we followed in the boat. As expected, Sickle and Bibi were tight side-by-side synching and Snubby was trailing 20 meters behind. So obviously, Sickle and Bibi would capture the next female together. Wrong. They spread out to fish and then came back into the shallows. Two hours later we watched Snubby and Sickle coming back in with Joy's Friend again. Who knows what had happened in the interim. They moved off and came in later with Wave. But Snubby, either excluded or having lost interest, remained inshore when Sickle and Wave left with Joy's Friend. I suppose it is also possible that Joy's Friend had been captured a third time; she was clearly being used as the "male bonding tool" of the day. Snubby then paired up with Bibi in the afternoon. The next morning Sickle and Wave still had Joy's Friend but Snubby and Bibi didn't come in with a female until the 14th. To recap, we had Joy's Friend herded by three pairs in one day: Snubby and Shave, then Sickle and Snubby, then Sickle and Wave. We also had periods where Sickle and Bibi, then Snubby and Bibi were paired without a female.

On 17 August, we hurried offshore to investigate a commotion and found Wave herding Surprise with Spud. Wow, I thought, as if relationships among SSB, Wave and Shave weren't complicated enough already, now we might have to add this guy to the equation! I was giddy just thinking about it. I hoped we would see more of Spud. We did.

Wave and Shave were clearly growing up. On the 18th we found them herding a maturing female all by themselves. Up until this point, they had only herded females with one of the Beach Boys. We were also starting to see Spud more often. He was with Wave and Shave offshore on the 19th and then again on the 21st. Spud was becoming much more relaxed around us as well. I assume that they had known Spud for years; he lived to the southeast, where they traveled often but we went infrequently. His reticence around people and boats had kept him from their company near Monkey Mia, but perhaps his maturation and need for an alliance was forcing the issue now. However, Spud had a lot of speckles, so another possibility was that he was a mature male that had lost a partner and was now seeking a new alliance.

On 7 September Snubby and Bibi were herding a female for a fourth consecutive day, Wave and Shave had Joy, and Sickle came in with a female along with his partner Spud! With Spud in play we had an incredible three pairs of males with females. Initially Spud wouldn't come into the shallows near people but he later steeled himself for the task and swam within two meters of people, but only for a few minutes.

Shave, Sickle and Wave, surfacing synchronously in "sardine" formation on 10 September. Wave was soon excluded from the consortship with Surprise. © Dolphin Alliance Project

Offshore on the 10th we saw a group porpoising and sped over to find Wave, Shave and Sickle with Surprise, whom they had evidently just captured. Snubby and Bibi were there also with the same female they had been herding now for a week. During the next half-hour there was a surprising number (39!) of triple synchs among Wave, Shave and

Sickle, with Sickle or Shave occupying the center position. They were very tight together and often looked to be touching. At one point Wave was trying to angle in toward Surprise's genitals, but Shave and Sickle, very tight side-by-side, appeared to push him away. Later Wave managed to get between Sickle and Shave, but it seemed as if they would not give him room; his flippers were over their backs when they surfaced! Shave and Sickle synched on either side of Wave and did tail-slaps on the way down. They had been moving steadily back toward the park while Snubby's group moved ahead toward the shallows. Wave persisted for about 25 more minutes; then there were no more triple synchs, only Shave and Sickle. Shave and Sickle got after Surprise, popping and charging at her. Wave finally moved off. Sickle and Shave kept Surprise for the next two days. I was fascinated by what we had just seen. Sickle and Shave had not been overtly aggressive to Wave; other than pushing him away from the female, they seemed to just let him know that his presence was not desired. I remembered a similar case from August when we saw Sickle and Bibi "shoulder" Snubby away from a female.

The next time we saw Spud was on September 13th, herding a female with Wave. We had three pairs again as Sickle & Bibi, and Snubby & Shave each had a female consort. Spud didn't become a regular visitor to Monkey Mia, but offshore he was one of the gang. On 16 November, we found the whole group together. Snubby and Sickle were herding a female, Bibi and Shave were acting like a pair and Wave was tight with his bud Spud. They were traveling when we found them, but shortly they increased speed, and then began porpoising toward a group of fishing dolphins. A female with a large infant was the target and after a short chase Wave and Spud had her, but everybody was excited as they charged around after the female. It was in that excitement that Spud really surprised us; he surfaced and then leapt with a sponge on his snout! What? It was a bizarre context for any dolphin to be carrying a sponge, especially a male. I guessed that perhaps the female had dropped the sponge when they captured her and Spud thought it would be fun to parade around with it for a bit.

§

Dolphins and People

If you visit Monkey Mia today you will find the people-dolphin interaction tightly regulated. You are not allowed to touch the dolphins and the only way you can give them a fish is if you are selected by the rangers to do so at feeding time.

People love dolphins. From all corners of the globe, they flock to Monkey Mia to see them. But before the current regulations were instituted, it was often sheer chaos in the shallows. At feeding time, tourists would purchase buckets of fish at the ranger center and everybody, several hundred during the school holidays, would rush into the water. Now it was most important to get that picture of your friend or family member feeding the dolphins and the best picture was one with the dolphin's head out of the water. So hold that fish up higher; no, wait a minute, don't give it the fish yet, the sun is bad from that angle, let me move over here. Now, ok, no wait, that child got in the way, ok, now give it the fish. Damn, the pelican snatched the fish; so try again. While all this crazy feeding was going on, people were trying to touch and pet the dolphins.

To touch a wild dolphin; now there's something everybody wanted to do. People would try to pat the dolphin on the head as they would the family dog. Only the dolphin's blowhole sits on top of their head so, for obvious reasons, they won't tolerate being touched there or anywhere around their head. The rangers explained that to the tourists and encouraged them to only stroke the dolphins gently down their side. But the tourists then reached over the dolphin's head to stroke it down the other side. The dolphin saw a hand reaching over its head and threatened the offending person with a snap of its jaws. The tourist ignored this obvious threat and proceeded, only to get a nasty bite. This scene was repeated daily.

The strange psychology of people in this situation was fascinating and was really driven home to me one day in late August. A burly 60-something Aussie bloke entered the water and approached gentle old Snubby, who was just resting at the surface. Now a dolphin's skin feels like soft rubber and the last thing you would want to do is scratch it. But this old gent didn't know that, and perhaps only having a butch Aussie dog as a reference, he muttered something like "give ya a good scratch" and dug his claws into Snubby's side. Snubby, shocked out of his slumber, lunged a good two feet in the air to clamp his jaws around the man's ample, fleshy bicep. Snubby then ripped away, tearing the man's skin with his back teeth—his front ones were worn flat.

Rivulets of blood streamed down the man's arm. He quickly dunked his arm in the water to wash off the blood and continued to act like he was having fun with the dolphins. The blood kept flowing. "Sir," someone offered, "you should go up to the center and get that taken care of." "It's just a scratch," he replied, quickly dipping his arm again. The blood kept flowing. Finally, with his attempts to conceal the bite having failed miserably, he sheepishly retreated up to the center to have his bite cleaned and bandaged.

Snubby receives a fish while ranger Tom Pepper looks on. © Dolphin Alliance Project

Why do people ignore a dolphin snapping at them, the same threat that would cause them to recoil from a dog? Why did the man work so hard to pretend that he had not been bitten by Snubby? I think it goes something like this. People like to imagine that dolphins are not only very intelligent (they are) but that they are all sweetness and light and incapable of aggression (they aren't). So, a dolphin snapping its jaws at you can't have been making a threat because dolphins are never aggressive. And if you have just provoked the most gentle, loving creature in the world into ripping a bloody gash in your arm, what does that say about you? An awful thought! So it didn't happen.

The conclusion I came to is that, while people love dolphins, they show them an unfortunate lack of respect. Making a dolphin crane its neck out of the water to get a fish is disrespectful, as is just walking up and pawing a dolphin anywhere on its body, behavior the same person would not dream of doing to an unfamiliar person — or dog for that matter. The key is fear. People don't respect what they don't fear. While the "no touch" rule now in play at Monkey Mia might be good for other reasons, such as inhibiting disease transmission, peoples' behavior made it absolutely necessary. Given the sheer numbers of people and frequent language barrier, it was impossible for the rangers to train the humans how to properly interact with the dolphins.

Given that you can't touch the dolphins and your chances of giving one a fish are miniscule, is it worth visiting Monkey Mia today? Absolutely! Nowhere else in the world can you watch wild dolphin behavior from the beach like you can at Monkey Mia. The dolphins put on a show nearly every day, especially the infants and juveniles. You have a front row seat while wild dolphins play and romp in the shallows. You can watch infants prodding their mothers for a feed or learning to hunt on their own by "snacking" on little fish that jump in the air. Larger fish try to escape the adult dolphins by fleeing into water only inches deep right by the beach, water too shallow for the dolphins. It is a frequent and amazing spectacle to watch as a dolphin tries to provoke a fish into fleeing into deeper water, then watching the explosive chase and capture when they succeed.

§

The Triangle in 1988

Through 1987 we had documented the remarkable friendships between alliances, like that between SSC and Steps and Kodoff, and SSB with Wave and Shave. We were fascinated by the "triangle" that developed between RH, CBL and TBC after RH lost Hack and Patches in 1986.

In seeking a new buddy alliance, RH had disrupted the friendship between CBL and TBC, seemingly playing them against each other.* The situation seemed volatile and unstable. Certainly by now, after a year had passed, the TBC-RH-CBL alliance triangle should have been resolved. We were anxious to find them, but through July we had yet to see Real Notch and Hi. Finally, on 6 August we followed RH and Two-scoops, who were with TBC off and on. It was often a fuzzy matter as to whether Two-scoops was being herded by RH, as they really did seem to have a different kind of relationship with her.† But herding or not, RH certainly got excited when Two-scoops caught a nice fish. As she lay on her side at the surface with her prize, one of the males nosed within an inch of the fish but didn't touch it. Then one came up underneath her, pushing her up as they do when mounting from that position. She polished off the fish but RH were not done; they mounted Two-scoops from either side, then turning out away from her, looped around behind, turned in and nuzzled into her genital area, all in perfect synchrony. In formation behind Two-scoops, I saw strange wriggling by the males before they synchronously mounted her again, crossed sides and turned out and away from her. The mounting continued, no longer in tandem, from above or below if she rolled belly-up to evade their advances. Then they settled down and started fishing again.

Two days later, on 8 August, TBC came in suspiciously close to Monkey Mia. They must have been disappointed because the Beach Boys were herding a female that was quite small, and while she might have been an adult runt, knowing their history we were probably safe in assuming that she was immature. The first six hours were uneventful as TBC traveled and then spread out to fish. Then Pointer joined and traveled with them. The older males did not get after him. I wondered if Pointer's wimpy friend Lodent could join and travel with older males like that. After a time, we saw that TBC and Pointer were approaching a rowdy group of leaping and chasing dolphins. We popped over; it was RH with CBL and some females! Ours were clearly interested; they were oriented toward the RH-CBL group and approached to within 40 meters, but they did not join. It appeared that the alliance triangle was still unresolved.

* See "An Alliance Triangle"
† See "Female Dolphins: Different Personalities and Lifestyles"

If watching Pointer traveling in a relaxed manner with the big boys tempted us to imagine that he might now be accepted as more of a peer, we were soon disabused of the notion. On the 13th Peter Tyack, from Woods Hole Oceanographic Institution, arrived for a visit with his graduate student, Laela Sayigh. Out with Rachel and Barb, they soon found TBC with Snubby, Bibi and a varying assortment of females and juveniles, including Pointer. Members of TBC and the Beach Boys synched together, and Pointer served his usual useful role as a bonding toy for the adult males. We all sat around that evening watching the day's entertaining video of the big boys mounting Pointer, a synchronous "butterfly" display and a puzzling but comical "head-out" behavior that had us all in hysterics.

CBL were still with Real Notch and Hi on the 18th and 19th of August. CBL had a female consort, Fickle, but RH did not, and on the 18th they were not far west of Monkey Mia. SSB and Wave and Shave, who were herding alone for the first time, likely noted their presence also. We had remarked on their unusual behavior: how Wave and Shave had huddled all morning with a young female in the dead-end channel east of the Monkey Mia jetty, and they left with SSB as soon as the incoming tide offered enough water to slip across the shallows to the east, missing the afternoon feed.

RH and CBL were still together on the 22nd; RH had a new female now, and CBL still had Fickle.

TBC were with Lucky and Pointer and some females on the 18th and with a bunch of females again on the 22nd. We wondered if TBC, as the odd-alliance out, weren't trying a different strategy with females, like being nice.

Things had flipped again the next time we saw those males; on the 27th RH were with TBC, who had Fickle! Again, we were left to wonder if TBC had caught Fickle after she left CBL, or if there had been a transfer "encouraged" by RH when they switched partners.* RH had no female but got into formation behind Fickle. A minute later Trips and Cetus lined up head-to-head against Hi; then a tiff broke out between Cetus and Hi. They squawked at each other, then Hi raised his open mouth out of the water and turned away. Immediately after that, Hi and

* *See a similar case at the end of "This is Like Science Fiction!"*

Trips synched several times, and a few minutes later Real Notch and Bite did likewise. They probably wanted to reinforce their friendship soon after the squabble.

Later when TBC were spread out feeding, Real Notch, Hi, Lucky, Pointer and Two-scoops gathered around the young female Scratches who was lying on her side with a bony herring. She threw the fish, lazily picked it up and threw it again. Nobody touched her fish. She was smaller than most of the dolphins around her; they could easily have snatched the fish but didn't. The dolphins often linger with a large fish that they must break up to eat, but this fish was small enough to swallow whole, yet Scratches toyed with it for several minutes. Not only is there an ownership rule where dolphins don't take another dolphin's fish; the dolphin with the fish seems to rub it in sometimes, as though saying, "Look at me, I have a nice fish. Oh, you don't have one? That's too bad."

We stayed with TBC for well over six hours, recording lots of pops in air, all by Trips or Bite. And, as was typical, Trips and Bite were side by side surfacing synchronously much more than either did with Cetus. Yet, as I watched TBC, I was struck by the fact that Cetus did have some synchs with both Trips and Bite, and all three did some triple synchs. That was something that I didn't see with Snubby, Sickle and Bibi; the odd-male-out in that trio was just not involved, and the trio rarely did any triple synchs.

Later, when I analyzed the data, I found that indeed, Cetus was the odd-male-out in the TBC trio, and Bottomhook had that role in the CBL alliance. The odd-male-out did not associate with the other two as much, and when he was present, he engaged in less synchrony. But that was just the overall pattern; on a given hour or day, one of the other males might be the odd-male-out. My impression of the difference between those two trios and SSB was also borne out. The odd-male-out in the TBC and CBL trios engaged in a lot more synchrony than the odd-male-out in the Beach Boys, and they performed a much higher percentage of triple synchs. Perhaps the "fish-female" conflict at Monkey Mia* kept SSB from forming a "proper" trio.

TBC and RH were together right through 1 October. TBC had Fickle for 26 days before trading her in for Square in early October and

---

* See *"Any Female Will Do"*

beginning 11 September, RH had a consortship for 22 days. We had noted last year how we started seeing longer consortships once the real mating season began in September. Then on 9 October we saw TBC sans RH engaging in rowdy socializing with Nicky, her pup Nipper, Joy and Joy's Friend. But the real surprise was when we found TBC and CBL together for two days in a row on 11 and 12 October! We had not seen them together in some time. I wondered where Real Notch and Hi were. TBC had Square on the 11th but traded her in for a new female on the 12th, and CBL were with Fickle.

Before we could get too excited about TBC and CBL renewing old vows, the pattern of the last two years was re-established. We found CBL with RH on three days from the 14th to the 19th. On the 16th we found TBC herding Yan and hanging out with a bunch of other females, including Crooked-fin and her brand-new baby, Cookie.

We had first seen Cookie on the 12th, and again two days later when we were distressed, but unfortunately not surprised, to find two of the Beach Brats, Sickle-fin and Wave, herding Crooked-fin and Cookie at Monkey Mia. I could not imagine TBC engaging in such behavior, so it was a hoot watching little Cookie, no more than 2 weeks old, bopping all around TBC and the others, tail slapping, whistling and mounting his mother. We could not know it then but Cookie would figure prominently in Real Notch's life over 20 years hence. By late October TBC was back with RH and in early November, they fought a pitched battle with SSB, Wave and Shave.

§

The Battle for Flo-Jo

On 20 October, the boys came into Monkey Mia with a female, accompanied by her older calf, that they herded for 17 days. For the first few days she was with Snubby & Shave, then she came in with Sickle and Bibi. I was reminded of a similar case in September when Snubby and Shave herded a female for a few days and then Sickle and Bibi had her for several more. In both cases I wondered if the female had escaped and been recaptured, or if she had been taken by Sickle and Bibi.

The 17 consecutive days the boys had her and the 13 days Sickle and Bibi herded the female set new records. One reason the boys may have been able to keep her for so long was that her escape attempts were pathetically slow. My assistant Scott and I were greatly amused by her sad attempts to flee from the males; it was like she was swimming in molasses. We named her "Flo-Jo," after the nickname given to the record breaking Olympian, Florence Joyner, widely considered the fastest woman of all time.

5 November was a nice day, so after checking on the boys and their consorts inshore we headed out and found Cetus for a follow, with Trips several tens of meters off to one side, and Bite tens of meters beyond that. They were spread out fishing in what we had come to call a "lateral line." Traveling close together was fine, but they could not fish like that or they would often find themselves chasing the same fish. Dolphins move so effortlessly in the water that it is easy for them to spread out to fish, then to come back together to travel, socialize or just rest.

They all came together and joined with Real Notch and Hi, who were herding Fatfin. While they were spread out fishing we had not paid much attention to the fact that they were moving steadily southeast in Red Cliff Bay toward Monkey Mia, but when they joined up with Real Notch and Hi, and kept moving that way, my heart rate jumped! I tried to conceal my excitement from Scott, but he had heard all the stories and was onto it as well. Only a few hundred meters northwest of the beach, Real Notch and Hi started to lag behind TBC, but the group drew closer, 300 meters, then 200 meters from Monkey Mia. I could see the fish window open at the center and tourists traipsing down with buckets of fish. Snubby, Sickle and Bibi were being fed as their rivals closed to within 100 meters. But there progress stopped. The group was very tight, but two individuals were snagging now, and one turned back to the northwest. They seemed indecisive! Then more snagged and two surfaced going back to the northwest. There was funny social behavior in the group as two surfaced synchronously and another came up between them and did a back-slap in the other direction. The whole group turned north, then two turned back south toward Monkey Mia and the rest followed suit. We ventured closer; TBC were snagging toward Monkey Mia a few meters ahead of RH. Trips turned around toward RH and then back toward Monkey Mia. Real Notch then turned away to the north. It seemed that TBC wanted to attack, but RH were reluctant. Maybe some of that social behavior, and Trips approaching RH, was an attempt by TBC to persuade RH to support them.

Trips went a few meters forward toward Monkey Mia and then returned to his mates. The whole group moved back north again. Trips, then Bite, turned back to-ward Monkey Mia, but Real Notch and Hi were still oriented to the north. Trips and Bite turned back toward Real Notch and Hi, who then turned back toward them. The whole group then moved north a very short distance and stopped. After all that back-and-forthing, they were still about 100 meters north of the beach. The entire group snagged toward Monkey Mia, with TBC lined up side by side in front of Real Notch, Hi and Fatfin. Suddenly, TBC went down and exploded toward the beach. It was an astonishing sight; TBC were side by side just under the surface and their flukes started pumping at full power in perfect synchrony as they accelerated from a stand-still to full speed in seconds. The assault was on! TBC leapt in perfect synchrony as they sped into the shallows, while Real Notch and Hi lagged behind. Inshore, the Beach Boys and their females moved in a very tight group down the beach in shallow water, then accelerated rapidly, leaping and porpoising as TBC chased after them. Then all turned out north away from the park. I got a better look at the Beach Boys; Wave and Shave were with them! TBC were right behind and RH were lagging 20 meters back.

Flo-Jo and her calf were still in a tight pack of the Beach Boys with TBC right on their flukes. TBC charged right into the SSB group and fighting broke out. The chase resumed, with much synchronous leaping and porpoising. Real Notch and Hi still lagged 20 meters behind.

Lucky and Lodent joined the mob. The group ground to a halt over the banks just north of Monkey Mia. Bibi and Sickle were on either side of Flo-Jo as Bite rushed up behind Bibi, who made intense pops in air. Real Notch, Hi and Fatfin plowed into the group and more fighting broke out; head-jerks and hitting and suddenly they were fighting all over the place, with dolphins chasing this way and that all around my boat in less than 2 meters of water. The fighting behind our boat was too close; "neutral" I yelled, so Scott would cut power to the propeller.

The group resumed chasing and again, Real Notch and Hi fell behind 30 meters. Then RH started closing the distance, to 15 meters, then they moved up into the group again before falling back. Lucky and Lodent were still there, but I had no idea whose side they were on, if any. There was fighting in the group ahead as RH trailed. TBC were right on the heels of SSB, Wave and Shave, who were all tightly packed around Flo-Jo. The group had charged north on the banks and then east to the eastern edge of the banks, moving rapidly along at 8-9 mph the whole time. Now they turned SSW back toward Monkey Mia. Real Notch and Hi had fallen back 40 meters then porpoised up into the group again. Two dolphins charged out ahead of the pack, and the pack charged after them. Real Notch and Hi fell back 30 meters again but a minute later charged up into the group. Real Notch went at a dolphin in the center of the group, then Real Notch and Hi moved up in front on the right side of the group, now bee-lining right toward Monkey Mia. Then, to our amazement, Real Notch and Hi turned back around right in front of the others, and the whole group then turned southeast and away from Monkey Mia. Real Notch and Hi had deftly redirected the group!

The chasing continued. Cetus head-jerked and side by side with another, charged into the pack. Real Notch and Hi, as well as Lucky and Lodent, dropped back 30 meters. Lucky and Lodent moved back up right behind the group as Real Notch and Hi continued to trail 40 meters behind. Everybody picked up speed as Real Notch and Hi closed to within 10 meters but remained behind the group for the next several minutes. I spotted a big new tooth-rake mark on Bibi's side; someone had really nailed him.

Suddenly Real Notch and Hi charged back into the group and intense fighting broke out again; in the chaos, I saw one go right at Bibi. TBC broke away from the group; they had Flo-Jo! The fighting continued as TBC moved further away with their prize, executing huge side-slapping breaches, the "victory leaps" that we had come to expect after they had stolen a female.[*]

TBC and Flo-Jo moved 100 meters away from the others, but the fighting continued. Wave and Shave were now gone, but Lucky and Lodent were still there. A big chase broke out; Real Notch and Bibi

---

* See "This is Like Science Fiction!"

were up in front of the chase. The only female in the group now was Fatfin, and Real Notch and Hi were outnumbered, but that didn't seem to matter. Suddenly, Sickle and Bibi were in front of Real Notch and Hi. Real Notch charged up from behind the group, snaked his way past the other dolphins and bit Sickle on his peduncle; Sickle whipped his head back like a dog that had just had his tail pulled. Then Real Notch charged up at them again. TBC, with Flo-Jo, had turned around and were coming back; they approached rapidly and rejoined. Perhaps they wanted to participate in the final reckoning. There was more chasing and fighting; violent loud hits were followed by SSB fleeing rapidly, but once clear they turned immediately back toward the group. They were still too excited to accept defeat and swim away. SSB persisted in following the group that stole their Flo-Jo, but Real Notch charged back at them whenever they came too close. Finally, SSB fell behind 30 meters. It was over.

The TBC-RH group was still terribly excited as they raced along, TBC with Flo-Jo and RH with Fatfin. Lucky and Lodent followed at 20-30 meters for a time. There were inter-alliance synchs, Hi with Cetus and Real Notch with Bite.

We broke off the follow as they moved off the banks into deeper water, in the now heavy chop. From beginning to end the chasing and fighting had lasted 70 minutes and covered 5 miles. I suspect the main difference between this theft and the ones we saw last year was in the numbers. This time SSB had Wave and Shave with them; they were all a year older and maybe a little tougher. We never saw runty Lucky and young Lodent get into the actual fighting, so probably at most they were cheerleading. As they were otherwise on friendly terms with both parties I could not begin to guess for whom they were cheering. What was most striking to me was the critical role Real Notch and Hi played in determining the outcome of the fight. Even though they lagged behind for much of the contest, the heavy fighting broke out each time they charged up into the group and the last time they did so was decisive. The way that they redirected the group away from Monkey Mia was astonishing. We replayed the video several times in slow motion and you could clearly see Real Notch and Hi, on the right front-side of the group, turn first, effectively blocking the rest, who then turned in the same direction. Also amazing was the fact that TBC, having left the group with Flo-Jo, suspended their celebration to rejoin Real Notch and Hi in the ongoing battle. Watching Real Notch move up through his group to bite Sickle, and then leave his group to go at the defeated Snubby, Sickle, & Bibi, reinforced my belief that it wasn't just about the females; these guys did not like each other.

Real Notch and TBC were sighted together until 23 November, when we found RH with CBL.

§

Play Herding

On 11 September we followed Lodent, Lucky and Pointer for a few hours. Just over an hour into the follow, they were with a large group of two females with their older calves and up to eight other male and female juveniles. It was chaotic and confusing as the juvies were extremely rowdy and I didn't recognize all of them. There were a couple of "clean-finned punks" as we called them, young dolphins without distinctive markings that were hard to ID in real time. For the next two hours they kept splitting up into smaller groups and converging into larger ones, raising hell the whole time. For 20 minutes I saw LLP getting after Tipless, a juvenile female. Then Lucky and Pointer were after Scratches, goosing her and performing butterfly displays, while Lodent and two others continued to get after Tipless. In another group, Natural Tag and Prima were after another, unfamiliar dolphin.

I was back with LLP and six other juveniles on 23 October. Again, I recognized some but not all. It was more of the same; they were rowdy, with subgroups forming and rejoining. LLP were chasing and goosing Joy's Friend; two of them did a butterfly display. Natural Tag, Barney and another were getting after Tipless. Then Pointer made loud pops at the surface; they were herding Joy's Friend! This was incredible. They were too young! More joined; we had 13 dolphins now. We saw erections and there was lots of mounting, goosing and chasing; I saw one mount Pointer. Males were after males and females were after females. Tipless mouthed Joy's Friend in front of her flukes, then they mouthed each other with heads raised in the air. Natural Tag and another got after Joy's Friend, mounting her, while Pointer and Prima were after another one.

We saw yet another juvenile orgy on 4 November. What was going on? Each time we saw many of the elements of herding: two or three would line up behind another in formation, goosing and mounting. We saw butterfly displays and chasing and we even heard pops. We also saw the "bonding" behavior, between juvenile females that were being "harassed" by the young males. One female would press her flipper against the side of the other and around they would swim, with a gaggle of boisterous boys right behind. But these weren't consortships. When the rowdy stuff ended they all went their separate ways. In real consortships the female remains with the males during all activities; including travel, rest and fishing. No, what we were witnessing was play; play herding if you will, by males and females that would be engaging in the real thing just a few years down the road.

It made sense. Play is common in mammals and the most widely accepted idea is that play is practice. Male and female sexual and consorting behavior in dolphins has many elements so it wasn't surprising (in hindsight of course) that they would have "play herding" sessions. Their hormone levels were probably up as well; after all, it was the peak mating season.

I suspect that another important aspect of juvenile sex parties is in relationship building. Most young males have many friends, and they may use such play sessions to test future alliance partners. That is not to say that they are objectively rating other males' ability to perform synchronous displays with them or chase a female. More likely, such compatibility would cause a male to like certain other males and want to spend more time with them. If the feeling is mutual, a future alliance may be in the offing.

§

Snubby, Sickle & Bibi

The record breaking Flo-Jo consortship reinforced what we had already noticed: that the same seasonal change in the pattern and duration of consortships and partnerships that we saw in the Beach Boys in 1987 was repeating in 1988. The winter months of July and August featured mostly short consortships (which we call "July things") and frequent partner changes. Once September set in, both consortships and partnerships lasted longer. It seemed obvious that the two factors were related; the greater stability of spring-time herding partnerships was due simply to consortships lasting longer during that time of year.

To my surprise we found that the seasonal change in consortship duration could not entirely explain the high rate of partner shifts in winter months. If Sickle and Bibi lost a female in October, we were likely to see them stay together and herd another female, but if they lost a female in July, we were more likely to see one of them pair up with Snubby to herd the next female. It seemed their social bonds were simply less stable in the winter months before the breeding season. Going back to our old friend Zahavi, and his ideas about "testing the bond,"* the winter time may have been the warm-up period for males to test and compete for mating season allies.

Yet all that business about male bonds didn't explain what was going on with the females, which was to me an even bigger puzzle. We knew from captive studies that female bottlenose dolphins ovulate up to seven times in the year they conceive. So it seemed obvious that the females being consorted each year, except for the Beach Boys' shenanigans with new mothers and such, were having multiple estrous periods. A female would be attractive for a time, herded by one or more alliances, and later we would see her in other consortships with the same or different alliances. What seemed especially strange, however, were those brief winter consortships. Yes, births can happen any month, but almost all the females that we watched in consortships during the winter and spring months gave birth in the spring a year later. Bottlenose dolphins

* See *"A Day with the Gerries"*

have a 12-month gestation period, so if a female gave birth in the spring, then she conceived in the spring a year earlier.

Given the extent to which females get harassed and even attacked by males during consortships, it would seem to make more sense for females to simply have one estrus period in the main mating season, ovulate, conceive, and get on with it! Because of the costs they suffer from obnoxious males, there had to be an important reason for natural selection to favor multiple estrus periods in female dolphins. Looking again to primatology, I came up with an answer: infanticide. In many birds and mammals, males that don't mate with a female may kill her offspring. Consider the example of lions. If a male lion alliance takes over a female pride from the resident males, they will kill the cubs. They are not related to those cubs, and by killing them, the females will cease to lactate and will conceive sooner with the new males. The result is more babies for males that commit infanticide. Of course, females are not happy about the situation and try to resist, but the males are larger and more powerful and they usually succeed in killing the cubs. Why would females mate with a male that had just killed their infants? We can't project our human psychology onto other animals; from the cold calculus of natural selection, a female lion that has just had her cubs killed should mate again right away to maximize the number of cubs she raises.

Infanticide in dolphins! What a thought. We had already besmirched their sweet reputation with our discovery of aggressive herding; now we were going to suggest to the world that dolphins might commit such a horror as infanticide! Hold on a minute, one of my Shark Bay colleagues objected, we have watched these dolphins for thousands of hours and have never seen an infanticide. Yes, I replied, but we have never seen a shark bite a dolphin either, but we know well that it happens from all the shark bite scars on the dolphins.* So, having no direct evidence, we published a paper predicting infanticide in bottlenose dolphins.

Within three years, evidence for infanticide was reported in several locations around the globe. Why did the discovery take so long? Often the infant victims washed ashore in seemingly pristine condition, with not a mark on them. However, necropsy revealed broken bones,

* See "Jaws"

ruptured organs and internal bleeding, wounds received from being battered by those powerful tails, and the occasional tooth-mark pattern on some victims matched those of male dolphins. It also turned out that even scientists were biased to interpret dolphin behavior benignly. In one study where they reported infanticide, they realized that they had a behavior in their catalog called "calf tossing," which they had assumed was playful!

In northern Scotland, researchers also implicated bottlenose dolphins in the killing of harbor porpoises. They could find no reason for such behavior, except that perhaps the porpoises were the same size as the infant bottlenose dolphins in that population. They suggested that groups of young males might be killing porpoises as a form of "practice infanticide."

Snubby, Sickle and Bibi © Dolphin Alliance Project

As in many birds and mammals, there are conflicting interests between male and female dolphins in Shark Bay. Males want to monopolize a female to increase the chance of fathering her calf. But that would leave the female vulnerable to infanticide because she would not have mated with other males. So females try to escape from consortships and have more than one estrus cycle. Females probably want to mate with as many males as possible, and during the year she conceives, we typically see a female in consortships with many males. There may still be conflict over how often she mates with particular males during consortships. While we see no evidence that males force copulations (females can just roll away from a mounting male), males may use intimidation and threats to coerce females into mating more often. Females might still be able to "choose" who fathers their infants by internal means, but we have no way to study that. The displays males perform suggest that it may still behoove males to impress the female whose company they have coerced.

The end of my 1988 field season was approaching rapidly. The Beach Boys were their usual entertaining selves through November and December, herding new females and old favorites. Snubby and Shave had been herding Flo-Jo since mid-December. Then, on 24 December, Sickle and Bibi had her; that was the third time I had seen Bibi and Sickle come in with a female that Snubby and Shave had been herding the day before. I was becoming more convinced that Sickle and Bibi were dominant to Snubby and Shave and that they were taking females from them, but I had yet to see it happen. Sickle and Bibi weren't the only ones that could play that game. Later that morning Real Notch and TBC came in and took Flo-Jo. This time, RH got Flo-Jo since TBC already had a female. Shave and Spud were also in that morning, so the fight was again a five-on-five affair, but the chasing and fighting this time lasted only 10-20 minutes. It was very choppy, so we could not follow the victors far offshore. Back at Monkey Mia, Sickle sported three new tooth-rake marks. Sickle and Bibi had Flo-Jo back the next morning and for two days after.

I packed up for my trip to New Zealand. I had learned so much from Snubby, Sickle and Bibi these last two years. They taught us about herding, male and female reproductive patterns and, as unwilling participants, helped us discover what friendships between alliances were all about. I owed them a lot and looked forward to learning more from "the Beach Boys" when I returned in February. I had no idea as I was leaving that I would never see them again.

§

Tragedy at Monkey Mia

I flew into Perth from New Zealand on 17 February 1989. Friends gave me the news that Holey-fin's new baby had died in the shallows at Monkey Mia a few weeks before. That was sad, but infant mortality is high, so it wasn't terribly surprising. I called Wilf to get the scoop and he mentioned that Puck's new calf was also missing. Next I called Sharon Gosper, who had become the head ranger after Tony left the area. Yes, she said, Puck's calf was missing, but she added that Nicky's 1.5-year-old calf Nipper was also missing. Sharon went on to say that Snubby had not been seen since Holey-fin's calf died and that Sickle was last seen two days later, and that Bibi had not been seen since the end of the month, and now beautiful 6-year-old Holly hadn't been into the park for a few days. An overwhelming feeling of dread set in.

I took the bus to Shark Bay the next day, stayed with Sharon in Denham and went out to Monkey Mia the following morning. We went offshore early and saw lots of dolphins but not the right ones. Tuesday the 21st I went out again and found RH herding Nicky and CBL herding Puck. Nick and Puck were cycling again; their infants were dead. On Wednesday Sharon dropped me off at Dubaut[*] point to the south. I walked back along the beach, looking for bodies, but found nothing. The next day I drove the boat as far as Dubaut but found nothing.

As the dolphins stopped coming in, Sharon had sounded the alarm but her concerns were largely ignored. A beautiful aboriginal woman, Sharon had a delightful way with people and dolphins and had been a real hit with tourists. She had also taken a keen interest in our research and elevated the rangers' record keeping to a new level, recording when the dolphins came and left, including herded females and which males had them. It was difficult not to conclude that her gender and race had something to do with the fact that she wasn't taken seriously by the authorities.[†]

[*] See map of Study area, page 138.
[†] The loss of her beloved dolphins and the unfortunate attitude of the authorities in this and other areas led Sharon to tender her resignation the following year.

I was able to get things moving. I called the regional manager of The Department of Conservation and Land Management (CALM), the Western Australian government department that had jurisdiction over the dolphins. He was unaware of the extent of the disaster and said he thought seepage from leach drains was a potential problem at Monkey Mia. I called other CALM officials in Perth.

Incredibly, Monkey Mia had just been sold. I spoke with the new owners who were up for the day. Reinforcing what the CALM officer said, they thought septic pollution was potentially a huge problem and that aerial photographs suggested an algal bloom.

Human waste? I was stunned. It had never occurred to me that a sewage problem existed here. Why now? Thinking about it, I realized that there had been major changes in the past year. The road from Denham to Monkey Mia was paved in 1988, allowing the tourist buses to visit Monkey Mia and visit they did. January saw a record crowd, more than twice the number as the previous year. Busloads of people arrived in the morning, had lunch, a colic reflex, and then used the one toilet in the ranger station that may not have been up to the task. The Department of Tourism had erected that building in 1986, well before CALM became involved and the tourist buses arrived.

The water was uncomfortably warm and unusually calm in January, with low tides that created a dead-end channel in front of the park, greatly limiting water flow in front of Monkey Mia. High water temperatures and minimal water flow would have created the perfect conditions for bacteria counts to rise in the shallows.

The tourist center toilet was not the only problem. Several leach drains had been put in around the park. Back in November, one of the pet dogs on site had dug through the hard pan by one of the ablution blocks and exposed a smelly cavern below. Then came the bombshell. I was discussing the pollution theory with Wilf and someone who was skeptical of the idea. Why this time of year, the man protested, tourist numbers are down in the hot months except for a "little" surge at Christmas (in fact they were quite high in January)? I suggested that it might take weeks for the waste to creep down into the water. Wilf countered, "No, we have a well in the back of the park that rises and falls with the tide. There is a layer of shell grit the water moves right through." I was shocked and said nothing. I'm sure Wilf did not appreciate the implications of what he had just said.

If there was any good news in the gloom, it was that the new owner of Monkey Mia, Graeme Robertson, was going to rip everything out and put in a proper waste-water treatment area up behind the park. The problem was going to be remedied almost immediately. I can only imagine what he thought, after spending a small fortune to buy this world-famous dolphin tourist attraction, upon learning that seven of the 10 Monkey Mia dolphins were missing and likely dead.

We were now moving into late February; the tides were higher and for some time the tourist numbers had been way down from the January peak. I was growing concerned that the evidence of pollution would be diminishing as the conditions that exacerbated the problem were alleviated. I spoke with people at CALM and the Environmental Protection Agency in hopes of speeding up the testing and learned that someone from the EPA would be up in a few days to conduct the tests.

Of course, there were some that weren't convinced that the missing dolphins were dead. A body would cure any skeptics. The odds weren't great for finding anything, but I had to give it a try. So, on the 25th I searched even further south, into Lahridon Bight and around to Petit Point. I found one dolphin skull but it was too old. Of course, sharks would likely scavenge a dolphin's body quickly, especially during that time of the year.

On the 27th the media learned about the disappearances; they were inundating the ranger center with calls and were on their way. Later that day I was asked by one higher official not to "play it up." Too late; I had already spoken to the West Australian newspaper. But I had no intention of playing anything up; as a scientist, I was interested in the evidence and the simplest explanation.

We did not have a body or bodies, so we could not do a necropsy. The first dolphin to go was Holey-fin's infant who died near the beach. Holey-fin was extremely distressed and kept pushing the infant's body to the surface. The rangers made the decision to let her keep it. That was the right decision as infants die often and there was no reason at that point to suspect anything else was going on.

Without a smoking gun, we were left with circumstantial evidence.

The too-often unaddressed question in such cases is where the burden of proof lies. Industry often plays that game, maintaining that there is no "proof" that their product has caused cancer or some such. But certainly, when enough circumstantial evidence accumulates, the burden of proof should shift to the other side. Then it becomes, "prove to me that your product is not responsible for this increased incidence of cancer."

To this point, what was the circumstantial evidence that something had happened to the dolphins at Monkey Mia? We had one new infant that had died at the beach on 23 January. Over the next three weeks, six more dolphins "went missing" on different days: two more dependent infants, including another newborn and a healthy 1.5-year-old, a healthy 6-year-old female, and three adult males. The males traveled together offshore but they had vanished on different days over an eight-day period. The males and females went in different directions when they left Monkey Mia; the females stayed to the northwest in Red Cliff Bay and the boys went southeast. The only thing they had in common was being together at Monkey Mia.

So the circumstantial evidence was pretty strong that something had happened at Monkey Mia, and right now, septic pollution was our best bet. I had talked to Sam Ridgway, the famous dolphin veterinarian and biologist, about the disappearances. He said fecal bacteria in the water can cause septicemia, blood poisoning, and kill dolphins quickly. Suddenly I recalled a conversation I had at the Atlantis marine park, just north of Perth, before heading off to New Zealand. I had popped in to visit the staff and see their dolphins. The head researcher and veterinarian, Nick Gales, was out of town. While I was there they received a call from a distressed mother whose family had been up to Monkey Mia. Her son had been bitten by Sickle and his wound had become horribly infected. She wanted to know what awful bacteria the dolphins had in their mouths. Nick wasn't there to take the call but I said I didn't know of any; the dolphins had nipped many visitors but I had not heard of any bite becoming infected. After the call ended, I remarked to the staff that I wondered where that kid had put his hand afterwards. Now, hearing what Sam said about septicemia, I realized that the boy may simply have dipped his wound into the water at Monkey Mia.

It occurred to me that if that boy's doctor had cultured the bacteria from the wound we might have the "smoking gun" or at least close to it. I called Atlantis but they had not recorded the name of the concerned mother.

I have always thought that CALM, now The Department of Biodiversity, Conservation and Attractions,* is a bit too motivated by PR. On the other hand, they have to deal with a sometimes-irresponsible Australian press. I became more sympathetic about the attitude of CALM officials after experiencing that irresponsibility first-hand. Channel 7 wanted to interview me about the situation. There had been a rumor that the dolphins might have been deliberately poisoned; it was rubbish and an unfortunate distraction from what was most likely, in my view, the real culprit. Before the on-camera interview, I spoke with the "reporter" about the various ideas and he bought that one up. I explained my position to him (not a shred of evidence, circumstantial or otherwise, for poisoning) and he agreed with me, saying he would not ask about it during the interview. Lights, camera, action, and the first question out of his mouth was about "deliberate poisoning." I was so stunned by his betrayal; the fact that he had just lied to my face, that I only managed to mumble a negative response, giving them nothing they could use.

I was pretty upset about the dolphin deaths, so it wasn't a good idea to approach me with notions of the dolphins simply taking a holiday or any other "she'll be right" bullshit. A leading local official tried that on me, suggesting in a jovial tone that the dolphins were probably just swimming around in the bay. I managed to suppress the choice words that came to mind and simply restated the overwhelming circumstantial evidence that the dolphins were dead. To this day I have no time for him.

Later I ran another search, this time driving the boat close to shore from Guichenault Point, about 15 miles northwest as the crow flies, back to Cape Rose, which marks the north end of Red Cliff Bay. We found CBL and RH still with Nicky and Puck.

On 1 March the EPA guy came up to do the testing. I helped him dig the holes in front of the center. A disturbing revelation: the too-small leach drain was right in front of the dolphin feeding area only 15 meters

* *This is only the latest in a series of name changes, so stay tuned!*

from the high tide mark! Unbelievable. The irony of it all is that the building that was erected to help protect the dolphins may have helped to kill them. He found that the salinity dropped sharply going up from the high tide mark toward the leach drain. I looked down one of the holes at the water; the surface appeared to have a film on it. And, as with Wilf's well behind the park, we could see the water level in the holes fall with the tide.

A week later Nick Gales had returned to Atlantis. I talked to him about the situation and he related a case from Hong Kong where dolphins died quickly of septicemia after exposure to septic pollution.

The EPA report was published in March. They found significantly elevated levels of fecal bacteria and nitrates; there was clearly pollution flowing into the waters in front of Monkey Mia. The report stated correctly that a causal link between the pollution and the dolphin disappearances could not be established, but it strongly implicated septic pollution as the culprit.

Why did the adult females survive while the others died? Nursing infants are more vulnerable and the males had fresh bite wounds from fighting, easy routes for the bacteria to get in. Also, with elevated mating season testosterone levels, their immune systems may have been depressed.

There were still some who wanted to sweep it under the rug, "move forward," not "play it up," etc. I viewed such an attitude as unethical and irresponsible. We had a duty to let the public and authorities know what happened at Monkey Mia, so it might not happen again somewhere else. On 1 April I was interviewed on the national ABC program, the 7:30 Report, and laid out all the evidence implicating septic pollution in the dolphin disappearances. The EPA report also did the job very well.

Several days later, on 5 April, Sharon alerted us to presence of a dead dolphin way down in Hamelin pool. We went to check it out. A gas induced erection proclaimed the dolphin a male that had been dead about a week. He had speckles around his genitals and on his belly up to the level of his dorsal fin. I found it fascinating that a young adult male was only a touch over 1.8 meters; our guys really were small! There was another dolphin that had been dead much longer. It was in an advanced state of decay and the dorsal fin was gone. Like Snubby, it had an underbite. Other dolphins had that feature, and way down there, it almost certainly wasn't him. But I had to wonder.

Years after the park had been cleaned up and rebuilt, I noticed that the sand under my feet at low tide had changed. In the 1980s, it was mucky at low tide. When I had to hop out and drag the boat in closer I used to sing a few of Judas's lines from *Jesus Christ Superstar*, "I shall be dragged through the slime and the mud." In later years, I noticed that the muck was gone. Without all that nitrogen input it had become sand again.

§

Sex at Monkey Mia

While Nicky and Puck were being herded, only Holey-fin was visiting Monkey Mia. But when Holey-fin came around, she usually had an entourage; Wave and Shave one day, TBC the next, then LLP the day after. All three females that lost their infants in the pollution disaster were attracting attention from males.

On March 5, Nicky returned to Monkey Mia with Holey-fin; they swam around the shallows, side by side, Nicky bonding to Holey-fin, then Holey-fin bonded to Nicky. Puck returned from her consortship on the 12th.

Given their 12-month gestation period, it is likely that at least Holey-fin and Puck had conceived by this time. Puck gave birth around 1 March 1990 but lost the calf within a week. Holey-fin was pregnant in late 1989 but disappeared from late January to early March 1990, and then came in without a calf. After March, Nicky was herded briefly three times in April (by CBL and RH) and gave birth in mid-April 1990. But males continued to flock to Monkey Mia to be with Nicky, Puck and Holey-fin through early June. Why were females still attractive if they were already pregnant? It gets back to fooling males about paternity to reduce the risk of infanticide. By continuing to be attractive after they have conceived, but before they are obviously pregnant, females can mate with more males.

However, it wasn't simply that the females were attractive to the males. Much of the time the females, especially Nicky and Puck, were clearly the instigators of the sexual behavior. They were attracted to the males, and sometimes each other. We had seen females excited around males before but nothing like what we saw over the next few months. I suspect that the females' attraction to males is often masked by the routine of being herded. When they were in heat but not being herded, the Monkey Mia females would go back and forth between the shallows for food and the channel for sex.

The males, also excited by the females, would get after each other as well. This months-long sex party, interrupted by the occasional herding of Nicky, was a nearly daily occurrence at Monkey Mia and in the nearby waters of Red Cliff Bay. Notes from a few days suffice to capture the range of interactions we witnessed from March to early June.

No males accompanied Nicky, Puck & Holey-fin to Monkey Mia on 23 March, but they made up for it by getting after each other. I was struck by how much more animated they were now, unburdened by the demands of nursing, and perhaps in estrus.

On 26 March Holey-fin and Nicky were with LLP, who were acting like a good trio, and TBC. Holey-fin was bonding to Nicky early on and then they reversed roles. Eventually LLP left the others, moving west of the park to hunt in shallow water where we could see them chasing fish. Lucky and Pointer took a break from fishing to engage in a little horseplay. Pointer became excited around a prone Lucky, rubbing against and mounting him, and at one point swimming around with his chin arched up out of the water, like a rooster strut without the head bobbing. Then it was back to fishing.

TBC, LLP and WSS all came in to Monkey Mia on April 1st with Holey-fin and Puck, but Nicky was absent. It was not hard to guess where she was and the next day we found her being herded by RH. They were with CBL, who did not have a female.

On 6 April we followed Lucky and Pointer who were with Nicky and Holey-fin. There was petting between Nicky and Pointer and then Nicky bonded to Holey-fin for 10 minutes, a long time for that behavior. Nicky, Puck and Holey-fin cruised into Monkey Mia for their fish, and when they returned, it was party time. Nicky goosed Holey-fin, then Lucky mounted her. The girls continued to raise hell with each other in the shallows while Lucky and Pointer waited patiently just offshore. Nicky bonded to Holey-fin as they rejoined the boys. Incredibly, the females continued to carry on as the males just followed along watching. Holey-fin and Puck took turns bonding to each other; Holey-fin bonded to Puck for an incredible 13 minutes. Suddenly RH and CBL came tearing into the group. Lucky and Pointer left a trail of flukeprints as they fled the scene. There were inter-alliance synchs as RH and CBL porpoised excitedly around Nicky. They were violent; there was hitting, and I saw fresh red rake marks on Nicky's lip and peduncle. They settled down and 40 minutes later let her go.

One young male mounting another. © Dolphin Alliance Project

Outside of RH and CBL, it was interesting that we were finding several alliances together with so little aggression. But there were sometimes indications of dominance relationships or aggression that was expressed subtly, at least to our eyes. On 8 April we were following SCC when LLP joined. LLP approached and then turned to the side and away from them. SCC went down and came up behind LLP. That was the submissive way for a female or young male to join an alliance, but I had rarely seen one alliance join another that way.[*]

On another day we followed SSC to the Monkey Mia channel where they joined Holey-fin, Nicky, Puck, Wave and Shave. Slash surfaced, his body jerked, creating a splash, and Wave and Shave left immediately,

For another example see "An Alliance Triangle"

moved off 30 meters, shadowing the group for the next half-hour. I suspect that Slash's body jerk was his way of telling them to get lost.

On 13 April Nicky, Puck and Holey-fin came in with their entourage of boys: SCC, TBC, LLP, Wave & Shave and even Fred made an appearance. SSC focused their affections on Holey-fin while the rest were after Nicky and Puck, but they found young Fred and Pointer pretty enticing too. While Wave and Shave goosed Nicky, TBC were goosing Fred. Then TBC started goosing and mounting their old favorite, Pointer. Wave back-slapped, then slide-slapped, and then repeated the sequence. Holey-fin's old friend Couch joined the group, and Nicky promptly bonded to her for over 10 minutes. Couch, who lived north of Red Cliff Bay, showed up at Monkey Mia to visit Holey-fin in the spring of 1987 and 1988. She was an old, heavily speckled female like Holey-fin. She swam side by side with Holey-fin during her annual visits, so they clearly had a history.

Puck was not involved in the rowdy behavior on 18 April, but a local juvenile female, Yin, substituted admirably, and Joy's Friend was around as well. It was the usual petting, goosing and mounting. Wave and Spud were goosing Yin initially and then Nicky was "it" for a while. Then several of the males got after Lodent, who bonded to Holey-fin! Someone goosed Holey-fin and Joy's Friend bonded to her. Joy's Friend appeared to solicit goosing from Puck and Holey-fin. As they sat there side-by-side she swam right in front them twice before they goosed her on the third pass. Nicky was clearly initiating a lot of the interactions that led to her being goosed. At one point Trips lay on his side and Wave and Shave came up on either side rubbing against him. Then we saw a wonderful display by Spud and Shave as Wave lay on his side. Spud and Shave swam in opposite directions perpendicular to Wave, passing each other right behind him. They mounted Wave from either side; then each came out of the water vertically on either side of Wave's peduncle and fell back into the water. They mounted him again, then synched. Later WSS, sporting erections, got after Lodent again, goosing and mounting him.

On the 28 April, we followed TBC and their frequent companions of late, LLP. Lodent started snacking on small fish and that apparently excited Trips. Trips performed a rooster strut right across Lodent's snout.

Lodent rolled belly-up and Trips chin-slapped in front of Lodent and then mounted him. A few minutes later Holey-fin and Nicky joined them. This excited the males, and there was a lot of intense social behavior, including aggression, but when the socializing was over, everybody just spread out to fish.

On a June day we watched Nicky stirring up the males who then turned their attention to each other. Wave and Spud chased Lodent. Wave and Pointer were head-to-head; then three were lined up against Pointer, including Nicky! Interest shifted to Holey-fin for a few minutes before she tired of the action and went back inshore. Lodent and Lucky formed a synch pair after Pointer, who lay on his side. Nicky seemed to compete for attention from the males who had gathered around a listing Pointer; she swam right in front of Wave and Spud and tilted her belly to them, then dove lifting her flukes up; then she surfaced and belly-slapped behind Lucky. Pointer synched a few times with Wave, then Spud and Wave got in formation behind Pointer. Pointer lay on his side again, jaw out of the water as the other males packed in tightly around him. Wave did a rooster strut and then mounted Pointer; then Spud mounted Pointer and we could see him thrusting. Wave and Spud synched and chin-slapped as they continued to mount Pointer repeatedly. Attention shifted briefly to Lodent as Lucky and Pointer mounted him. Wave lay on his side as Lodent, Pointer and Lucky rubbed against him. Then Wave and Spud had another session with Pointer before Lodent and another one mounted Spud. Then it was back to Pointer. Lodent and Spud synched five times so close they were almost touching. Wave and Spud did a butterfly display around Pointer before mounting him again. Pointer was "it" for another 15 minutes before they settled down. Later they moved back out into Red Cliff Bay and everybody spread out to fish.

§

Crinkle's Crush

During this period of autumn sex at Monkey Mia, the interactions between the males and females were clearly not entirely random. We were amused to find that one of the old geezers, Crinkles, was smitten with Holey-fin.

Lucky and Pointer came into Monkey Mia on 19 March, as did Wave, Shave and Spud. We went off to follow Slash, Crinkles and Chunk for six hours. They spent time spread out fishing, then joined up with Lucky, Pointer, Crooked-fin and Cookie. They spread out to fish again, then they resumed side by side travel until Holey-fin approached them head-on, turning around in front of the trio. They followed as she fished. Crinkles started to become excited around Holey-fin, crossing right under her jaw, then he approached again and tilted his belly toward her. Crinkles again approached Holey-fin, this time swimming over her flukes. He surfaced synchronously with her, close enough to be touching, then they were petting. As they moved toward Monkey Mia, no doubt at the discretion of Holey-fin, Crinkles became more excited, synching with Slash, then again with Holey-fin. All three males seemed excited behind Holey-fin, petting each other furiously as they sped in toward Monkey Mia. Crinkles sidled up beside Holey-fin, synched twice more, almost touching. Chunk was beside Holey-fin briefly, but it was clearly Crinkles who was most excited, porpoising beside her twice, going right over her snout the second time. Quite the opposite of herding, Crinkles seemed to be begging Holey-fin not to go into the shallows, but she did anyway, accompanied by intense whistling. When Holey-fin moved back into deeper water, Crinkles was waiting and sidled up beside her, almost touching, synching several times. He appeared to bond to her at one point.

We saw more of Crinkles' special interest in Holey-fin. On 21 April, when we were following SSC offshore, they returned to Monkey Mia to visit the girls. Holey-fin and Crinkles were petting, then Holey-fin rubbed under Crinkles. Nicky approached and bonded to Holey-fin. They all paused to chase tiny fish, then Crinkles did a rooster strut next to Holey-fin. He followed her around for the rest of the hour, even at the end, when she approached our boat, he was right behind her and they started petting again.

I remembered how violent SSC had been with the much younger Yogi in 1987,[*] yet here Crinkles was acting like a puppy around Holey-fin. He was clearly enamored of her.

* See "Reliving Old Glories"

§

Wave, Shave & Spud on Their Own

With the disappearance of SSB, Wave Shave and Spud had lost their older friends and "mentors." What would they do? We had plenty of opportunities to keep tabs on them as they visited the females at Monkey Mia.

On 7 March, Wave and Shave were following Nicky around in the Monkey Mia shallows. Wave did a rooster strut and more than once Wave and Shave synchronously charged at Nicky. But they clearly were not controlling her movements, as Nicky would just swim in and out from the people when she felt like it. Then Shave grew excited and rushed up and down parallel to the beach. He approached Wave, but Wave turned away. Shave bonded to Wave, and Wave kept turning away as Shave was tail-slapping excitedly. Around and around they went, in two and a half circles. Incredible! This was the same circle-swim that I had seen Snubby, Sickle, and Bibi perform when they were having partner disputes!* But there was no partner dispute here, or was there? I continued to watch them. After the circle-swim ended, they were no longer pursuing Nicky together. Shave left Wave and went offshore. Wave stayed around a bit and performed a solo display around Nicky, then he moved offshore. Later Shave came back in alone. I think Shave was entreating Wave to do something, perhaps to go after Nicky together or leave to pursue someone else, but Wave wasn't up for it and rejected Shave by turning away. The circle-swim was apparently more general than just a partner dispute among three males; it might occur when there was any kind of a dispute where one male refused another's "request" to partner with him for some task.

On 12 March Wave and Shave were after Puck, until Nicky arrived and they turned their attention to her. Wave and Shave performed an amazing series of rooster strut displays, with variations, around Nicky, including synchronous rooster struts. We followed Wave, Shave and Nicky when they left the park. After an hour or so they were joined by Surprise. Nicky and Surprise left the males, so this was clearly not

* See example in "Starving Dolphins"

a consortship, but the males were just as clearly interested and kept following them at a distance. Nicky bonded to Surprise for a few minutes. While they were bonding, Wave and Shave rejoined and TBC came on the scene, but Nicky and Surprise moved away from them as well. TBC only visited for a few minutes, and Wave and Shave just traveled along before abruptly turning east. Up popped Real Notch and Hi! Wave and Shave lined up head to head against Real Notch. Real Notch and Wave then got into a tiff; it was brief and they rubbed against each other when it ended. Wave lay on his side briefly and then Wave and Shave were again head to head with Real Notch and Hi. Hi moved a ways off then came back. Real Notch and Wave swam right by each other going in opposite directions, and then Real Notch and Shave did the same thing. Weird! Suddenly there was a chase; it was Hi and Wave, but I could not see who was chasing whom. Real Notch and Shave were sitting about 5 meters apart just watching the scene. They spread out to fish while Hi and Wave surfaced side by side a few times. In that position, Hi and Wave turned 180° to the southeast, then back northwest, then back southeast, then back northwest, then back southeast. They had turned 180° five times in a row! Shave rejoined Wave, and side by side, they left.

I had no idea what that bizarre direction-changing behavior was about, nor could I make sense of the entire interaction. There was aggression, a tiff and a chase, but no real fighting, and it all seemed kind of low intensity. Maybe RH and Wave & Shave were starting to recalibrate their relationship now that SSB were out of the picture. The next morning Wave and Shave were back inshore at Monkey Mia, strutting around and pursuing Nicky again, who stayed close to people, bonding with Holey-Fin when she wanted to avoid the males.

We enjoyed a relaxing six hours with Wave, Shave and Spud on 7 April. The only incident of note was when one of their friends from out east, Astro, joined them and promptly performed a tango with Shave. Otherwise, as WSS traveled alone, we were entertained by a lot of synchs, with many by Wave and Spud, some by Shave and Spud and hardly any by Wave and Shave. But there were also a fair number of triple synchs. Without SSB around to hijack one of them for partner duties, these guys were finally acting like a real trio. My impression was borne out in the analysis; the proportion of triple synchs among WSS increased after Snubby, Sickle and Bibi died, and was now in the range of "normal" trios like TBC and CBL.

On 1 June, we found WSS with the older trio Codon, Chewy and Judas. They found togetherness in getting after Lodent and Pointer. In the kind of interaction we had seen before, the two rowdy groups would split up and rejoin as Codon, Chewy and Judas were after Pointer, and WSS focused their affection on Lodent. Lucky, the older runt, just hung back and watched as his mates were goosed and mounted by the other trios. Lucky didn't hang back on 20 June. Lucky, Lodent and Pointer were with Wave, Shave and Spud who were performing impressive triple synchs, literally sandwiched together. The group became extremely rowdy with mounting, goosing and head-to-head posturing, then at one point Wave and Spud paired off to pursue Lodent while Lucky teamed up with Shave to "get Pointer."

§

TBC and CBL Reunited

On 15 March we found TBC with RH charging around the bay but later the same day we followed TBC with LLP. The next day, during a follow on Lucky and Pointer (Lodent was absent), CBL joined, as did Nicky and Puck a few minutes later. They engaged in petting and a few brief bouts of more intense socializing but mostly they rested. We noted petting in our group as another dolphin approached from 30 meters. It was Trips! He joined, followed by Cetus a few minutes later. Since RH divided them a few years earlier we had rarely seen TBC and CBL together. But the only noticeable reaction to their old friends was a spate of triple synchs by CBL. Otherwise they just continued to rest before Cetus, then Trips, peeled off to fish. That was anti-climactic! But as we soon discovered, RH were also in the area. After a leap-feeding bout, LLP and CBL approached a rowdy group, with CBL pulling ahead to join RH and some females. RH left and joined Lucky and Pointer, who were with Nicky and Holey-fin now. They displaced Lucky and Pointer from the position behind Nicky and Holey-fin and CBL rejoined. Then CBL and RH left together.

A month later, on 17 April, the girls came into Monkey Mia without any suitors. A few hours later LLP came in with Joy and one of her young female friends. They turned offshore and ventured out a few meters to meet TBC. Then I saw a trio only 40 meters away—it was CBL! TBC turned toward CBL and we scampered for the boat. By the time we got to them, TBC had joined CBL. LLP, sitting back 30 meters, had demurred. I looked around. No Real Notch and Hi. What would happen? I was excited. They were too. Chop performed two chin-slap-tail-slap displays, then he alternated chin-slaps with Cetus. Trips and Chop were intensely petting and rubbing each other; they rushed over and surfaced excitedly on our bow, even though we were barely moving. A tail-slap by Trips was followed by a series of Lambda-Cetus synchs. Puck, then Holey-fin, joined and several males started goosing Holey-fin, but they lost interest in the girls and just strolled around together in front of the park for the next half-hour. There were a few more synchs between TBC and CBL members but mostly they synched with their own. They moved further east, to the end of the dead-end channel and across the shallows into the channels out east. Given the windy conditions, that was not fun for us, but we were going to stick to them like glue anyway.

An hour of meandering was broken by a sudden acceleration. They charged into a group of Slash, Crinkles and Chunk, young Cookie, the female Nook and her infant Cranny, and the female Uhf. We didn't have time to identify a couple others as CBL and TBC clearly had designs on Nook and were excited around her. A minute or two of rowdy behavior and it was over. With Nook & Cranny in tow, and Uhf along for the ride, they left the others. As usual, in their excitement they got weird; Trips blew a big bubble under water, lifted his head up a bit, then bolted forward next to Bottomhook, and both took off and swam a fast circle, synched, and someone blew another bubble under water. There were several more inter-alliance synchs by Bite and Bottomhook. The level of excitement ebbed and flowed for a bit as they settled down, with CBL stationed behind Nook. Over an hour later we saw them on an intersecting course with another largish group; it was the trio Codon, Chewy and Judas with an eastern trio we had seen only a few times before and a female with her infant. The two groups joined; everybody was clearly excited, with dolphins surfacing at sharp angles to each other, singly and in pairs and trios. It reminded me of the time that Real Notch's group encountered the B-boys in 1986.* The groups separated, but Codon remained with CBL and TBC, who got after Codon, chasing and goosing him while CBL were still herding Nook! The socializing was intense and aggressive; there were hits, but it was unclear who was getting whacked. None of Codon's friends got involved; they just followed and watched. And just as the "get Codon" session got underway, another round of inter-alliance synchs started between Cetus and Chop, Cetus and Lambda, Trips and Lambda; Chop and Trips did several in a row; then Bottomhook got in on the act with Trips, and Bite synched with Lambda. Somewhere in the chaos Uhf had slipped away. After 20 minutes of giving Codon the business they stopped and left, still with Nook. Shortly after, in the heavy chop, we lost them.

What an incredible day! CBL and TBC found each other at Monkey Mia and went off northeast where I had never seen them go and, perhaps most importantly, where I had never seen Real Notch and Hi. I suspect that was intentional; CBL and TBC wanted to spend some quality time together and knew that RH would split them up. And apparently, among these males, there is no better way to rekindle a friendship than capturing a female and sexually harassing another male. I was fascinated that TBC and CBL dominated Codon like that, with his friends present. Codon was no young punk like Pointer or Lodent; he was at least their age and probably a bit older.

It was only a one-day affair for CBL and TBC as the next day Trips and Cetus (sans Bite) were back in the sex party at Monkey Mia with LLP and WSS.

§

Resolution

On 12 April, a few days before the great TBC-CBL reunion, we had followed CBL for nearly nine hours. Just after we joined, Bottomhook left. That wasn't unusual; often the odd-male-out would go off fishing

---

* See "Male Dolphins: The Politics Emerge"

alone. I was accustomed to seeing Bottomhook and Cetus off by themselves, tail-out diving to explore the bottom for a meal. Chop and Lambda joined up with several younger males to snooze for a few hours, but then they got moving again. As another dolphin approached rapidly, Chop and Lambda became very excited, increased their speed and raced excitedly around the bow of our boat. Who would it be? The dolphin surfaced; it was only Bottomhook. Chop and Bottomhook performed a striking tango, back and forth and back and forth they turned, four or five times, and suddenly Real Notch and Hi appeared. They were all extremely excited. CBL did a triple synch and performed another tango. They surfaced a couple minutes later petting. Real Notch did two tail-slaps and synched with Hi twice, and gradually everybody settled down. But Chop remained tight with Bottomhook and they synched a number of times. A few minutes later Lambda synched with Hi, then with Real Notch a few times.

Apparently, Bottomhook had been with RH and then he sped ahead of RH to rejoin his mates. But why the excitement and tango between males that were so familiar and that had only been apart a few hours? I had no idea, but it was fascinating.

A bit later, the two alliances separated but then came back together. Lambda and Real Notch synched and increased their speed. Real Notch and Lambda synched again, then RH and Lambda did a triple synch with Lambda in the center. Lambda and Real Notch petted; Chop was briefly on his side and everybody was excited as they moved in toward shore just west of Monkey Mia. They accelerated, porpoising toward a rowdy social group ahead. They closed in rapidly and a chase exploded out of the group; they had captured Nicky again. Not only had they captured her, they had taken her right out of the group of TBC, LLP, and Wave and Shave. Real Notch and Bottomhook synched twice. Wave and Shave synched twice as they followed RH & CBL with Nicky, but TBC and LLP stayed away. Wave and Shave followed our excited group for another 15 minutes before leaving. A half-hour after capturing Nicky, RH and CBL again picked up speed and moved toward a rowdy social group. It was TBC, LLP, Wave & Shave again, but now they were carrying on with Puck and Joy. As RH & CBL closed to 30 meters, we could see TBC split off from the group ahead and move away. Wave and Shave, with LLP, turned toward our group, then back toward TBC, and followed them away as ours joined Joy and Puck. TBC had clearly avoided RH & CBL, and the younger males had decided to follow suit.

Joy was bonded to Puck when RH & CBL arrived. The males were excited, synching side by side so close they were almost touching. Then Nicky bonded to Puck for a few minutes before Joy resumed bonding to Puck. There were displays and aggression among the males who seemed more excited around Joy now; Chop mounted her while she was bonded to Puck and somebody else rubbed her from below. Then Nicky mounted Joy! The males and Nicky were all after Joy while she remained fastened to Puck's side. This was amazing. Then Chop mounted Joy again. Lambda and Bottomhook synched. Then the females traded off bonding positions, Puck to Nicky, then Joy to Puck, and finally Joy to Nicky. CBL swam very tightly together synching, and RH got in formation behind Nicky. Wave and Shave were watching the action as they followed 30 meters behind our group.

TBC were with RH on 29 April, but three days later RH were back with CBL, charging around the bay causing trouble. Their first stop was with the young females Scratches and Flip, a runt, whom they goosed and mounted. Real Notch synched with Lambda twice. They sped away from Scratches and Flip to capture a female who had been peacefully fishing with her infant. They raised hell with her for 10 minutes, with synchs between Real Notch and Chop, then they left, traveling excitedly toward a rowdy group a few hundred meters to the southeast. Their flukes were kicking up in the air as they blasted into the group of Holey-fin, Nicky and Puck. Intense splashing and chasing erupted; we saw Bottomhook and Chop after Holey-fin. Real Notch was tail-flailing, as the males were excited behind Nicky and Puck. Real Notch and Hi performed a stunning series of alternating side-slapping displays. Real Notch synched with Chop, slapping his flukes on the way down, then they synched twice more. Nicky bonded to Puck.

Wave and Shave came close; they had been parked nearby watching. I suspect they had been with the females but cleared out when they heard the train coming.

The Real Notch group left 10 minutes after they arrived. Much of what we had seen today, I suspect, was simply RH and CBL targeting others as part of their male bonding exercises.

Twenty minutes later they were excited again; Hi lay on his side at the surface with his eye closed. Chop and Lambda gently pushed him up from below, then CBL, sporting erections, mounted him from below and above as he lay there. Then they settled down and resumed traveling.

We had a period of wind, then I left Monkey Mia and returned in the latter part of May. Back offshore on the 21st we followed TBC, who were with RH again. There was nothing unusual about that, nor our discovery on the 29th of TBC with Wave and Shave, but it certainly was entertaining. Wave and Shave were petting when TBC joined, and in the company of an excited Nicky. The two alliances launched into a series of inter-alliance synchs, Wave with Bite, then Cetus then Trips; Shave with Trips, then Bite, then Cetus! It seemed as if they were making sure that they covered all possible combinations. Some of the petting was inter-alliance as well; Cetus with Wave, then Trips and Bite petting Wave, who was between them.

Wave made a bizarre vocalization, then did a series of chin-slap-tail-slap displays. For the next hour, they remained excited around Nicky, but synched and petted with their own alliance partners. Then it started again, petting between Wave and Trips, then Cetus and Bite joined in. Puck and Holey-fin joined the group, and Puck jumped right into the petting, as Cetus stroked her. Trips snagged and Shave got excited, rushing around him. Trips lay on his side, then Wave and Shave swam forward past him on either side, and turned in and swam back past Trips; looping out and in toward his flukes; they did synchronous chin-slaps and dove steeply, flukes out of the water as they made another sharp turn to the back and forward again. A butterfly display around another male!* Later they did another butterfly display around Trips & Bite. The funny interaction between RH and Wave & Shave that I observed in March† had made me wonder if RH were renegotiating their relationship with Wave and Shave in the absence of the Beach Boys. Now I wondered if TBC were doing the same thing.

Our first sign that something was amiss came on the 30th, when TBC came into the Monkey Mia area with RH and Bottomhook! RH

* See "Wave's Bud Spud" and "Sex at Monkey Mia" for examples of males performing butterfly displays around Pointer.
† See "Wave, Shave & Spud on Their Own"

and Bottomhook were acting like a trio and had a female consort; they even did several triple synchs behind her. The next day we were in the boat watching a snoozing group of Wave, Pointer, Puck and Joy's Friend, when they turned toward a group coming in from the northwest. Wave and Pointer left the females just before the new dolphins arrived; it was Real Notch and Hi, and Bottomhook was with them again. Amazing; I wondered where Chop and Lambda were.

Real Notch and Hi showed up inshore again on 2 June with Trips and Bite. Nicky and Holey-fin would go back and forth between the shallows for fish and the channel for the boys. Most of the synchs were inter-alliance as the males chased around after the females.

On 5 June we saw Real Notch and Hi with Bottomhook again, fishing out in Red Cliff Bay. Then we had a period of bad weather and were stuck inshore for several days; male visits to Monkey Mia were waning during this time. Back offshore on the afternoon of the 12 June we found TBC herding Goblin, and Real Notch, Hi and Bottomhook with Two-scoops although, as usual, they didn't seem to be herding her.

It was now becoming clear there had been a change. What had happened? I hadn't seen Chop and Lambda since just before I left Monkey Mia in early May. I checked the records. We had TBC with RH and no Bottomhook during a follow on May 21, so maybe whatever happened occurred after that date. Were Chop and Lambda still around? Were they dead? Had they been driven from the area? I remembered that strange observation on 12 April when Bottomhook had been with Real Notch and Hi, then did that really exaggerated tango with Chop when they met up again. Were Real Notch, Hi and Bottomhook laying the groundwork for the change?

I would never know. And I never saw Chop or Lambda again, even when we expanded our study site several years later to cover a much larger area. Anything could have happened. They could have been killed or chased away. Dolphins or a shark might have killed Chop or Lambda, leading to the other being expelled from the group. The possibilities were endless, but the outcome was clear: the triangle among RH, CBL and TBC, which had started when Hack and Patches went missing in 1986, was finally resolved.

§

This Bonding Business

I'm not sure if I first noticed bonding among males or females, but by now it was clear that it was common among females but rare among males. We had seen bonding clearly during male circle-swims but that was about it. On the other hand, over the past few years, we had seen bonding quite often among females, especially when they were being herded or harassed by males.

12 June was a great day for bonding. We were with the new trio RHB and TBC, who were herding the female Goblin. Two-scoops was also there. Ten minutes after we started the follow, amidst rowdy social behavior, Nicky and Uhf suddenly appeared in the group. Nicky was bonding to Uhf, then a few minutes later to Two-scoops, and Uhf bonded to Goblin. Real Notch, Hi and Bottomhook split from the others as they chased, goosed and mounted Nicky. RHB did some triple synchs, and Bottomhook was in the center in a few. When they got back together a few minutes later, Nicky bonded again to Goblin, and Two-scoops bonded to Uhf. Hi rolled belly-up and did an upside-down rooster strut, then rolled right-side up, ending with a tail slap on his way down. Uhf bonded to Nicky for the next five minutes. The males continued to be excited around the females, and the females continued to switch off bonding partners for the next hour. There were several inter-alliance synchs, Hi and Bite, Real Notch with Cetus, and Bottomhook with Cetus and Bite. Real Notch and Cetus even did a butterfly display around Two-scoops and Nicky while the females were bonded! A bit later Two-scoops left and for the next half-hour Nicky and Uhf took turns bonding to each other. Uhf then snagged away from the group and left.

The bonding party on 12 June illustrates nicely how bonding commonly occurs between females when they are being herded or harassed by males, and that it occurs not only between females that know each other well, such as Nicky, Uhf and Two-scoops, but also between females that don't, like those females and Goblin. Goblin was not a Red Cliff Bay female. The males likely captured Goblin in her normal range north of Red Cliff Bay and brought her down to our area. Now it is highly unlikely that Nicky and Uhf had not met Goblin previously; we had never seen them together, but we only see the

Young Holly bonds to Puck. © Dolphin Alliance Project

dolphins for a tiny fraction of their lives. Their ranges overlapped at least part of the year, so they likely knew each other. But we saw enough of Uhf and Nicky to know that they were not regular associates of Goblin. Some females in Shark Bay have an extensive social network and, as our bonding observations illustrate, they can express friendly behavior to other females they rarely encounter. Why females might want to maintain such an extensive array of female friends is still somewhat of a mystery.

The female that plays the active role in bonding, by laying her flipper against the side of the "bondee," also positions herself slightly behind the bondee. This is close to the "infant position," and we know that infants enjoy an energy savings when they ride in their mother's slipstream. Now we don't think that the benefit of bonding derives from any energy savings; it is usually a short-lived behavior anyway. But bonding may be derived from the protective "infant" position, as an expression of support by one female for another.

§

RHB & TBC

I was interested to see what kind of role Bottomhook would take in his new trio. The bonding party on 12 June provided such an opportunity when we discovered that RHB weren't merely harassing Nicky, they were herding her. Nicky and UHF joined the group of TBC and RHB with Goblin and Two-scoops, so we didn't suspect that Nicky was being herded until she made a run for it, not long after UHF left the group. It is possible RHB hadn't decided to herd her until that point, but it was clearly a decision that Nicky found unacceptable. The males had just started to get excited behind her again when Nicky bolted. Real Notch and Bottomhook chased her and the rest of the dolphins trailed behind. Nicky had a 20-meter lead, but the males closed the gap and caught her, at least for the moment. She took off again and they chased; a pattern repeated several times: they would catch up, the group would slow down briefly, then it was off to the races again. The chasing went on for an incredible 14 minutes. Bottomhook seemed to be losing his enthusiasm for the chase, as he fell back 25 meters, but Real Notch was still right behind Nicky and caught her. She lay on her side as Bottomhook and Hi caught up. Real Notch popped in air as Nicky was four meters off to his side, but she did not approach him. They continued to swim excitedly around her. A few minutes later she came over to our bow with Bottomhook following about 4 meters behind. Nicky ducked under the bow and took off again, using the same maneuver that Square had employed to flee the Crunch Bunch in 1986!* The males chased briefly but soon gave up and moved into the shallows to fish. The next morning Nicky had fresh tooth-rake marks near her blowhole.

We followed RHB and TBC for several hours again on 17 June and again at the end of the day on the 18th. On the 23rd we found the two alliances together again, and RHB were herding the female Holey-hole, whose name was a play on Holey-fin.†

---

* See "Female Dolphins: Different Personalities and Lifestyles"
† Holey-Hole had a hole in roughly the same fin location, but it was open to the trailing edge of her fin; hence there was a "hole" in her "hole." That Australian sun again.

On the 26th we found RHB with Holey-hole, traveling with TBC. After a time they joined with a group of females to drive a school of fish. The feeding was followed, as was often the case, by a bout of intense socializing. One female remained in the group after the other females left and the males seemed interested in her, angling in to "inspect" her genitals. Evidently, she wasn't "there" yet, as they didn't persist and she left. The female moved into the shallows to fish and RHB must have decided that was a good idea and went in there to fish also, but TBC didn't follow. When feeding in the shallows one male would often go off to chase fish while the other stayed close to guard the female. As Real Notch ran off to chase a fish, Hi, who had been some distance away, immediately swam to Holey-hole's side. After fishing successfully, the males got excited and packed in close behind Holey-hole. They blew bubbles while doing rooster struts underwater, their snouts popping up as they surfaced. Real Notch chin-slapped as Hi and Bottomhook, side by side, shouldered him out of the way. Hi and Bottomhook oriented to Real Notch and blew more bubbles as Real Notch did a belly-slap. Hi and Bottomhook synched, and as Real Notch moved back in, they shouldered him out of the way a second time.* It looked like there was conflict in the new trio. Then it was back to fishing for the next hour.

They were soon joined by their old friend Two-scoops, and Real Notch and Hi immediately got in formation behind her before Real Notch and Two-scoops started petting. After the greetings were finished, it was back to fishing. Shortly thereafter Hi caught a Spanish mackerel. He lay on his side at the surface, holding the fish by the head, allowing the rest of the 15-inch body to dangle off to the side. Real Notch, Bottomhook and Two-scoops were beside themselves with excitement, zooming in close behind him doing three triple synchs with Two-scoops in the center. Bottomhook rubbed up against Hi, then nearly mounted him while Real Notch displayed on the other side. As Hi righted himself, a dolphin blasted right past him, then another pushed him up from below and he flopped on his side again. The intense socializing around a prostrate Hi lasted for seven minutes, and the entire time the long skinny mackerel was hanging like a lure for any taker. But Hi did the fish no damage and no one else touched it. Finally, Hi dove with the fish and when he

---

* See "Wave's Bud Spud" for similar cases of two males "shouldering" another away.

surfaced again it was gone.

Of course, we had seen this sort of behavior before, where a dolphin lies on its side with a fish, or throws it, and the others get excited but do not touch the fish.* But no observation before or since compared to this case in the level of excitement shown by the other dolphins or the length of time Hi lay on his side holding it. Neither have I seen a dolphin catch a Spanish mackerel again, so it seems safe to assume it was a real prize!

The 28th presented us with another twist in the RHB-TBC story. We found RHB with Trips only. The same female RHB had been herding, Holey-hole, was still here, but Real Notch and Hi had her, and Bottomhook and Trips were a pair, herding a female! They only kept her a bit under two hours, and when they launched into an area with leap-feeding dolphins, she was gone. After the feeding session, Trips and Bottomhook captured Nook. Amidst the usual excitement Trips and Bottomhook did synchronous belly-slaps. Trips popped in air and they got in formation behind Nook. As they settled down and traveled along, there were lots of synchs between Trips and Bottomhook and a surprising number of synchs between Real Notch or Hi and Holey-hole.

Hi came to the surface, popped, head-jerked, charged and hit Holey-hole with his flukes. To this point we had followed Real Notch and Hi with Holey-hole for 11 hours over two days and had seen no aggressive behavior whatsoever. Then in the space of two seconds Hi threatened, charged and hit her. In general, we see evidence of aggression in about half the consortships. But because the aggression can occur so quickly, and often underwater where we can't easily see what is going on, we suspect that the actual percentage of consortships maintained by aggression is much higher.

A bit later Trips became excited and swam two full circles around Nook while arching his head way up out of the water. This was followed by a butterfly display by Trips and Bottomhook. Twenty minutes later Trips was at it again, arching and tail-flailing, followed by another butterfly display.

We didn't get back offshore for a while but when we next found them, on 8 July, RHB and TBC were proper trios again and RHB still had Holey-hole.

* *See example with Scratches in "The Triangle in 1988"*

Then on the 12th Bottomhook was a no-show for a six-hour follow with RH and Holey-hole. TBC were present with a new female. We heard later that Bottomhook was with a group of juvenile males and females.

Things got complicated for TBC when the group joined a large mob of females and young males. Uhf was there and she was evidently pretty interesting. Cetus goosed Uhf, then he performed a genital inspection. Uhf rubbed under his flipper. A few minutes later Bite goosed Uhf. They were chasing fish, so Uhf moved away from the males. Then she came back. Hi approached Uhf and did a genital inspection. They commenced chasing fish again, then a large social group formed with over 20 dolphins. A chase exploded out of the group; it was Bite and Cetus after Uhf. The others just sat and watched. Bite and Cetus caught Uhf, but in minutes she bolted and they caught her again after a 60-meter chase. Trips had gone nowhere during all of this; he was still with the female and infant that TBC had been herding to this point. The observations lasted two more hours and TBC had the two females the entire time. When Real Notch and Hi took their female into the shallows to fish, they split from TBC, who still managed to keep both females. It was the first and last time I ever saw an alliance herd two females at the same time.

The absence of Bottomhook on the 12th may have reflected conflict in the new trio, or just the fact that it was July and the males were exhibiting the usual pre-mating season craziness. The double herding by TBC suggests the latter.

I would not know it until later, but the new second-order alliance of RBH and TBC was short lived. TBC were not seen after July 1989. Perhaps they went off somewhere to join their old buddies, Chop and Lambda.

§

A Female Coalition

We spent five hours with Wave, Shave, and Spud on 15 July. For the first 40 minutes or so they were socializing with the usual crowd of females, including Nicky, Scratches, Surprise, Uhf, Puck, Joy, Yin and Holey-fin.

After a while it was just the boys and little Yin; they were excited, chasing and mounting her. Yin's mother Yan and two little dolphins joined and Yan left with Yin. Then WSS got excited behind the little ones. It was hysterical; this tiny twosome could not have been more than 2 years old yet they swam side by side and even synched once. Where were their mothers? WSS were tight behind them for 20 minutes, following the tiny tots and even getting in formation behind them a couple of times. Yin and Yan came back around and Shave became very excited around Yin. He left his mates to follow Yin and Yan, racing all around them, rolling on his side and arching up, rushing in circles around them, then arching up on his back and side again.

Finally Shave left Yin and Yan to rejoin Wave and Spud. They traveled around at a leisurely pace for a time, then took off like a shot, racing toward dolphins ahead. They flew into the group and two dolphins took off at full speed. WSS chased, leaping side by side after their quarry. One of the dolphins ahead fell back, but WSS kept after the other. From tiny splashes nearby, we could tell it was a mother with her infant. They caught up to her with intense thrashing and splashing. We saw Shave charge the dolphin, who promptly blasted off again. They caught up to her again and were excitedly trying to mount her. I could see that she was all scratched up along her side. Her baby was still ahead of the pack 30–40 meters, keeping its distance from the melee. The mother was still trying to escape, porpoising along when we saw a group leaping in from the southeast. Then the groups were lined up, with the larger group chasing WSS, who were chasing the mother and infant. The males slowed down and the group behind closed in quickly. We drove over expecting to see male alliances so I was surprised to find Uhf, Joy, Puck, Scratches, Nicky and Surprise! The males were very tight together as the females simply snagged around them. Wave did a few chin-slap-tail-slap displays but there was no other interaction. WSS were packed tightly together. After five minutes like that, the two groups separated.

It was tempting to conclude that the females had come to the aid of the female that WSS were after. For the most part, it was the same set of females that the males were romping around with earlier, but the nature of their interaction here was decidedly different. And all six of the females were cycling. I never saw another event like this one. We had the case in 1987 of Nicky and Puck helping Poindexter escape from the Beach Boys,* but they did not accomplish that feat by confronting the males, as seemed to happen here. This remains the best possible example of females forming a coalition against males in Shark Bay. I doubt females could form an effective alliance against adult males in their prime, especially those with second-order alliance friends around. WSS were young and had only begun to herd females on their own in late 1988.

We had seen WSS herd mostly young, maturing females like Surprise and Joy. On the 27th we were with Wave, Shave, LLP, Joy, Surprise and Joy's Friend when E.D., Ceebie and Uhf joined them. Wave and Shave immediately became excited by Uhf, started synching, and charged her. They followed her closely as she moved away, then she rubbed under Wave's flipper. They moved away from the others, but Joy's Friend stayed by Uhf's side. Wave head-jerked, Uhf took off, and they pursued her. Shave popped in air, but Uhf ignored him. A few minutes later Wave popped, but again, Uhf did not respond. LLP joined the group. Joy's Friend bonded to Uhf. Wave followed them around, and there was a brief petting session between Uhf and Wave. A few minutes later Uhf and Joy's Friend just swam away from the group. Their departure elicited no reaction from Wave or Shave. Had Wave and Shave simply lost interest, or had Uhf just said "no", and the boys weren't quite big and old enough to do anything about it? Perhaps the support of Joy's Friend was critical. I recalled how she stayed with Uhf during her trying episode on 31 July of the previous year when Uhf was chased by Wave and Shave, but perhaps protected by TBC.† I saw no overt joint aggression by the girls against the boys so I can't say it was a coalition, but neither do I know what was communicated.

Harassment from juvenile males can be very costly to female mammals, so it might pay females to support each other against young males, and help in other ways against mature males, as illustrated by the Nicky, Puck and Poindexter case. We have few observations of such behavior in Shark Bay but we see a lot of bonding between females during harassment by males. At this point, we can't say that resistance

---

* See "This is Like Science Fiction"
† See "Wave's Bud Spud"

against males is the reason females have friendships with each other, but I suspect it is a factor.

§

The End of the 80s

I was winding down to the last days of data collection for my Ph.D. thesis. I had the data I needed on my main study males and took the opportunity to learn more about some familiar and less familiar males.

On 21 June we were following SCC when they blasted off toward a commotion ahead. It was their friends, George and Elroy, who had helped SSC steal Yogi from Snubby and Shave in 1987.* George and Elroy had evidently just captured a female. They were all very excited and Chunk and Elroy did a synchronous chin-slap-tail-slap display, then Slash and Crinkles did the same. Elroy made pops in air. SCC enjoyed the excitement of the moment with their friends, then traveled with them for a time after everyone had settled down.

On 13 July we found Codon, Chewy and Judas herding a female, and

A trio of males from the "Crunch Bunch" dive synchronously
© Dolphin Alliance Project

* *See "Reliving Old Glories"*

in the company of eastern friends, a male trio that we had seen a few times since 1987 and a younger male pair. We knew that we would eventually expand our study area to include these eastern alliances.

The Crunch Bunch lived to the northeast but visited Red Cliff Bay several times in July, likely attracted into the area by fish or estrus females. They were a young maturing group of 10 males and we hadn't sorted out their pairs and trios. We knew that juvenile males usually didn't have stable partners, so maybe they would be forming those soon and break up into smaller groups. But during my last week we saw them herding the adult females Uhf, E.D. and Nook. On the 21st we were watching the Crunch Bunch out northeast where they met up with other alliances. They would certainly be worth watching more in the future.

On the 23rd I had my last look at RHB before leaving. They no longer had Holey-hole but were acting like a good trio. They joined the Crunch Bunch, all 10 of them. This will be interesting, I thought, and it was. I was always impressed with how tough RH seemed to be, and these were younger males certainly, but there were 10 of them. Still, RHB totally dominated. They goosed and mounted members of the Crunch Bunch, whose only response to the abuse was to lie on their sides submissively.

RHB left the Crunch Bunch and headed south over the Monkey Mia banks. There was a dolphin ahead; they swam right past but I stopped. It was the old male Steps and he had a small shark, only a foot long, wiggling in his mouth! This was too strange to pass up, so we ditched the follow to watch Steps. He carried that shark around for 45 minutes, often working it into the bottom as dolphins do to break up larger fish. But other than killing it eventually, I saw no damage. Then he dove and when he came up it was gone. I guess he swallowed it. An hour later we saw Steps with another shark. It was yet another case of something I saw for the first and last time. I can only imagine that old Steps was having a tough time catching fish, so he opted for the sharks, which were clearly much harder to "process." Steps had lost his partner Kodoff and, as it turned out, he was in his final year.

As I was packing to leave, I could not help reflecting on all I had learned over the last several years. Obviously, the highlight was our discovery of two levels of alliance formation, the stable pairs and trios that herded females and teams of two alliances that fought against others. I remembered when SSB brought that female with the new infant into Monkey Mia in early March of 1987. And I thought back to that incredible day in August of the same year when TBC recruited RH to help them steal a female from SSB.

I was very fortunate, during my Ph.D. thesis years, to be able to watch Snubby, Sickle and Bibi at Monkey Mia, while the alliance triangle of RH, TBC and CBL was playing out offshore. The SSB relationships illustrated the cooperative-competitive relationships among individuals, while the triangle showed us that there were complex relationships between alliances, something that was unheard of outside of our own species. The synchronous surfacing and displays among allies was another area where human and dolphin male alliances had converged. The 1980s had been an incredible crash course in dolphin social intelligence. So much had been laid out before me, and all I had to do was watch and keep my boat motor running. I was one lucky dolphin watcher!

I also thought about the future and what new dolphin discoveries Shark Bay might yield to the persistent observer. I found myself fantasizing about yet another level of alliance formation in the bay. We had seen the B-boys and Sharkies together; maybe they formed a third level of alliance to rule the north. Maybe the Crunch Bunch would cooperate with other eastern alliances. Now that would be amazing! I had to get back here, but for now, I had a lot of data to analyze and a Ph.D. thesis to write.

Part II

Beyond Red Cliff Bay

1990s

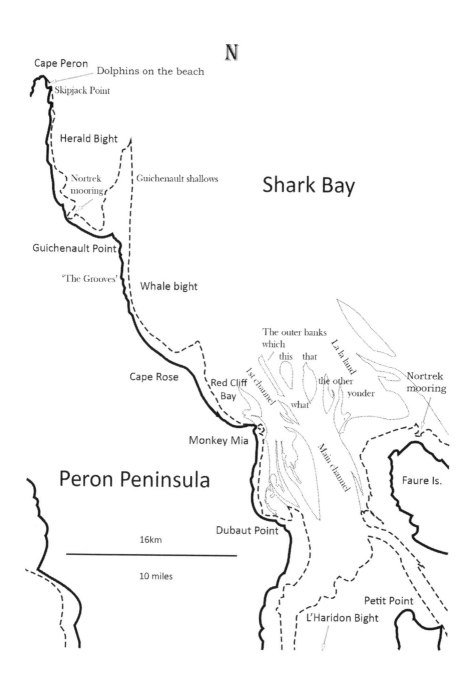

N

Cape Peron — Dolphins on the beach

Skipjack Point

Herald Bight

Nortrek mooring

Guichenault shallows

Shark Bay

Guichenault Point

'The Grooves'

Whale bight

The outer banks which

this   that

La la land

Nortrek mooring

Cape Rose

Red Cliff Bay

1st channel

the other

yonder

what

Monkey Mia

Main channel

Faure Is.

Peron Peninsula

16km

10 miles

Dubaut Point

Petit Point

L'Haridon Bight

Interlude: Nortrek & NOVA 1991

Into the Frying Pan

After successfully defending my thesis in December 1990, I returned to Shark Bay twice in 1991. Neither trip was for my research on the male alliances. I went down for three months to help start another project, then returned later in the year to help with a film on our research that was being made for NOVA, the well-known scientific documentary series.

I landed in Perth on 22 February and was joined by the leader of our new effort, the Swedish biologist Per Berggren, and Jeff Skelton, an assistant from Canada. A life-long sailor, Per was a tall, lanky good-natured man who worked hard but was easy-going; just the kind of person I enjoyed working with. Coming from the frigid northern winter, our timing could not have been better as the next day broke the record for Perth at 116° F (46.2° C). Welcome to the summer in Australia!

As we drove up Peron Peninsula on the evening of the 28th we were treated to a light show from thundershowers just north of us. We pulled into Monkey Mia just as one of those beautiful mothership clouds arrived, with a gust of wind and a spit of rain, its layers glowing in the moonlight.

Early the next morning we strolled down to the beach to see the newest addition to the Monkey Mia dolphin crew, the young female Surprise. With the addition of Surprise and Crooked-fin's return, there were now five hand-fed dolphins visiting Monkey Mia, plus their always-entertaining infants.

But we could not lounge around watching the beach dolphins; we had work to do. Our attention shifted quickly to Nortrek, the 36-foot catamaran that would be our home for the next three months. We had acquired Nortrek from Paul Anderson, an older Canadian biology professor, who had used it for his dugong (think manatee but a bit sleeker) studies in Shark Bay, but was now wrapping up his career. The National Geographic Society funded both projects, so it was a case of great timing, and they simply transferred the boat to us.

Until now our work had been confined to Red Cliff Bay and surrounds. We had come to know a lot of dolphins but wondered how big the community was and whether the dolphins were doing the same things up and down the Peninsula. Nortrek was to be our mobile home; we would tow our little boats to each new location, then spend a few days checking out the local dolphins before coming back to Monkey Mia to resupply. I was excited at the prospect of exploring parts of Peron Peninsula that I had never seen.

We thought we might find dolphins doing things differently elsewhere because the ecology of the bay is not the same everywhere. There is a strong salinity gradient along the length of Peron Peninsula, from super-salty water at the bottom of the peninsula to oceanic salt levels off Point Peron. Not much lives in the really salty water; it is as clear as a swimming pool. And coral can grow only when salinity values are not much higher than in the open ocean, so the only decent reef is at the top of the Peninsula.

Unfortunately, it looked like we had a reef on Nortrek. She had been sitting on her mooring for some time and all sorts of marine life had found her hull to be very accepting. Colorful fish darted in and out of the aquatic jungle that covered every inch of Nortrek below the waterline. With all those extra passengers Nortrek was none too fleet; we had to jibe to change direction as she refused to tack.

Monkey Mia was not the place to clean Nortrek. It would require a trip across the bay to Carnarvon, the town due north of Monkey Mia across the bay. There we could haul Nortrek out of the water, clean her hulls and apply a fresh coat of antifouling paint.

We could not make the trip to Carnarvon for two weeks but we had plenty of other work to do to get Nortrek ready for use. The summer heat in Australia didn't make our job easier. The wind at that time of the year isn't cooling; you feel like an oven is blowing on you. And the Australian desert sun is not to be trifled with.

Despite my warnings, Jeff was determined to get a nice tan. He worked deliberately toward that goal, exposing his pale, innocent winter skin for brief periods to the sun. He thought he was being careful. After a few days he announced that he had enough of a base to lie out in the sun for a bit at mid-day. Twenty minutes to be exact, but that was enough to put him in sun-poisoned agony that night. He broke out in a rash and was itching so bad he literally could not sit or stand still. Fortunately, I remembered the hot water treatment. We boiled water and poured it on a cloth that he could apply to the rash. His relief was so great I could almost feel it.

Australia is a black person's continent, so it is no wonder that the skin cancer rates among the white population are the highest in the world. During the Austral summer I had taken to wearing long white martial arts pants and a long-sleeved shirt that covered my fingers. On bare skin the sun hurt. I used to joke that I covered up so much because sunscreen would just sizzle on my skin. I received one of my worst burns in Shark Bay after an 11-hour boat day in July, the middle of winter. It may have been understandable that I would forget to slap on sunscreen on a cloudy, cool winter day, but I paid for it with a painful burn.

About the time Jeff got burned I was on the beach and saw a middle-aged couple, fresh from England, lying out on the beach at mid-day. The wife had removed her top and was lying face down with her back fully exposed. Her skin was that pasty white, almost pinky color, of a baby who had never seen the sun. I could not believe their stupidity. I walked up and spoke sternly to the husband, "20 more minutes like that and you should just drive her straight to the hospital because that is where she will need to go." He scowled at me and I walked away, not looking back to see what they did.

Once we had the boat ready, we sailed to Carnarvon to give Nortrek her makeover. With her reef slowing us down, the trip took twice as long as it should have. I had been to Carnarvon once before, in 1988, to give a talk to the Rotary Club. The town fathers were concerned that the young people left at the first opportunity. That was, perhaps, not surprising. The shoreline had also shifted over time so the once 2-mile jetty was now a 1-mile jetty. It seemed as if even Shark Bay itself was trying to escape from Carnarvon. As low as my expectations were, the reality of our visit was even more dismal.

We had been warned not to steer into the Carnarvon channel at night, but there we were, in a raging southwesterly. After entering the channel, which was an obstacle course with unlit poles failing to announce sharp turns, the inevitable happened. We ran aground. As we bounced around, a large cracking sound elicited heightened concern. Per got the motor going and used an anchor to swing us into the wind, and eventually, off the sandbar. But the damn wind pushed us right back onto the bar and we had to repeat the procedure. We finally got away from the bar and threaded our way into the harbor.

We hired the slipway to pull Nortrek up on the rusty jinker and dug into the miserable task of cleaning the reef off in 100-degree heat. We worked hard and got it done by sunset. The people we interacted with were no more pleasant than the heat. The next day, 3 April, we sanded and painted, then put her back in the water on the 4th. We sailed out on the 6th, thrilled to be leaving that place* and heading home. We were sailing into the wind, so we had to tack back and forth all night. Dawn greeting us with the visage of Monkey Mia; it had never looked so nice.

§

Dolphins on the Beach at Cape Peron

Our first data collection trip was on 10 March, going north around Guichenault Point to Herald Bight, where we nestled into a wonderful pool near shore. That night, too-close-for-comfort lightning roused us to put out some jumper cables that would direct any strike to the water. I learned that Per, who had a sailor's superstitions about the weather, did not appreciate it when I teased and dared the nearby storms to "mess with us."

The next day Per and I surveyed to the top of Peron where, just north of the lighthouse, we were greeted by a stunning orange bluff that, set against the blue sky and water, still ranks as one of the most beautiful natural sights I have ever seen.† We also saw and photographed lots of dolphins, including one with a sponge. Of course, I scrutinized every dolphin group for any indications of male alliances!

We went back to the top of Peron the following day. Per was scanning

* *I understand that Carnarvon is now a much nicer place to visit.*
† *And that bluff graces the cover of this book!*

close to shore and spotted a large group of at least 10 dolphins clumped near the beach between the lighthouse and the orange bluff at Point Peron. He shouted excitedly that a dolphin had beached itself! I grabbed binoculars and saw a second dolphin launch halfway out of the water. What were they doing?

We drove into shore for a closer look. A dolphin was swimming slowly along the beach, patrolling right at the water's edge. A spray of water signaled a sudden acceleration and the dolphin was flying along, hydroplaning on a cushion of water only a few inches deep. A quick turn and the dolphin came partly out of the water onto the beach with a prized fish in its mouth. The dolphins were beaching in pursuit of fish!

We kept watching, mesmerized by the spectacle before us. The dolphins stranded and caught more fish. We watched a beautiful and majestic black and white Sea Eagle swoop down and snatch a fish off the beach just before the dolphin could grab it.

A dolphin beaches in pursuit of a fish at Cape Peron. © Simon Allen

Yet another exciting discovery in Shark Bay! Similar beaching behavior or "strand-feeding" is common in the southeastern U.S., where groups of dolphins drive schools of small fish onto mud banks exposed at low tide. However, in Shark Bay, single dolphins perform strand-feeding in pursuit of larger, single fish. The beautiful hydroplaning by the Shark

Bay dolphins is, to me, more spectacular than the beaching itself.

The Peron beaching behavior appeared to be another specialized feeding tactic, like sponge-carrying. This was demonstrated in later years by Per and others. Like sponge carrying, beaching seems to be a mostly female habit; although there are only a few beaching dolphins and many spongers.

The morning after we returned to Monkey Mia from Peron, I stood on the jetty watching the beach dolphins accepting their daily regimen of fish-handouts. I realized that accepting dead fish from people in the shallows at Monkey Mia is also a kind of specialized feeding tactic, just like sponge carrying and strand-feeding, albeit one practiced by males and females. We had wondered if any dolphin could join the Monkey Mia club, or if the beach dolphins maintained an exclusive membership. So it was interesting that Surprise had joined the club. Maybe she was allowed in because she was friends with the beach dolphins. She lived in the area and loved to ride our bow as we left the park heading west into Red Cliff Bay.

I also thought about why we saw strand-feeding at Peron but not elsewhere. We often watched the beach dolphins chase and catch fish in the shallows at Monkey Mia. When chased by a dolphin, a frantic fish would often seek refuge at the water's edge where the dolphins could not follow. This made for great comic theatre as the fish would just sit there, bathed with sonar by a frustrated dolphin who was undoubtedly trying to figure out how to scare it back into deeper water.

But the Monkey Mia dolphins never beached in pursuit of the fish they chased. The reason seemed obvious. The beach at Monkey Mia is not as steep as the one up at Peron, so a dolphin that strands at Monkey Mia or any similar beach might have a hard time getting back into the water. It is simply too risky to strand-feed in most Shark Bay locales.

§

Beyond Red Cliff Bay

Our first dolphin-watching trip out of Red Cliff Bay had certainly been fun, so we were anxious to explore other areas. Our next venture was to the east of Monkey Mia, across the channels to Faure Island, which was used to farm Angora goats. We parked in another nice pool set in a broad expanse of shallows off the north end of the island. With the southerly wind coming off the island, we were treated to the sweet fragrance of a cormorant rookery in full bloom. While Per and I tooled around the banks looking for dolphins, we came across the biggest shark I have ever seen; an over four-meter tiger, with its back exposed and a huge tail fin standing high in the air but flopping over with every sideways stroke. I could not believe that such a monster was in water so shallow. With an oar, we estimated the depth at about a meter. Ridiculous!

Two days later we motored way out northwest, which was far to the northeast from Monkey Mia. We saw a large group of dolphins, blasting along as we tried to snap pictures. Where were they going at such speed? I looked ahead but could not see any leap-feeding or social group. They continued to leap along at high speed, gradually turning in a large circle, then started another, and it hit me. They weren't running toward anything, they were fleeing from us! Their evasive behavior was so contrary to my experiences in Red Cliff Bay, and even Peron, that it had taken me a while to see the obvious.

We later found that many of the dolphins we encountered in that area were strongly allergic to our presence. I think they were just not familiar with boats. Smallish recreational fishing boats regularly visit many areas along the peninsula, but not the area to the northeast of Monkey Mia that I came to call "La-La Land." It still amazes me that we have in Shark Bay some of the tamest dolphins in the world, but out in La-La Land they flee as though we are invading aliens.

We spent the next day in our little boat, circumnavigating Faure. The scenery was beautiful and we practiced slowly easing closer to skittish dolphins so we could photograph their fins.

Our next destination was closer, just the other side of Cape Rose, which marked the northern end of Red Cliff Bay. We would survey from there up to Guichenault. This meant running into familiar dolphins. Seeing a trio of the Sharkies, Snap, Crackle and Pop, was most exciting for me. Just south of Guichenault bluff, we pulled into a lovely beach by two beautiful, closely spaced gullies that perforate the towering bluff there in a blaze of yellow and orange. "The Grooves," as we would come to call the gullies, was inaccessible except by boat. The Grooves offer a delightful beach for a respite, and the climb up the side of one of the gullies is rewarded with spectacular views. I have tried to stop there at least once every season since 1991.

We went back to Herald Bight and Peron on 9 April, this time with marine mammal photographer Flip Nicklin on board. Flip was traveling all over the world on an assignment for a National Geographic article on dolphins. Flip and I spent a day on the "beaching beach" so he could photograph the strand-feeding behavior, but the dolphins mostly snoozed in the shallows. As we stood there, silently urging the dolphins to strand-feed, two stonefish came clumsily bopping along the water's edge, standing out dramatically against the white sand. Stonefish, which look like algae-covered versions of their namesake, are perhaps the deadliest fish in the world, with an array of sharp dorsal spines that would inject highly toxic venom and searing pain into anyone unlucky enough to step on one. This was just not fair, I thought, stonefish were supposed to confine themselves to rocky and weedy habitats where they blend in so well they are nearly invisible. Yet, here they were, swimming over beautiful white sand. The pool by the beach had seemed inviting until they swam by.

The next morning we were sitting in the galley when a red-faced Flip poked his head in saying there was someone who wanted to speak to us. While doing his morning business off the end of the boat he had somehow failed to notice the massive Australian coast guard vessel sidling up alongside Nortrek. I'm sure they got a laugh out of catching Flip unawares. Now, there had been some drug running in Shark Bay, so they may have been suspicious about two Americans, a Canadian and a Swede up at the top of Peron, but they bought our story and went on their way.

I had discovered on the previous trip that squid were abundant up at Peron. I had never fished for squid before but I love calamari so wanted to give it a try. As the sun touched the horizon I tossed out the squid jig and felt a tug. I yanked hard and as the squid came flying out of the water, it let loose a cannonball of ink that clipped my shoulder, sprayed the mainsail and absolutely nailed Jeff, who was standing in the cockpit wearing his favorite shirt. He was not a happy man!

But everybody enjoyed the several squid I caught each evening. Eventually, after decorating the side of Nortrek with dark splotches, I learned that one didn't have to pull so hard when the squid latched on. A slight tug and the squid would shoot their ink out underwater, sparing Nortrek and its inhabitants from being splattered with each catch.

After a nice dinner of squid and being gently rocked to a good night's sleep on Nortrek, we were ready to survey lots of dolphin groups each day.

The surveys were fun, but it was a bit frustrating for me because we weren't really watching the dolphins; we just went from group to group spending little time with each. Once we photographed a social group where sharp jerks of the fin indicated head-jerks, a clear sign of aggression. They were probably males. How I would have loved to stay and follow them around, but that was not our mission. Per's study was focused on surveying dolphin groups along the entire length of the Peninsula, and time spent watching any one group meant fewer groups sighted.

Our next trip was back east to Faure Island. We saw a dolphin with a shark bite scar so fresh that it was still oozing white blubber. Then in the shallows we happened upon a single dolphin poking around the seagrass looking for fish hiding there, a behavior we call "bottom grubbing." Suddenly it lifted its flukes high the air and brought them down forcefully, producing a nearly 3-meter high spray plume. Why did it do that? Maybe it was irritated by our presence. Perhaps the fluke-slaps were part of a hunting strategy. The dolphin did the same thing five more times: flukes raised high, then "kerplunk" as the flukes hit the water. I knew that sound. Way back in 1982 an older couple traveling around in a cement hulled sailboat had taken us out for a little tour and we had stayed overnight in this same spot on the north end of Faure. As we sat on the deck on that perfectly calm night Rachel and I heard strange "kerplunk" sounds carrying across the still water. At the time, we deduced that dolphins were making the sound by slapping their flukes, but we had no idea why. Now that I had seen the behavior it was still a mystery, but one to be solved in the future.

After the Faure trip, Per and Jeff traveled up north to visit Coral Bay and I set out to test an idea I had a few years earlier. On a walk along the ocean face of Peron in 1988, I saw what I thought were large, offshore bottlenose dolphins like the large dolphin that had stranded in Red Cliff Bay back in 1987.* The large-looking dolphins were just lounging in the shallows. The different detritus I found along the beach there also impressed me, bits of coral and different types of shells. Even the sand felt different, coarser, between my toes. I figured that our small dolphins were more abundant in the seagrass-based habitat south of the ocean face but up there, with oceanic salinity levels allowing coral to grow, maybe the big dolphins predominated. Perhaps they enjoyed the reef fish they might catch around coral. I would head up to Peron in my little boat, survey along the ocean face, then travel down the other side, ending my trip at Denham. I would find small dolphins along either side of the peninsula, but the big ones along the ocean face. The theory was perfect; it couldn't miss. But it did. All I saw on my four-day excursion were our smaller dolphins. Oh well, other than being ambushed by hordes of mosquitoes at night, I had a great time, enjoying stunning scenery and beautiful solitude.

When Per and Jeff returned we headed back up to Herald Bight. Our first day out we found a large group with Two-scoops, the Red Cliff Bay regular and the masculine female friend of Real Notch and Hi! We hadn't seen any of our Red Cliff Bay dolphins in Herald Bight, so that was exciting. Another distinctive dolphin in the group looked like one we had photographed at the top of Peron on an earlier trip, so this one group may have linked dolphins from Point Peron to Monkey Mia! A couple days later we saw Couch, the old female that came into the shallows to visit Holey-fin in 1987 and 1988. Herald Bight was her winter home but, as we would later learn, the northern dolphins moved southeast in the spring. So when Couch was "in the neighborhood" she would pop into Monkey Mia to visit with Holey-fin. It amazed me that

*See "Stranger in a Strange Land"

some females had seasonal social relationships.

That was our last trip. Per would return to continue his Nortrek study several times during the 1990s. I would get back to my study on the male alliances, but not before returning in August to help make the NOVA film.

§

NOVA: Filming the Boys

Only three months after leaving Shark Bay, I was back to help with the NOVA film. Although I wasn't there to do my own research, part of the focus of the film was my male alliance research, so I would get to watch the boys again. Since I left in 1989, there had been a few big changes. After Trips, Bite and Cetus vanished in July of 1989, Real Notch, Hi and Bottomhook had formed a new second-order alliance with Lucky and Pointer. Lucky and Pointer's old friend Lodent vanished a month after TBC. Two of the old guys, Steps and Chunk, had also "gone missing," but Slash and Crinkles were still around, sometimes with George and Elroy.

On 15 August we found Wave, Shave, Spud and their eastern friend, Astro. On this day Wave and Shave were clearly a pair as were Spud and Astro. After a time the two pairs split, with Wave and Shave racing ahead of the other two. They entered a group, then exploded out chasing a female. The chase covered a mile and a half but that didn't make the film. Weighed down by the film crew and their equipment, and running on the 6 hp motor, we could not keep up. Wave and Shave were still very excited around the female when we caught up. Five minutes later Spud and Astro slammed into the group and two tiffs broke out! It was Shave against Spud and Wave against Astro, both pairs lined up head-to-head jawing at each other. That part did make the film, along with my excited jabbering, as I had never seen a "double-tiff." Probably Spud and Astro were upset that they had not been in on the capture, but they calmed down after a few minutes and the same males that had been arguing minutes earlier were now petting each other. Social mammals often reconcile after spats and we had just seen a great case of that in our dolphins.

Two days later we followed Real Notch and Hi for eight hours. They joined up with Lucky and Pointer and later Bottomhook. They traveled north and ran into a trio of B-boys who were herding Munch. Aggression broke out and they chased one of the B-boys and mounted him repeatedly. Real Notch's crew then left the B-boys and went north to another group, and as they entered the group all hell broke loose again. There was more aggression, including side by side head-jerks by Real Notch and Hi. Bottomhook performed an apeshit display, arching up on his side and tail-flailing. Then a big chase broke out, and Real Notch, Hi and Bottomhook captured a female from the group. It might have been a theft since some members of the group were males who may have been herding the female. Later they rejoined the B-boys, but this time the interaction seemed friendly and they continued to shadow each other for some time. Perhaps the earlier interaction, when they were mounting one of the B-boys, had been a demonstration of dominance, and RHB didn't need to remind the B-boys who the boss was so soon after.

A male careening around during an "Apeshit" display.
© Dolphin Alliance Project

A few days later we found Fred and Barney with a female. Pointer was hanging around as well. We heard pops on the hydrophone, that aggressive herding vocalization we had discovered in the 1980s at Monkey Mia,[*] but the males weren't doing much. I found myself wishing that RHB would come in to spice things up a bit and five minutes later they did! I saw them approaching side by side in glorious synchrony. Our group turned away from RHB, who came within a few meters and floated at the surface, snagging. Apparently in a show of "respect," Fred and Barney approached and rubbed under their snagging seniors. Then they all became excited, and in that context, Fred got angry with Barney and chased him around. I remembered the day in 1986 when Snubby and Bibi got into a fight after joining with CBL.[†] Fred and Barney had given us another example of a spat between friends that occurred because of something that happened when they joined with other males.

These observations also showed me that, despite the changes in their second-order alliance partners, RHB had not lost a step and still dominated Red Cliff Bay politics.

But what happens when they go outside of Red Cliff Bay? The group, still excited, traveled farther north past Cape Rose into Whale Bight. There was a breeze, so it was moderately choppy. The group slowed a bit, then sped up again. I saw a fin ahead and thought we were going to see a capture. Sure enough, a chase broke out; but then another chase started and suddenly tons of dolphins were blasting around all over the place. It was total chaos; we ran around trying to identify dolphins and saw five of the Sharkies with the female Munch, but there were other dolphin groups charging around. We found our group again and the female that had been with Fred and Barney was gone, but they were all ganging up on Hi! They lined up behind him, charged and literally threw him out of the water. What had happened in all the chaos with the other dolphins to cause Hi's friends to become upset with him? Hi must have blown it in some way. Maybe it had to do with the loss of the female, but she wasn't being herded by RHB anyway. Well, all that seemed to be forgotten soon enough as they spread out to fish again. Shortly after, RHB captured another female who lived in the area.

I still wanted to sort out what had happened in that mob scene, so we went back to find the other alliances. We found the five Sharkies and

[*] *See "Pop Goes the Dolphin"*
[†] *See "Male Dolphins: The Politics Emerge"*

three B-boys with a different female. Nobody had the female that Fred and Barney had been herding, so we had not seen a theft, at least not by those guys. But then I didn't know how many males had been involved; it had happened so fast we were caught off-guard and the sea conditions were lousy. What I did know is that it was a bigger affair than I had ever seen, with more dolphins chasing around than in the Battle for Flo-Jo in 1988. I had left in 1989 wondering if there might be a higher level of alliance formation, or something else beyond what we had been able to see in Red Cliff Bay. I had an unsettling feeling that something important had just happened right in front of our eyes, but we missed it.

The filming was over and I went with the film crew back to Perth. However, Andrew called from Monkey Mia to announce that Holey-fin had a new baby! She had been huge for a few months so we knew she was due any day. This would be too good to miss, so we went back up. The film crew got the shots they wanted and left later that day, but I stayed on a bit longer. I'm glad I did because I was treated to an interesting insight into relationships between females. We had rarely seen aggression between females, but the next morning, about 10 minutes after coming in, Puck got into a tiff with Surprise. The tiff was very different from those I had seen between males. Instead of lining up head to head and shaking their jaws up and down, they angled in at about ninety degrees to each other and made little back-and-forth head-jerks as though they were taking turns making their points. It soon escalated, but instead of full on fighting with hitting and whirling around to avoid strikes, Puck and Surprise were pushing and shoving. We saw several rounds of Puck and Surprise tiffing over a few days. Surprise clearly initiated a few of the tiffs and Puck initiated the shoving match in one case. It was fascinating, and got us thinking again about female pecking orders and whether the beach dolphins defended their "resource" from others. Surprise was the new addition to the group, so maybe she had to endure some aggression. On the other hand, she was younger than Puck but also bigger, so maybe she decided it was time to assert herself.

My time with Per and Jeff exploring the east side of Peron Peninsula and the "mob scene" we had witnessed with the NOVA crew (but not sorted out) convinced me that I needed to extend my work on male alliances significantly beyond the confines of Red Cliff Bay. So it was back to the US to a post-doctoral position at the Woods Hole Oceanographic Institution and a lot of grant writing. In 1992 we published our first major scientific articles, including one in *The Proceedings of the National Academy of Sciences*, describing the two levels of male alliance formation. That one attracted the attention of *The New York Times*, leading to a headline article in the weekly *Science Times* section. The NOVA film aired in the U.S. that year and was later adapted for broadcast in the U.K. Our study was on the map!

The Wow Crowd

1994-1997

The Cast

Male Alliances:

The **Wow Crowd** were a group of 14 males inhabiting the area between Cape Rose and Guichenault. **Latch, Hobo & Gripe** formed the most stable and successful male trio in the group. The rest of "the central committee" included **Myrtle, Pik, Roleypole, Veetop, Wow** and, for a time, **Anvil**. Other group members included **Ajax, Krill,** the old male **Vax**, his friend **Horton**, and the youngest member, **Wannabee**.

The **Prima Donnas** were an alliance of seven males that "crystallized" over a 3-year period, 1995–1997, and included several individuals that we knew well as juveniles in the 1980s **(Fred, Barney, Natural Tag, Prima)** as well as **Big Midgie Bites** and **Ridges & Wabbit**.

The **Kroker Spaniels** were a large loose group of at least 12 older juvenile/maturing males that lived in Whale Bight. Members of this group included **Ceebie** and **Skini**, who were seen often as dependent calves with their mothers in the mid-1980s.

The **B-boys** were two trios in the 1980s, but were now 5 strong: the trio **B-jay, BamBam & Bumpus** and the pair **Bo & Biff**.

The **Sharkies**. The 1990s incarnation of this group included **Sharky, Crackle, Sylvester, Fang & Terra,** and the infrequently seen **Sly**. We suspect that Sharky, Crackle and Sylvester formed a relationship with Fang and Terra after the disappearances of 1980's members **Snap & Pop**.

Peace, Love & Understanding were a trio of males seen rarely in Whale Bight. They probably lived mostly further north or offshore.

The Females of Whale Bight:

Bad Ghost, Dent (Duchess), Dunce, Goblin, Holey-hole, Kwisp, Mini, Nip, Square (Peglet), Tab, Tryky, Tuck (Nip's oldest daughter), **Wanda**

Juveniles & Maturing males of Red Cliff Bay:

Urchin (son of **Uhf**), **Jessie** (son of **Joy's Friend**), **Cookie** (son of **Crooked-fin**). **Captain Hook** and **Bly** came into Red Cliff Bay from the east.

§

A New Project

After three years in New England, at Harvard and Woods Hole, I returned to Michigan in 1993 - 1994 to start a three-year stint with their "Society of Fellows," an inter-disciplinary post-doctoral program. I was excited about the new dolphin project we were starting that next summer. Over the years I had noticed that males in the same alliance or in buddy alliances would coordinate their movements around the bay at distances where vision was not an option. They had to be communicating by sound, but we knew little about dolphin communication.

Dolphins make two general kinds of sounds, clicks and whistles. Each dolphin makes its own distinctive "signature" whistle, which we now know they use when separated or when meeting up at sea. Dolphins are superb mimics and there is evidence that they copy each other's signature whistles and respond with their signature whistle when another dolphin calls them by "name."

Dolphins also use rapid-fire trains of clicks, focused like a flashlight beam, to see objects in their habitat. The returning echoes from this dolphin sonar reveal exquisite detail about the size, shape and even density of objects in their path. Clicks are also packaged into a variety of social sounds. Some click-based sounds, like growling and screaming, are clearly aggressive, while others may be friendly.

Rachel and I decided to try to find out what kind of sounds dolphins were using to coordinate their movements in Shark Bay. This would not be easy. There was a reason we knew so little about dolphin communication. Humans are adapted to hear sounds in air; put us underwater and we can't locate the source of sounds, and if you can't tell where sounds are coming from, you don't know who is talking, so good luck learning about communication. Other mammals, like your cat or dog, might help us out by moving mouthparts when they make sounds, but dolphins don't avail us with such clues because they produce sounds inside their head and don't have to open their mouth to "speak."

While we could not just put a hydrophone in the water and tell where dolphin sounds were coming from, we knew that a dolphin whistle or click would sound louder if the animal producing it was close to a hydrophone compared to an animal that was far away. This fact gave us the basis for a plan. Using two boats equipped with identical video and sound-recording systems, we would simultaneously record the sounds and behavior of alliance buddies when they were separated but coordinating movements. If two buddy males separated for a time, I would follow one and Rachel would follow the other. Sounds made by "my" dolphin would be louder by my boat and sounds made by Rachel's dolphin would be louder at hers.

Our plan was great in theory, but a nightmare in practice. There is an old adage about any system involving electronics: the number of problems goes up exponentially with the number of connections. We had a ridiculous number of connections. Our video camera, powered by an inverter that fed off the boat battery, fed into a recording deck that also received the hydrophone input. We used an early model GPS to get exact universal time off a satellite so our recordings would be synchronized. Well, the information from the GPS had to flow into a time code reader to be stamped on the video. There are two kinds of time code and of course we had to put the other kind on the video. So we had the time code reader transfer information to the time code translator for conversion before it went into the video recording deck. The GPS ran off the boat battery and the time code devices were each connected to their own battery packs. Whew!

Since we were going to be expanding our study area considerably beyond the confines of Red Cliff Bay, we needed at least one bigger boat. So after arriving in Perth, I went shopping with my new assistant, Mike Heithaus,* a tall, blonde 19-year-old from Oberlin College who had the energy of five people. After poking around boatyards, we checked the used boat ads and found a gem being sold by an older gentleman living in a suburb south of Perth. His 15-foot yellow fiberglass boat was much better than anything we had seen in the boatyards, so we pounced on it.

I dubbed my new boat "Bony Herring" after the dolphins' favorite fish. It came with a noisy two-stroke motor but we needed quiet for our recording. Fortunately, much quieter four-stroke motors had just come on the market in Perth so we put in an order for one.

Mike went on to have a stellar career in Marine Ecology.

We towed Bony Herring up to Shark Bay on 5 June, arriving in the early evening. We were greeted by the body of a dead dolphin that had just been recovered from a beach nearby. I knew the fin; it was the young female Tatters. My first full day in Monkey Mia was spent standing in a pool of blood dissecting Tatters. We simply wanted to learn what we could.

Tatters looked as if she had been healthy; she was not at all emaciated. I made a mid-line incision from the genitals up to the level of her flippers. Yellow fluid that looked like pee came spurting out, and I thought I had cut into her bladder. More fluid gushed out, way too much to be urine. Then I saw a tiny dorsal fin, folded over; Tatters had been pregnant! The fetus was a female and 51 cm long. I was amazed as Tatters was only 180 cm. Our dolphins can exceed 2 meters but here again was evidence that mature animals can be considerably smaller. We did not have the skill or knowledge to determine why Tatters died, so that would remain a mystery.* We buried Tatters and her fetus up behind the park, but not before collecting and preserving bits for later DNA analysis. Tatter's tissue was the first contribution to the study of dolphin genetics in Shark Bay, an area of research that would become a major focus in the years ahead.

The month of June was much like starting out in 1986; we were setting up a new project and there was a lot of work to do and problems to sort out, with new and old equipment. Even three of the four tires on our car went flat that month, so we had to get a new set. In fact, everything seemed new; the park had been completely rebuilt and was now run by a really professional operation. The new owners valued our presence and did not charge us rent for campsites. That was, and still is, a financial lifesaver. Additionally, researchers were now giving weekly talks to any interested members of the public, a tradition that continues today.

We did manage to get out on the water that first month. My dolphin ID skills were rusty, so I needed to start looking at dolphins again in the bay and the catalog to get back up to speed. Seeing Real Notch, Hi & Bottomhook for the first time on 7 June was like running into old friends. Other researchers had been keeping tabs on them the last few

---

* *Now when dolphins die we send them to Perth for a proper necropsy.*

years and they had observed Real Notch, Hi & Bottomhook maintaining a steady relationship with Lucky and Pointer. Only Pointer was with them today. I didn't realize it at the time of course, but that was a hint of changes to come.

I thought about how much had changed in the Bay since the 1980s. So many of the males that had been central to my Ph.D. study were now gone. Snubby, Sickle and Bibi had died in the 1989 pollution disaster. We had witnessed the mysterious disappearances of Bottomhook's mates, Chop and Lambda, amidst the political changes orchestrated by Real Notch and Hi. TBC vanished a short time later. The old "Gerries" that I had followed, Spike, Slash, Crinkles, Chunk, Steps and Kodoff, were all gone as well. Only George's boy Elroy was still hobbling around. Pointer and Lucky's young friend Lodent was not seen after 1989. Shave was not seen after 1991.

Wave was still with his bud, Spud, but not for long. We saw Wave and Spud together for the last time on 8 June. We saw Wave a few more times, alone, surfacing in a very odd fashion. When dolphins look for fish near the bottom, they take four to five breaths, then dive, arching their tailstock up or lifting their flukes out of the water as they descend at a steep angle. But Wave was arching like that with every breath in only 12 feet of water, and his breath smelled awful. We last saw him on 8 August. Spud had now lost Shave and Wave, but he would soon join Captain Hook and his friends, a group of mature and maturing males whose main residence was just to the southeast of Red Cliff Bay, in the area where we had first seen Spud in 1988.

With the loss of so many of the males we had studied in the 1980s, we needed to find new alliances, so we decided to expand our range from Dubaut Point to the southeast and northwest to Guichenault.

On the 8th we learned of another dead dolphin near Cape Rose. We went looking for it with David Charles, a ranger at the Dolphin Information Center. We didn't find the dolphin but did manage to run out of petrol. I was still using the gas-guzzling two-stroke at that point; it was the first and last time I would run out of petrol. Fortunately we were near shore and Mike was quite the athlete so he jogged back to get help. A new tourist operation had started up to take people out to see dolphins, dugongs and other wildlife on board a big beautiful catamaran, "Shotover." Harvey Raven, the owner, kindly came out to give us a tow back to Monkey Mia. Harvey has helped us in countless ways over the years.

On the 9th I read a fascinating letter from Bob Warneke, a biologist with the South Australian museum. They had found two male bottlenose dolphins stranded together on the coast there. The dolphins had been battered to death, likely by members of their own species. I thought about Chop and Lambda and wondered again what had happened to them.

We saw RHB on the 14th, briefly with Uhf. Her infant, Urchin, was born in 1991 so, I thought to myself, Uhf should be "coming on" this year. The males were probably checking her out. We saw RHB with Lucky and Pointer again on the 17th, but Bottomhook was tighter with Lucky and Pointer. They traveled three abreast with Lucky in the center. Most of the synchs were between Lucky and Pointer or Lucky and Bottomhook. That was interesting, but I remembered from watching TBC, CBL and others that on any given day the males might deviate from the "normal" pattern of association and synchrony.

Of course, we weren't there just to study the same males I had watched in the 1980s, and most of those guys were gone now anyway. We were making jaunts out to the east and north to find new alliances and to become more familiar with males we already knew, albeit not well. Out east one day, Rachel and I followed an intriguing group of unfamiliar males that were evidently herding a female. Listening with our hydrophones, we heard the strangest—and creepiest—aggressive vocalizations either of us had heard before or since. It is possible that groups in different areas of the bay produce different variants of particular vocalizations, but more likely the sounds were made by an individual whose sound producing structures were abnormal. After all, we have heard strange whistles out there, including one individual who sounded like a cicada.* In the next decade, we would come to know that eastern group as the Exfins, but our destiny in the 1990s would be just to the north of Red Cliff Bay, in Whale Bight.

On 23 June we found a group of eight dolphins including one female, but most of the rest were suspected to be males, including Wow, a

* See "Real Notch Meets the Wow Crowd"

"Wow" was named after our reaction to his shark bite scar.
© Dolphin Alliance Project

dolphin Rachel and I had photographed in 1982. We had named the dolphin "Wow" because that was our reaction to seeing the large shark bite scar behind his dorsal fin. Wow and his friends didn't live too far north, so they were good candidates to include in our new study. Just how good would become evident later that year.

§

Jaws

Now I would think twice about jumping into the water if I was visiting a place called "Shark Bay," but I am constantly amazed to see people flopping around in the channel in front of the park, doing what looks like their best imitation of a dying fish. Only one small area, where the dolphins are fed, is off-limits to swimmers. Otherwise, you can take your chances anywhere you like. Nobody has been killed, yet. And yes, large sharks have been seen in the channel and occasionally they swim right into the shallows.

I recall an incident from the late 1980s when an Englishman walked down to the water's edge and saw his girlfriend swimming in the channel. He ran into the water, swam out and almost literally dragged her back to shore. Following an animated conversation on the beach, he left her and stormed up to the ranger's center where I was chatting with the head ranger Sharon. He burst through the door and angrily confronted Sharon. "You said she could swim out there and there are sharks in the bay!" Sharon shot him an exasperated look and replied, in a slightly irritated voice, "I said she *could* swim out there; I didn't say it was a good idea." It took every bit of self-control that I could muster to not burst out laughing.

What about the dolphins; do they have to worry about swimming with sharks? We haven't seen a shark attack a dolphin, but judging from the shark bite scars we see, the answer is an emphatic yes. Inspired by the movie "Dances with Wolves," we named a dolphin that was sporting a substantial bite scar, "Swims with Sharks." Once, while Holey-fin was being fed by people in the shallows, a 2-meter tiger shark killed her infant, who was mucking around in the channel. We didn't see it happen, but tourists witnessed the attack. Holey-fin and the other dolphins chased the shark, but it was too late for the infant, who was killed almost instantly.

We also just missed seeing another dolphin infant killed near Monkey Mia. As we were coming back into Monkey Mia on 10 July, Nicky approached our boat, mouth open, begging for a fish. That was typical of Nicky; she begged from all the boats, but what caused us alarm was the absence of her 7-month old infant. Our concern was justified; the infant was gone. Nicky had left the Monkey Mia beach with her infant within a half-hour of our finding her alone. The crew on Shotover had seen a 3-meter shark in the area the day before. As for Nicky, well, her reputation toward people and other dolphins extended to her mothering skills; to this day she has never had a calf survive to adulthood.* We joked that Nicky may have encouraged the shark.

A week later, Mike and I were cruising around on a glassy calm Red Cliff Bay when we came upon a skinny 8-foot shark with big black eyes cruising lazily at the surface. To our surprise, it did not flee or sink out of sight when we approached, as the tiger sharks do in deeper water. It clearly wasn't a tiger, but we had no idea what it was. When I splashed

---

* Nicky died in 2014 but her last calf, born in 2008, is not yet mature but is still alive so we are hopeful!

my hand in the water the shark approached and it seemed fascinated by our motor. This was one weird shark.

So what were we going to do about this shark? Let's follow it! We could follow and videotape the shark just like we did the dolphins and maybe we would see something interesting. It didn't take long. The shark veered and swam slowly toward a snoozing group of eight dolphins, all females, including three who were with their 3-to 5-year-old toddlers.

The shark swam directly into the group. The dolphins dove abruptly then came up leaping, and did not stop leaping for nearly 12 minutes! Nobody was hurt, but those dolphins certainly got one hell of a fright. We know that even tame dolphins flee when they are with scared, evasive dolphins. Dolphins simply stay with their friends. So it seems likely that the only reason that the adults kept leaping for so long was that the little ones were scared.

The snoozing dolphins obviously had no idea the shark was approaching them. Tourists often make the comment that you are safe in the water if dolphins are around because dolphins are aware of any danger. Maybe not.

Looking at our video and photographs, I tried to "key out" the species of shark from a book at the information center, but I kept coming up with species that were one or two feet long. I sent everything to Perth for a proper shark expert to evaluate. A few days later I received the verdict; our skinny 2.5-meter shark was a great white; a juvenile great white, but still a great white! I didn't recognize it as such because I had never seen a picture of a juvenile, only big fat "Jaws." The shark biologist further explained that the big black eyes, lack of fear and fondness for our motor were typical of a white shark. Next time, I thought to myself, I won't wiggle my hand in the water.

Although white sharks are not common in Shark Bay, tigers are and they clearly are a problem for our dolphins. Mike went on to do his Ph.D. on the dolphin-shark interactions in Shark Bay and found that tiger sharks are incredibly abundant, at least during the warm months. For some reason, judging from the appearance of fresh wounds, March seems to be a favorite time for sharks to bite the Monkey Mia dolphins, but I have seen a fresh bite in July so no month is completely safe for the dolphins.

A fresh shark bite in July. No month is completely safe.
© Dolphin Alliance Project

That point was driven home again several days later. On 20 July, we followed Real Notch & Hi for nine hours. In the morning they were roaming over the Monkey Mia banks where Nicky and Surprise were poking around. Lucky and Pointer came on the scene and suddenly a chase erupted; Real Notch and Hi were blasting after Nicky, who was racing to Monkey Mia. Nicky made it into the shallows and was lounging among the people while Real Notch and Hi watched from just offshore. They waited and waited and seemed ready to give up and leave when Nicky finally sauntered out with the rest of the Monkey Mia females. We were excited, anticipating the start of a herding event, but nothing happened. Nicky rubbed up against one of the boys and that was that. Real Notch and Hi followed her for a while, then seemed to lose interest. However, the next morning, when Nicky was a no-show at Monkey Mia, we knew where we would find her. Sure enough, we found Nicky with Real Notch and Hi, and Bottomhook was present but he was herding the female Pseudopee with Pointer. Lucky was not around. They headed north and crossed over the Cape Rose shallows. In only half a meter of water, there was none of the familiar up and down surfacing of dolphins; instead their dorsal fins sliced menacingly through the water like sharks.

We found the same group the next day, but Pointer and Bottomhook had traded Pseudopee in for Wanda, a deep-water female who lived north of Red Cliff Bay. Bottomhook was unusually aggressive to Wanda, popping at her constantly, perhaps because she stayed closer to Pointer. As the sun dipped low on the horizon, RH and Nicky moved into the shallows to chase fish. Nicky caught one, broke its head off but left the fish at the surface. Real Notch and Hi investigated, coming within inches of the fish, but did not touch it. Nicky came back and ate the fish. Another example of that fish ownership thing.

Perhaps encouraged by the fish captures inshore, Bottomhook and Pointer started to move into the shallows toward the RH group, which panicked Wanda's 2-to 3-year-old. The tiny tot would not follow mom into the shallows, remaining back at the deeper water's edge, whistling frantically, sometimes coming over to the relative comfort of our bow. Bottomhook and Pointer came back out with Wanda but the scene was repeated several times. I was looking over at the RH group, heard the whistling start up again and knew that Bottomhook and Pointer had turned back into the shallows with Wanda. Poor Wanda was caught between a rock and a hard place. At one point, as Bottomhook and Pointer had led her into the shallows 30–40 m from her infant, Wanda stopped, torn between the demands of her frantically whistling calf offshore and the threats from Bottomhook, popping at her from the other side. Finally, all the males came back out from the shallows and Wanda's little one nestled up under her, not just in the infant position, but pressing into Wanda's belly. Why had Wanda's infant been so afraid? Other females swam in the shallows with their infants routinely. But Wanda was a deep-water fishing "specialist," so her infant had probably never experienced the shallows. It was a new and scary experience for the young one.

As it was getting dark we left the males with Wanda and started for home, but just as we got underway we saw the signature "V" ripples of a small shark's fin slicing the glassy calm surface. We went over for a look at the little guy and were startled by a 3-meter tiger shark. Only the tip of the fin had been protruding above the surface. Wow. While we had been watching the drama with Wanda, forced by the males to leave her youngster in deeper water during the dangerous sunset hour, this large predator had been lurking nearby. The entire scene was a fascinating illustration of the coercive nature of herding and the potential costs to the females and their young. I remembered a day from November 1988 when we happened upon a smallish tiger shark, and then only two minutes later we encountered the female Munch with her brand-new infant and Holey fin's juvenile daughter Holly. The company of female friends, young and old, may be especially important for mothers with newborns.

As part of his Ph.D. study, Mike also checked carefully for shark bite scars and found that over 70% of our dolphins have been bitten at least once, and some more than once! That is an astonishingly high percentage, greater than any other population studied so far. Most of the shark bites are on the top half of the dolphin as they are unlikely to survive if a shark opens their belly. If a dolphin can't avoid being bitten, the best it can hope for is to take the bite on the back, so we suspect they roll their back toward the shark just before impact.

A few years later we found a recently killed dolphin that didn't make that roll fast enough. We were cruising through the middle of Red Cliff Bay on a nice July day and talking about a dead dolphin someone had sighted over the banks north of Monkey Mia when we nearly ran over it. A shark had removed a good portion of the dolphin's peduncle. Mike came over with his boat; we managed to hoist the body onto the side of his boat for the tow home. We estimated the dolphin's age, based on a few speckles, at around 8–9 years. Much of his genital area was missing but a stump of his penis remained; it had been cleanly cut through. Ouch.

Another thing I hear tourists say is that they would love to be a dolphin. Maybe not.

§

A New Bond

We found RH with Nicky again on the 24th, but this time Pointer and Bottomhook did not have a female. We saw Lucky nearby. He approached to within 30 meters of his buddies, but did not join. For a while, Lucky was shadowing the group, moving parallel at about 100m. What was going on with Lucky? Why didn't he join his mates? Later in the afternoon, Bottomhook and Pointer charged into a group of females, capturing Square who was with her calf Peglet, her older daughter Squarelet and another female. Again, Bottomhook was quite aggressive; at one point he head-jerked and charged Square. We next saw them on 2 August, just as Bottomhook and Pointer were capturing E.D.* We had seen Bottomhook and Pointer as a pair now on four consecutive sightings and each time they herded a different female. And still... no Lucky. We found them again on 8 August and this time Bottomhook and Pointer had Tryky. While they were in the shallows chasing fish, Lucky was shadowing them again, lurking out at the edge of the deeper water. On each of the next three sightings Bottomhook and Pointer had a different female and RH still had Nicky. On the 21st, Puck was the "female of the day" for Bottomhook and Pointer. During the follow the two alliances approached and joined a group of three females with infants. Lucky was snagging 30 meters away. We suspected that he had been in the female group but had to move away when his "friends" approached. After the follow we found those same females again and Lucky was with them.

Over a three-week period, Bottomhook and Pointer had herded a different female on each of the eight days we found them. But why did they herd Puck?

Puck was almost certainly not in estrus; her calf was only 20 months old at the time. While we have had a few three-year intervals between births in Shark Bay, most females don't begin cycling again until their calves are at least 2.5 years old. Indeed, Puck did not become pregnant again until December 1996. I realized that it was not about Puck, it was about Pointer and Bottomhook's new and fragile bond with each other. I thought about all the herding of non-estrus females by SSB in the 1980s.† I had concluded that some of their herding was more about male bonding than the female. Real Notch and Hi had apparently excluded Bottomhook from the Nicky consortship, so he formed a new bond with Pointer, at Lucky's expense! Bottomhook and Pointer

---

E.D. had a large range and a lot of dolphin friends, hence her name which stands for "Enigmatic Dolphin."

† *See "Any Female Will Do"*

probably had an unrelenting need to reinforce their delicate new bond by herding a female together, and whether she was actually in estrus was of little consequence.*

After 35 days with Real Notch and Hi, Nicky came back to Monkey Mia on the 24th. Incredibly, exactly one year later, on 24 August 1995, Nicky came into Monkey Mia with a brand-new infant. Our DNA tests showed that Real Notch was the father.

Things went back to normal after the Nicky consortship ended. Bottomhook was free to join RH again and Lucky would return to his friend Pointer. For the last month of our field season, RHB herded several females and were often in the company of Lucky and Pointer, who herded females also.

On September 12, we started a follow on Lucky and Pointer who were soon joined by RHB, who were herding Square. The meeting was marked by inter-alliance synchs, a tango by Lucky and Hi, then a profusion of inter-alliance petting. A need to reinforce their bonds may have been the motive for an excursion to Monkey Mia, where they engaged in an intense but brief herding of Nicky that included hits, synchronous displays and very bizarre and intense synchronous buzzing sounds. It was not at all clear to us which males had Nicky, and at one point we thought that RHB had Square and Nicky! We were probably more concerned about which males had Nicky than they were, as they abruptly let her go but continued with the inter-alliance love fest.

§

Kerplunk!

We went southeast looking for "east-side" gangs on 20 August. Not finding much, we turned back north. Scanning ahead with binoculars, I saw whale spouts! My heart raced; I had rarely seen whales in Shark Bay, so we sped north for a closer look. However, when we arrived at the location where we had seen the whale spouts it was only 1.5 meters deep and there were just a few dolphins poking around. Suddenly one of the

---

* For other examples of "male bonding" herding and harassment of females by non-provisioned males, see "Resolution" and "Poor Vax".

dolphins lifted its flukes high out of the water, then drove them down, "kerplunk," and up rose a 3-meter "whale spout." Then I remembered seeing the dolphins making similar "whale spouts" with their flukes while working with Per out on Faure in 1991 and hearing them at night while anchored at Faure way back in 1982.*

Another of the dolphins arched its flukes high out of the water and kerplunked. This was fascinating; we had to figure out what this kerplunking business was about! We watched and videotaped a mother fishing with her infant for an hour and a half. The water was clear; the bottom was covered with seagrass and the dolphins in the area were bottom grubbing, poking their snouts into the seagrass as we often see them do when looking for fish hiding there. Occasionally the mom would catch and toss a large chunky brown fish, together with seagrass that she had grabbed with the fish.

The following year we went looking for kerplunking armed with an underwater camera in addition to the regular one. We followed a female for five hours and she kerplunked over 200 times! She was totally unconcerned with our presence. Once she kerplunked so close to the boat that the splash got us; I had to quickly jerk the camera out of harm's way. Looking closely at our video, frame by frame, we saw that the dolphin pivots as it raises its flukes, lifting them so high that the peduncle comes out to the level of the back of the dolphin's dorsal fin. Then the flukes descend, hitting the water at a 45–80 degree angle, producing a small but inconsequential splash. But the flukes continue to drive into the water in a cloud of bubbles and the water collapsing in behind the flukes creates the "kerplunk" sound and the subsequent whale's spout. You can do the same thing in the bathtub or a swimming pool by slapping your hand in the water, making a little splash or driving it in, making your own little kerplunking whale's spout.

Our star kerplunker caught 10 of those same browny fish during those five hours. The fish captures occurred while she was bottom-grubbing; she would lunge and wheel sharply around with powerful fluke strokes, then surface with the fish and a mouthful of seagrass, often tossing the fish a few times. The sonar she emitted during bottom grubbing was punctuated by a squeal and bite sound when she caught the fish. Her

* See "Beyond Red Cliff Bay"

calf made a few appropriately small kerplunks. At one point two dolphins chased and captured her, in what we think was a herding attempt, but the interlopers left when we approached; they were unfamiliar to us and were likely afraid of our boat. Later two juveniles joined her and began fishing and kerplunking as well.

Since observing kerplunking the previous year, I had read up on fish to figure out what might be going on. I discovered that some fish have a big nerve cell that produces a dramatic startle response when a predator is closing in. The pressure wave from the attacking fish triggers the startle, which is an automatic reflex much like the way our knees jerk when tapped by the doctor during check-ups. The fish startle response causes big muscles to contract and the fish to jump forward a bit, just ahead of snapping jaws, buying it a split second to make an escape. Intriguingly, a range of stimuli can trigger the startle response; even tapping on the side of an aquarium or dropping a ball into the water might do the trick.

We think the dolphins use the sound produced by kerplunking to startle fish hiding in the seagrass. If we are right, it is an extraordinary trick, as the dolphins are eliciting one fish predator avoidance behavior (startle response) to defeat another (hiding in seagrass). The kerplunking dolphin startles a fish, whose sudden movement gives away its hiding place, and then it's lunchtime for the dolphin. This idea explained why some kerplunks occurred after a failed fish chase and others seemed to occur randomly. The dolphin might kerplunk to find fish in the seagrass or to relocate a fish it had missed.

Someone once asked why the dolphins didn't simply use the almost magical powers of their sonar, which can easily "see" through seagrass, to find the hiding fish. But dolphin sonar is narrowly focused like a flashlight beam. When a dolphin is in less than 2 meters of water oriented to the bottom, its head is in or close to the seagrass. The sonar beam, so close to the bottom, will cover only a tiny area. To search even a modest area for a hiding fish using sonar would require an energetically costly and time-consuming search.

Kerplunking looks and sounds like it takes a bit of work as well. A remarkably high percentage of the dolphin's body is lifted out of the water during a kerplunk. And, most amusingly, the ongoing click trains are accentuated dramatically as the flukes are driven toward the water, as though the female is constipated and straining, until the moment of impact.

We have seen both males and females kerplunk, so it isn't a mostly female behavior, as are the sponging and beaching hunting techniques. Kerplunking is much more common over the banks to the southeast and northeast of Monkey Mia. When looking over my data, I discovered that I had seen kerplunking only once on the banks just north of Monkey Mia, even though we drive over those banks all the time. It may be that the fish species that are hunted with kerplunking are more common on the banks out east, or that the dolphins that live there have such a large area of banks in their range that it pays for them to put in the time to learn the behavior.

Kerplunking has since been described in a few other locales, notably Florida. I saw film of kerplunking dolphins in Florida Bay. They lifted their flukes only a short distance out of the water, so the behavior there is not nearly as dramatic as in Shark Bay. It may be that our diminutive dolphins must put more of themselves into a kerplunk to achieve the requisite effect on hiding fish.

§

The Wow Crowd

On 19 August we found Wow and his friends in a big group. We were familiar with several of the fins from past surveys. We watched them for a few hours. They were separating and coming together in trios and a pair, and one trio was consorting the female Holey-hole, whose infant came and went. Latch, Hobo and Gripe were behaving like a good trio, swimming side by side synchronously. Our friend Wow was with Myrtle and Roleypole, also clearly a trio. Evidently, when doling out new names we had thought Myrtle was a female, but he was certainly acting like a male today. Vax, with his chopped off fin, was paired up with Horton. There was another trio, and still another suspected male, Veetop, joined. We had four alliances, at times joining into one big group!

Everybody in this "Wow Crowd" seemed to get along. Were second-order alliances of this size possible? Maybe this huge group was just a temporary association between smaller second-order alliances that simply happened to tolerate each other fairly well. I would have to find these guys again soon!

A week later we found the Wow Crowd again, and they were still in their huge group! The day revealed another startling surprise; Latch had been in a trio with Hobo and Gripe previously, but today he was herding a female with Hobo and Pik! Gripe was herding a female with Myrtle and Veetop.

We found them one more time during the 1994 season, on 9 September. Now there were four trios and each was herding a female!

And again, to my utter amazement, the trios had been reshuffled again. None of the trios were the same as any that we had seen during the previous two sightings. Hobo, Myrtle and Veetop were one trio; Wow, Pik and Roleypole were a second trio, Gripe, Horton and Vax were another trio and the final trio featured Ajax, Anvil, and Krill. Latch wasn't around this day. I cannot overstate how startled I was. We were so used to stable pairs and trios, to calling out names of trios, like "CBL" and "TBC" as though they were single individuals. Yet here was a group of clearly adult males that was not only considerably larger than any other group we knew, but their trios were so labile that they seemed to be playing the alliance equivalent of musical chairs.*

I was sold on the Wow Crowd. Somehow, I was going to find a way to focus more on these guys. I had to. They did not fit "the model" that I had established in my Ph.D. research, that male pairs and trios, or "first-order alliances" were strong and stable and that teams of pairs and trios, or "second-order alliances" were composed of two first-order alliances. Sure, some relationships within and between these groups changed over time and we saw the occasional odd herding partnerships, such as Bottomhook and Pointer this year, or Trips and Bottomhook during the 1980s,† but the overall pattern had been pretty consistent. In the 1980s I had watched SSB with WSS; SSC with Steps & Kodoff; there were the two B-Boy trios and TBC with CBL. When RH moved in on the TBC-CBL relationship it became an unstable situation, basically proving the

---

* *When reviewing survey records, we discovered that we had photographed ten Wow Crowd members together in 1987, along with some females that they consorted frequently in the 1990s.*
† *See "RHB and TBC"*

importance of two alliances together. And RHB had formed a new second-order alliance with Lucky and Pointer the past few years. Of course, sometimes alliances seemed to have more than one alliance friend, as we saw with SSC and George & Elroy, but the pattern seemed to hold reasonably well. But did it? There was that funny group, the Crunch Bunch, who were 10 strong in 1989.* They were just maturing then, so we figured that they would break up into stable trios or pairs. However, in 1994 we still had eight members of the Crunch Bunch and no matter how you sliced it, they had at least three alliances' worth of males.

Those few days of watching the Wow Crowd had shattered my confident sense of understanding. In fact, I felt quite the opposite, almost clueless. That wasn't right either, but when I left for the U.S. in late September 1994, I knew that I still had a lot to learn about male dolphin politics in Shark Bay.

§

The Death of Holey-fin

After the 1994 field season I interrupted my three-year stint with the Michigan Society of Fellows to help some colleagues at the Center for Advanced Study in the Behavioral Sciences at Stanford write and assemble what we hoped would be a cutting-edge review of whale and dolphin societies. So when I arrived in Shark Bay the next July, I was carrying a lot of unfinished chapters that would occupy many a windy day.

The first morning I was greeted by ranger David Charles, who related disturbing news. Holey-fin was not surfacing normally. I went down to the beach for a look. David was not kidding; Holey-fin was surfacing just like a newborn dolphin, popping up to the surface, lifting her snout out of the water for each breath. This could not be good.

I watched her for some time. What a terribly inefficient way to breathe; it looked like she was exerting herself with each breath. And she looked really thin. Holey-fin was clearly in trouble. We talked it over

* See "The End of the 80s"

and decided to increase the amount of fish she was given significantly. I spoke with a dolphin vet in Perth who suggested that we soak her fish in fresh water and give her nutritional supplements.

The next day I called Sam Ridgway, who had counseled me when Holey-fin had been burned so badly seven years earlier.* Sam listened closely as I described Holey-fin's odd surfacing, then replied that he had seen that in other dolphins minutes or hours before death. He tried to soften the news by suggesting optimistically that she might just have an inner ear problem, perhaps an infection, causing her to over-compensate when surfacing. At least that sounded like something that might right itself over time or be curable. For the time being, we could do no more than offer her extra fish and hope for the best.

The top dog in the West Australian Department of Conservation and Land Management (CALM), Sid Shea, happened to be visiting Monkey Mia. Sid was not the sort to commiserate with me over Holey-fin's condition, so I focused my conversation with him on general issues, like the dumping of fish offal in the channel in front of Monkey Mia.

In addition to Holey-fin, I was trying to sort out myriad equipment problems, so when Sid invited me to join a group that was going to explore Dirk Hartog Island, I jumped at the chance. It was just the sort of distraction I needed.

Dirk Hartog reaches further west than any other part of Australia and fortifies the northwest side of Shark Bay against the Indian Ocean. The island was named after a Dutch sea captain with the East India Company who was only the second European to touch Australian soil, at least without crash landing, at Cape Inscription on the top end of the island. He landed there in 1616, over 400 years before the publication of this book!

The plane only held six people, so the pilot would make two trips to ferry the group over. I was in the first group. We flew in a squally southwesterly wind that raged over the island dunes toward the salt pan that was our landing strip. Our small plane was buffeted quite a bit and the stall warning buzzer kept going off as the pilot attempted to circle in lower to land. He was so calm that I was not as nervous as I should have been. After several aborted approaches, we touched down. The pilot said

---

* *See "Burning Dolphins"*

he would not go back for the others.

We set off on the long and bumpy ride around the island, stopping at Cape Inscription to see the commemorative plaque that few Australians have seen. Another highlight for me was Mystery Beach on the ocean side of the Island. The sea there was wild, with waves stumbling all over each other to see which could crash onshore with more force, depositing all manner of detritus. Not a good place to go swimming.

Sid Shea was quite the character. He had managed to stay in his position through several changes in government, in spite of a temper that, I was told, would light up his Irish face in a glowing shade of crimson. Australians are brilliant at assigning appropriate nicknames to challenging personalities, and Sid's was "the exploding tomato." I assume that it was never said to his face. To my surprise, he brought up and discussed with candor his ability to remain in power through successive administrations. How did he do it? "I suck up," he proclaimed, laughing at the notion.

Back at Monkey Mia, our equipment set-up was still not working properly, so we continued testing it with endless permutations of connections to find the source of the problem so we could start collecting data on the boys offshore. I would check on Holey-fin occasionally and imagine that her surfacing looked a little more normal. Then, on 26 July, Holey-fin did not show up for the morning feed. In fact she had not shown up after the early feed the day before.

I knew she was dead. I also knew that she would have sunk to the bottom until gasses of decomposition refloated her, most likely by the next day. I advised the local head of CALM to wait a day to search for Holey-fin, but he was going on about being "proactive" and went spinning around Red Cliff Bay in their ugly new banana shaped boat, accomplishing no more than running aground on the banks offshore.

Once refloated, the prevailing southeasterly winds would push Holey-fin's body northwest. The next day, we went looking along the shallows and the beach toward Cape Rose. As we searched in our two boats I was waylaid by males and started a follow, so Mike decided to go inshore and walk the beach up to Cape Rose. He found her body, bouncing in the shallows just south of the cape, probably having arrived there in the few hours before we found her.

We loaded Holey-fin into my boat and bought her back to Monkey Mia where we photographed and measured her (207 cm). I made calls to Perth to arrange for a necropsy and called Bill Sherwin at the University of New South Wales to see what he wanted for DNA analysis (some kidney and cubes of skin and blubber). The local CALM director obtained permission for us to cut the required samples from Holey-fin at the fish factory, but that did not seem appropriate; I was sure that the fish factory folks had no idea about what we were intending to do. We headed off to the town offal pit instead where we extracted the needed bits and pieces before sealing Holey-fin in a body bag and placing her in a cooler prior to shipping her south.

We found Holey-fin's body as it was washing ashore south of Cape Rose.
© Dolphin Alliance Project

We went out to watch dolphins the next day while Holey-fin's body was flying to Perth. By the time I got back inshore late that afternoon, the shocking results were in. They found a stingray spine embedded in the left ventricle of her heart. I was astounded; I had never heard of such a thing. A stingray spine?

There are lots of string-rays in the shallows of Shark Bay. One of the important cautions I stress to all new assistants is that when they are wading in the shallows to watch carefully for stingrays and to do the

"Shark Bay Shuffle," rather than lifting their feet up and stepping down on who-knows-what. The dolphins often blast around the shallows chasing fish, whirling around, bottom grubbing, racing this way and that. In hindsight, it seems obvious that stingrays might pose a threat to them but it had never occurred to me before.

Stingray spines are serrated. Once broken off inside her, it would have moved slowly in deeper and deeper, propelled forward in the tiniest of increments by her own movements. Holey-fin may have been stung by the ray months earlier, as there was no longer any sign of an external wound where the spine had entered. But once the spine was inside, its trajectory was clear and her fate was sealed. Holey-fin was about 35 when she died. Had the spine been pointed in a different direction, missing her heart, she may have lived a few more years.

Poor Holey-fin died a slow, agonizing death. As the spine penetrated her heart, interfering with its ability to pump blood, fluid would have backed up into her lungs. The infant-like pop-up surfacing was a frantic gasping for air as she died slowly of congestive heart failure, drowning in the fluid in her lungs.

It was a sad time at Monkey Mia, and they flew the flag at half-mast. Holey-fin had been the best-known of the Monkey Mia dolphins for two decades. Hundreds of thousands of tourists from all over the world had met Holey-fin and her sweet, even-tempered disposition had made her a tourist favorite. She would be missed.

§

Real Notch Meets the Wow Crowd

Things were looking up for Lucky in early 1995. We first saw Real Notch, Hi and Bottomhook on 21 July, herding Wanda. They still had her on the 25th but let her go, then captured another female who soon bolted. The males did not chase after her. Pointer was not present on either day, so I thought he was probably with Lucky.

Then on the 27th and 28th we found RHB with Lucky and Pointer! Lucky and Pointer were now herding Wanda, while RHB had Goblin. It was pretty evident that Wanda had failed to get pregnant last year or had lost the fetus at an earlier stage. We often see females being herded in consecutive years. Lucky and Pointer astonished me with their level of violence toward Wanda; they were after her with a lot with pops and "crack" sounds (the vocal signature of the head-jerk threat) and hitting. The two groups didn't stay together much but shadowed each other around the bay, ending up well north of Red Cliff bay about halfway to Guichenault.

We first encountered the Wow Crowd on the 23rd. We were up north of RCB and had found a few Sharkies and started a follow on them. After an hour and a half, the Sharkies approached a larger group; there was a growl underwater and the Sharkies turned abruptly and left the area. The group they were not anxious to meet had seven Wowsers and a female. The Wowsers spread out, but Myrtle, Gripe and Wow stayed with the female.

On 2 August we found five Wowsers up by the Grooves, which we would come to recognize as the core of their range. Myrtle, Gripe and Anvil made a bee-line toward some dolphins and rushed in excitedly at a female. We heard pops. Then the female continued to fish as the males meandered after her in a behavior I simply call "follow the fishing female." She always popped up in their midst, until she didn't, after 45 minutes. The males showed no interest as she swam away. A "July thing"* in early August. But wait, hadn't Myrtle been with Gripe and Wow the last time we saw them? Well, neither observation lasted very long but it was an early indication that the musical alliances we had tasted in 1994 were still being played by the Wow Crowd.

Then two days later we found them again. Now there were 10 members of the Wow Crowd together, and Myrtle was with Roleypole and Veetop herding Wanda! We had seen them three times this year and Myrtle was with a different trio each time.

After another one-day interlude we found the Wowsers again. Myrtle, Roleypole and Veetop still had Wanda but now Latch, Hobo and Gripe had Goblin. Wow was hanging out with a younger, non-descript looking male who would turn out to be the 14th member of the Wow Crowd. Because of his apparent youth, we initially doubted that he was old enough to participate in an adult alliance and christened

See "Snubby, Sickle & Bibi"

him "Wannabee."

7 August was a disappointing day, for Lucky that is. We went up to Whale Bight and found Bottomhook and Pointer together herding Kwisp, a female from the Guichenault area. They were with Real Notch and Hi, who did not have a female, for the moment anyway. Shortly the whole group began to move deliberately and rapidly toward another group to the north. Real Notch and Hi captured the female Pseudopee; there was excitement and popping, then everybody settled down and turned back to the southeast. But we noticed that three dolphins were following them. Mike went back for a look; it was three very "male looking" dolphins. They were traveling side by side and had great fins; really tough looking guys. They turned toward ours, then away, then back again; seemingly indecisive. Then they left, or so it appeared. Mike stayed with them. Over two hours after we started the follow they started approaching our group again from a kilometer away. As they came closer, our group, who had been resting, stirred to life and turned toward them. We saw nothing at the surface but heard a brief aggressive interaction underwater. Then the three strangers surfaced going back northwest and ours came up going southeast, excited at first but soon settling down again.

The behavior of that trio, following and approaching ours just after RH obtained the female, was like that of males that have had their female stolen. We may have just missed seeing a theft rather than a capture of Pseudopee. What was unusual about this case is that our group let Pseudopee go an hour and a half after they got her, so she was no longer with them when the trio returned later. Perhaps the trio was still stewing over losing her. We would see that trio of "strangers" occasionally over the next few years. Because our first observation of them was in a conflict, we named them Peace, Love and Understanding. It seemed terribly funny at the time, but perhaps that was the effect of the Australian sun. I have developed the habit of blaming that sun for any failed humor, faux pas, malapropisms, forgetfulness, etc.

On the 10th we found Bottomhook, Pointer and Kwisp with Real Notch, Hi and Wanda. Listening through the hydrophone, I heard Wanda's now familiar but odd whistle, which sounded like a cicada. RH & Company seemed to be trading Wanda back and forth with the

Wow Crowd. Wanda's range was more in the Wow Crowd area to the north, so it seemed likely that our Red Cliff Bay boys were going into the enemies' backyard to get her. As we drove home that evening it was glassy calm with a beautiful full moon hovering just above the horizon in a layer of pink sky. I thought about this group I knew so well and the large mob to the north that I was just beginning to get to know. Real Notch and Hi had proven to be the tough guys of Red Cliff Bay, but I wondered what would happen if they ran into a huge alliance like the Wow Crowd. I would find out the next day.

Early in the afternoon, the southeast wind dropped and the bay turned into a sheet of glass. We went north and found a trio of Wowsers: Horton, Krill and Vax, who were herding Goblin off the Grooves. They joined with a trio of the Prima Donnas: Prima, Wabbit and Natural Tag, who were with a female. Prima and his friends had been juveniles in the 1980s but were looking and acting much more like adult males these days. A few minutes after the two groups came together there was a tiff in the Prima group: Natural Tag and Wabbit against Prima! They started fighting and a resounding whack underwater was followed immediately by a vocalization that I would not be surprised to find was a dolphin version of "ouch!" Prima seemed quite interested in Goblin during the affair and somehow that may have precipitated the aggression, but why with members of his own alliance? It was yet another case of aggression between friends in the context of joining another alliance. I recalled how Snubby and Bibi had gotten into a fight after they joined Chop, Bottomhook and Lambda back in the 1980s[*] and how, in 1991, Fred had chased after his best mate Barney after they joined Real Notch and Hi.[†] After their squabble, the Primas left our group.

As we continued the follow, another Wow Crowd trio of Wow, Pik and Veetop joined us. Wannabee was bopping around in the area and we had seen Anvil as well, so we had eight members of the Wow Crowd nearby. Mike was doing a follow on Anvil when the Wow trio suddenly began bee-lining toward shore. I knew that when males began traveling in that deliberate manner that they were going to cause trouble, so I asked Mike to drop Anvil and follow the Wow group. Anvil had been pretty boring so he was only too happy to oblige. The Wow trio traveled

[*] See "Male Dolphins: The Politics Emerge"
[†] See "NOVA: Filming the Boys"

well over a kilometer northwest then stopped, lingered for a minute, then started rapidly porpoising southwest toward the shallows. They stopped again. Mike saw another group snagging back to the southeast of his group. It was Real Notch & Co.! If that was the target, the Wow trio had overshot the mark.

Wow, Pik & Veetop turned back toward the Real Notch group and suddenly began porpoising in their direction. The Real Notch group turned to face them. As they met, fighting and chasing broke out with dolphins leaping out in three directions at once. A cacophony of whistles broadcast the altercation and a Wow Crowd trio that had been approaching ours from the south turned and blasted off leaping in that direction, as did another dolphin to the north. Our trio began rapidly traveling in that direction as well, but lagged behind the others, probably because they had Goblin. The Wow Crowd reinforcements were racing in toward the fight!

The Real Notch group broke off from the conflict and fled toward the shallows. My heart was racing; my Red Cliff Bay males were outnumbered and far away from home. If this huge mob caught up with them things could get ugly.

As we approached the shallows I could see the Wow Crowd trio just sitting at the edge, watching the RH group blast south, now far in the shallows close to shore. Our group arrived at the edge and stopped also. Eventually the Wowsers coalesced into a single group; 11 males strong plus Goblin.

It had been a close call. What were Real Notch and his friends doing up there? When Mike went to check them out he saw that Bottomhook and Pointer still had Kwisp, but RH had a new female. Perhaps they had come north to capture that female, but captures are noisy affairs and the Wow Crowd, alerted to their presence, attacked. Fortunately for RH, the other Wow Crowd members were not close by, so they had time to escape into the shallows.

Real Notch and Hi were the masters of Red Cliff Bay politics, but up here it was entirely another matter. The Wow Crowd was a huge group that, as we were learning, dominated this part of Shark Bay.

Why did the Wow Crowd hesitate at the edge of the shallows? They were deep-water fishers and maybe, like for Wanda's calf the year before,[*]

See "Jaws"

the shallows were not a comfortable place for them. Real Notch and Hi, as we knew, would fish in the shallows up to the water's edge and were even observed to belly bump, partially exposed, across a sandbar once. It was fascinating to think about. Real Notch and Hi could sneak up north along the shore and make guerrilla raids into deeper water to capture females, then flee back to the safety of the shallows before heading home to Red Cliff Bay. But I would not want to be in their fins if ever they were caught out in deep water by the Wow Crowd.

§

The Rulers of Whale Bight

Over the next few days we learned that Real Notch & Co. were not the only dolphins to flee from the overwhelming force that was the Wow Crowd. On 15 August we found Latch, Hobo and Gripe without a female and started a follow. Shortly, Wow, Myrtle and Roleypole, who had Goblin, and Anvil, Pik and Veetop, who were herding another female, arrived. Wow's trio was really getting after Goblin; they hit her, she bolted, they chased and we could hear more hits on our hydrophone.

When you find a trio like Latch, Hobo and Gripe without a female you know it's a temporary condition that they will act to cure swiftly. They didn't disappoint on this day, capturing Nip. The excitement of the capture drew in Horton, Krill and Wannabee who were also without a female.

Not far away a large group of young maturing males that we were calling the Kroker Spaniels were harassing a female with a calf. The Wow Crowd moved toward them at moderate speed; the Krokers ditched the female and fled. The Wowsers weren't interested in the female; they apparently just wanted to show the Kroker Spaniels who was boss.

Latch, Hobo and Gripe had let Nip go after a short time, but she didn't run far. We could see her fishing nearby. The Wow Crowd had a huge range, from the northern part of Red Cliff Bay all the way north to at least Guichenault, and at any given time Wow Crowd males could be spread over a wide area. The ranges of many of the females up that way were fully contained within the Wow Crowd range. A female that escaped from one Wow Crowd trio would likely run into another, so maybe there was no point in running far away, and on this day we saw a benefit of remaining close. The Wow Crowd trios had been fishing apart. They came together, changed direction and swam fast for a while.

It would have simply been another "what the hell was that about?" observation had I not seen the tip of what was likely a large shark at the surface briefly. Tellingly, Nip, who had been fishing with her calf about 30 meters from the males, quickly joined the fast-moving group and only gradually moved away from them after they slowed down a couple miles later. There is safety in numbers, even if those numbers are obnoxious males. Incredibly, after the group slowed down I saw another shark fin in the distance. I scooted over for a look and, to my amazement, saw that it was another juvenile great white about the same size as the one that had scared the dolphins the previous year. We see largish sharks infrequently, so two so close together in one day was very unusual. It wasn't surprising that Mike thought I was kidding when I radioed, in a casual voice, that we were going to check out another shark.

Before we left the Wow Crowd that day, Latch Hobo and Gripe had caught Nip's oldest daughter, Tuck.

The next day we looked all over the place for the Wow Crowd but could not find any of them. Finally, Mike had to run in for more fuel, so I turned offshore. Scanning in the binoculars I saw huge splashing in the distance. We blasted out there and found the entire Wow Crowd chasing the Sharkies. After we joined, the chase continued for 15 minutes and covered nearly 3 miles, going all the way into the top of Red Cliff Bay. Of course, our recording deck picked that moment to misbehave.

After everybody slowed down to go their separate ways, we had a close look at each group. The Sharkies had one female and the Wow Crowd had two that were not with them the day before. Latch, Hobo and Gripe had one of the new females. While it is possible that the Sharkies had stolen their female from one of the Wow Crowd trios and managed to keep her after the chase, the most likely scenario is that the Wowsers took one of their new females from the Sharkies. When we join a conflict mid-stream, without knowing who had which female before, we can't know who stole from whom. But one thing was clear: the Sharkies were fleeing from the Wow Crowd. So far this month, we had seen the Wow Crowd chase off Real Notch and his boys, the Kroker Spaniels and the Sharkies. More and more, I was deciding to focus my effort on these guys.

We found them again a week later, on the 23rd. It was an astonishing sight. All 14 males were present and accounted for. Four trios had females with calves, so we had a tight group of 20 dolphins! Latch, Hobo and Gripe had a new female, as did Pik, Krill and Wannabee; Wow, Myrtle and Roleypole still had Goblin, and Anvil, Horton and Vax were with the popular Nip. That evening I looked over our Wow Crowd observations from this year. From our first sighting of them, a month earlier on 23 July, we had eight days of observations. In only those eight days we had seen several Wowsers herd females in three different trios! For example, Wow herded a female with Pik and Veetop, then another with Gripe and Myrtle, and then with Myrtle and Roleypole. Clearly, those few observations from 1994 were no fluke; these guys were a different beast from the stable pairs and trios I knew before. Only Latch, Hobo and Gripe, remaining together through several consortships, seemed to be a somewhat stable trio.

I had a month left in my field season. We would enjoy the company of the Wowsers on five more days. When we found them on the 27th, the Wow, Myrtle, Roleypole trio with Goblin had broken up. Wow had joined with Anvil and Veetop, yet another new trio, to herd a female, and Myrtle and Roleypole stayed together but brought in Ajax to herd a female. The Latch and Pik trios still had the same females, so we again had this "super-alliance" with four females. Roleypole caught a large fish, which excited Ajax to mount him. Two of the Wow trio males did a bizarre display where they squeezed their heads together and came up out of the water in that position several times.

We found them again in a group of 20 on 2 September. Wow was into his fifth different trio of the year and Latch, Hobo and Gripe were still together. Ajax caught a big fish today, but it was a species not found often on the menu of dolphins or people. Locally called a "Nor'west Blowie," it was listed in fish books as a silver toadfish. Ajax was shaking it and, in blowfish fashion, it inflated. We had seen juvenile males tormenting a Nor'west Blowie last year, but they were treating it like a toy rather than trying to eat it. Ajax dove with the fish for a long time, so maybe he was going for a little Fugu buzz. Nor'west Blowies don't look dangerous but they are. After hearing dugong researcher Paul Anderson describe how two Blowies attacked him while snorkeling, and how he had to fend them off with his dive knife, I came to think of them as Shark Bay piranhas. In the 80s I was astonished to see one chase a person out of the water, nearly beaching itself in the process. Nor'west Blowies have a pair of chisels for teeth and could nip off a finger or toe with ease. While I would not encourage anyone to swim in Shark Bay, if one must, I would sternly caution men against skinny-dipping.

Our last day with the Wow Crowd in 1995 was on 24 September. Myrtle won the prize for being the most "flexible" member of the Wow Crowd this year. He had herded females with seven different trios and partnered with seven of the 14 males in the group. Latch, Hobo and Gripe were continuing to be the most stable trio. It was also becoming clear that some males didn't get to play as much as others. We had recorded eight to nine herding events for males like Gripe and Myrtle, but only three for Horton and Wannabee, and two for Vax. While most of the Wow Crowd acted like tough, prime-age males, Vax seemed much older. It was like the difference between old Slash and tough young Real Notch in the late 1980s.

As we sought out the Wow Crowd we still kept tabs on Real Notch and Hi. Bottomhook and Pointer had been herding Kwisp since 7 August. When we saw them on 27 August they had been with her for 21 days, but on 2 September, Real Notch and Hi were with Kwisp, and Bottomhook and Pointer did not have a female. I remembered how Sickle and Bibi used to take over females from Snubby & Shave in 1988,* and that bizarre sequence in the 1980's TBC-RH-CBL triangle when a female passed back and forth between TBC and CBL based upon which was in the company of RH.† Maybe RH had been happy to let Bottomhook and Pointer keep Kwisp until they wanted her. Whatever the case, Real Notch and Hi kept her through at least 24 September; between the two groups they had Kwisp for a record 49 days.

Now that Kwisp was with Real Notch and Hi, perhaps there was an opportunity for Lucky to rejoin the group. Maybe he had been excluded

---

* See "Snubby, Sickle & Bibi"
† See "This is Like Science Fiction!"

only for the duration of that long consortship. Alas, Bottomhook and Pointer continued to herd females without Lucky, whom we sighted occasionally in groups of females.

I left Shark Bay to conclude my stint with the Michigan Society of Fellows. I had left some of my things stored with friends in Ann Arbor, but shipped the rest from California before leaving for the 1995 field season. By now I was tired of moving around. After getting my degree at Michigan in 1990, I had moved every year, not counting the trips to Australia. I wanted to start a permanent job, so I applied for the few assistant professor jobs that opened in New England. I had fallen in love with that region, with its four seasons, beautiful rural areas, access to big cities and the ocean. If I failed to get a job in New England, I would have to apply anywhere and everywhere the following year. I saw an advert for a molecular ecologist at a small branch campus in the University of Massachusetts system. I was intrigued by the school's location, near a splendid coastline south of Boston between Rhode Island and Cape Cod. A phone call to Peter Tyack at Woods Hole sealed it. He knew the area and said it was stunning. I had never heard of the school, and nobody could accuse me of being a molecular anything, but what the hell. As luck would have it, the department chair liked what I did and they ended up making two hires: a real molecular ecologist and me. My first year as an assistant professor at UMASS-Dartmouth would fall between my last two field seasons in the 1990s.

§

Keeping Up With Old Friends

I returned in early June 1996 with two seasons of funding left. Mike ran the 2nd boat in 1995 and 1996, then started his Ph.D. research on sharks, so a wonderful assistant from 1996, Lynne Barre,* returned in 1997 to captain the other boat. 1995 had only whetted my appetite for the Wow Crowd; I was determined to go north at every chance to find them. The Wow Crowd were so different than the groups I studied in

---

* *Lynne wrote an amusing "Day in the Life" of our research, which she has kindly allowed me to reprint here (see appendices.)*

the 1980s and I knew I had to get a lot of data on them to erase any doubt. I was also anxious to see if such a large group could persist for more than a year.

Of course, to get to the Wowsers up north we had to traverse the ranges of other alliances, some familiar, some not. When we found unfamiliar groups that acted like males, we made note of it for future reference. Some of these groups, whose ranges were mostly further offshore, did not appreciate our presence and were evasive. One amusing encounter involved a putative male alliance that was skittish and evasive but who were apparently consorting a female who was anything but; she raced over eager to ride our bow. These "tough" males were afraid of our boat but were not going to leave her and stayed off at a distance. Seeing that she was having a roaring good time on our bow, they seemed to become gradually emboldened and one even cautiously approached and acted like he was riding the bow. I say "acted" because he remained at a distance where he could not possibly have felt the pressure wave generated by the boat! We were in hysterics watching his antics.

More often we encountered familiar groups like the Sharkies, the B-boys and the newly formed Prima Donnas. Real Notch and his mates were always going to be a welcome sight. The longer we have been watching dolphins the more valuable each observation becomes. This is because we can interpret each interaction in a richer historical context, and we had more historical detail on Real Notch's crew than for any other group.

During our first day on the water in 1996 we found Lucky with Pointer and Bottomhook, herding the ever-popular Kwisp. Everybody likes to cheer for the underdog, so we were happy to see Lucky with his old, but not very reliable friend, Pointer. And Lucky seemed to be playing a key role, as he was side-by-side with Pointer behind the female while Bottomhook was off looking for fish. We found them again two days later, this time with Real Notch and Hi. So maybe Lucky was back! Maybe Bottomhook and Pointer decided that a trio with Lucky would work for them.

Or maybe not. After a week of wind and rain the weather settled and we shot right up to the Grooves looking for the Wowsers. Instead, right in the core of the Wowser's range were Real Notch and Hi. Bottomhook and Pointer were there as well, still with Kwisp, but Lucky was nowhere to be seen. Oh well.

The Real Notch crew seemed to be living dangerously by swimming these waters with a female, but even though they were in deep water they also remained fairly close to shore should the Wowsers come after them. With their keen hearing, maybe they knew the Wowsers were elsewhere. We would have to discover that the hard way, looking all over the area for Wowsers before giving up and going back to relocate Real Notch & Co. Instead, we found the trio with whom the Real Notch crew had a little altercation last year, Peace, Love & Understanding.*

Bottomhook and Pointer still had Kwisp near the end of June. Looking around the area, we found Real Notch and Hi within shouting distance of their friends. Two days later we found the two pairs again, this time in a tight group, and now Real Notch and Hi also had a female. Peace, Love and Understanding were traveling in the area with other tough-looking dolphins. We had only seen Peace, Love and Understanding alone and had been wondering if they had a buddy alliance. Maybe their presence was why Real Notch and his friends were staying close together today.

It was tempting to wonder if Peace, Love and Understanding were still upset about their encounter with the Real Notch crew the previous year. They certainly could have been. We know that dolphins can remember associates they have not seen for 20 years. But in this case, I doubt it. The social lives of these dolphins are intense and relentless, and we see a tiny fraction of their interactions. More likely, that 1995 episode, which is so prominent in our memory, was a blip in theirs, crowded out by numerous conflicts with other males that had occurred since. Possibly some of those interactions were with Real Notch & Co.

On 3 July, we found Real Notch and Hi, still with their female, but Bottomhook and Pointer no longer had Kwisp. They rapidly approached a group with a few females, chased and caught one, harassed her for a short time, then let her go. It was July.†

Lucky did get to enjoy more time with the Real Notch Gang in 1996; it was certainly a rebound from the year before. However, his time with them was scarce thereafter; mostly he was found in groups of females or

---

* See "Real Notch Meets the Wow Crowd"

† See "Snubby, Sickle & Bibi;" July consortships," which we playfully call "July things," are often very brief.

juvenile males. However, Lucky was a persistent fellow and we would hear from him again.

Through 1997 we continued to see Real Notch and Hi with Bottomhook and Pointer; often one or both pairs had a female consort. One observation in 1997 stands out, if only in hindsight. On 27 June that year it was too windy to venture up north to find the Wowsers, so we sneaked in a follow on Real Notch and Hi. They were doing their usual thing, fishing in the Red Cliff Bay shallows, which allowed us to get good data even though it was choppy offshore. Along the way they ran into some Red Cliff Bay juveniles, including Urchin, Cookie and Jessie. Cookie was now nearing his 9th birthday and Jessie and Urchin were nearly 8. Real Notch got excited around Cookie and mounted him. Cookie lay on his side at the surface. Real Notch approached from below and hooked his penis into Cookies' genital slit. It was one of the first clear cases of intromission that I had seen.

Amy Samuels, now in her mid 40's, was studying the Red Cliff Bay juveniles. Starting in the 1970s, Amy had "been there" on some of the most famous primate and dolphin cognition and behavior projects, both in captivity and the wild, and had conducted her own ground-breaking research on dominance relationships in captive bottlenose dolphins. All that experience and years in the African sun gave Amy a wizened, weather-worn look and the kind of trained eye that was absolutely required to keep up with the crazy antics of juvenile dolphins, whose fins are not well marked. She had taken to calling Urchin, Cookie, Jessie and their friends the Red Cliff Bay Rascals, or just Rascals for short. I could not know in 1997, watching Real Notch mount Cookie, just how important Cookie and the Rascals would become to Real Notch in his later years.

§

A Crack in the Armor?

Although we found the Real Notch crew up in Wow Crowd territory on occasion, we saw only one other interaction between the two alliances. Actually, it was more of a non-interaction, but it was interesting.

We had our first sighting of the Wow Crowd in 1996 on 14 June. Not surprisingly, the first trio we encountered was Latch, Hobo and Gripe, south of the Grooves with a female they'd had a couple times last year. Mike found a few more Wowsers spread out fishing; I found another trio, then a few more members. We had everybody in the area but Horton and he was probably somewhere around diving for fish. Only the Latch trio had a female, but it was just mid-June and things didn't usually heat up until August. Perhaps because they were consorting, the Latch group seemed to be the group's center of gravity. Two of the groups finished fishing and joined Latch, Hobo and Gripe to form a group of 10 Wowsers.

We then suffered a windy stretch, but on the 28th we found Horton with several members of the Wow Crowd. So we still had all 14 present and accounted for. I was surprised but relieved that none had "gone missing" and looked forward to an exciting season with them.

The Wowsers next made an appearance on 7 July. Ajax, Krill and Wannabee had one female, and Wow, Myrtle and Roleypole had another. Sans a female, Latch, Hobo and Gripe made a brief appearance. Maybe that was the reason they didn't linger; they were on the prowl for a female. Veetop and Pik were fishing nearby when Pik appeared to cause trouble in the Wow trio. He joined and became tight with Roley and Myrtle. He had a bit of a kerfuffle with Wow, and then Pik left. Was he trying to take Wow's place or just stirring everybody up?

A few days later we saw some Wowsers avoid a conflict with the Real Notch and crew.

Michael Krützen, a German in his mid-20s, was visiting from the University of New South Wales. He had become intimate with the dolphins' DNA while doing his honors thesis under the supervision of Professor Bill Sherwin, and he wanted to meet the dolphins in person. Michael had a nasty cold, but I rousted him out of bed early on the 11th and he mustered himself for a day on the water.

We found Myrtle and Roleypole with Horton, yet another new combination. Horton was usually with old Vax. They seemed to be consorting Nip for a time but their interest level was low and she was soon gone. At one point, off the Guichenault shallows, they were traveling on a collision course with another group over 100 meters away, but then they turned in a different direction as if to avoid the encounter. We went over to see who they were avoiding; it was Real Notch, Hi, Bottomhook and Pointer! Real Notch and Hi had Kwisp; it wasn't the first time these guys had traveled so far north to find her!

The Myrtle trio's retreat smudged the gloss of invincibility surrounding the Wow Crowd. Evidently the Myrtle trio didn't have the numbers to take on the Real Notch crew. The only other Wowser we had seen around was young Wannabee and he would be of little use in a fight with Real Notch & Co. These weren't the toughest members of the Wow Crowd. I wondered what might happen if they met with equal numbers and the Wow Crowd was represented by members like Latch, Hobo, Gripe and Wow. A tough call, but looking back from the present, I would never bet against Real Notch.

For me, 11 July was a normal day watching males; nothing exceptional. But Michael Krützen has always said that this day changed his life. He had finished his honors degree and was thinking about returning to Europe to work on something else. But after a day on the water with us watching Real Notch and the Wow Crowd he was sold. He went on to do his Ph.D. and a post-doctoral study working on Shark Bay dolphin genetics. He would join me to work on our next male dolphin project in the early 2000s, and we still work together today. From his position at the University of Zurich, he works on the genetics of primates and cetaceans.

§

Poor Vax

Latch, Hobo and Gripe were the most stable trio in the Wow Crowd and they spent more time consorting females than any other members. Vax was at the other end of the scale, consorting fewer females than anybody. On 23 July we saw just how quickly hope could turn into disappointment for Vax.

The 19th, 21st and 23rd were July craziness, Wow Crowd style. On the 19th we found all 14 Wowsers together for the first time this year. They had three females; Latch, Hobo and Gripe were herding together but the other two trios with females were new combinations: Anvil, Pik & Krill and Wow, Ajax & Wannabee.

On the 21st we found the whole group again. Latch, Hobo and Gripe still had their female. Wow had changed trios; he was now herding a different female with Myrtle and Veetop. Anvil, Pik and Krill caught a new female, let her go, spanked the Kroker Spaniels,* then caught another female. Ajax, Roleypole and Wannabee herded a clearly pregnant Wanda for over an hour; she would give birth a few months later in November. The way Wow Crowd members switched partners was reminiscent of Snubby, Sickle and Bibi in the 1980s, so we were not surprised to see them engage in "male bonding" herding,† especially in July. The bonding exercise apparently didn't satisfy Roleypole who, after they let Wanda go, tried to buddy up with Vax and Horton.

Male dolphins often spread out to fish alone, and sometimes surprise us with what they find, like this male who has captured a snake eel.
© Dolphin Alliance Project

The Wowsers were in close to Guichenault on the 23rd. They were spread out all over the area, fishing. We saw Vax tail-out diving for fish near the bottom. The Latch and Wow trios still had the same females. I started a follow on the Wow trio and the Latch group soon joined them,

---

* *See "Terra Becomes a Troll"*
† *See "Any Female Will Do" and "A New Bond".*

followed a bit later by Roleypole, Ajax and Horton who did not have a female. Pik and Krill were around as well, but without Anvil, who was absent for the day. Wannabee was there in his place. Intriguingly, they had the second female we had seen them capture on the 21st when Anvil was with the trio. I would have loved to have seen how and why Wannabee replaced Anvil. Maybe Anvil lost interest and the others, needing a third, deigned to let lowly Wannabee join them.

The Wow trio snoozed for a while. The calf of the female they were herding would come and go from Mom and we saw her nursing twice. Then the males woke up and started petting. The Roleypole trio and Vax began traveling deliberately toward another dolphin; we heard lots of aggressive sounds on the hydrophone and, when they came back to the main group, we saw that they had a new female, Tab. Vax seemed to be in on the action along with the other three males. All four males were tight around her; this was interesting, was it going to be a consortship with four males? That would be amazing; I had never seen a clear case of four males herding a female.

Sometimes it looked that way, especially in the excitement just after a capture, but if you watched long enough it always settled down to two or three males with the female. Maybe this would be the exception to the rule. After all, Vax's regular buddy Horton was there, so maybe they would let him join the consortship. Indeed, as we watched we saw that Vax was close to Tab a lot and often tight with Horton. Alas, it was not to be. Vax was suddenly "uninvited" when his group rejoined the other Wowsers. Mike stayed with Vax for the next 50 minutes. Vax kept his distance from the group and sat there snagging for long periods with no real dives that would indicate fishing. When we listen to fishing dolphins with our hydrophones, we can hear their echolocation clicks and feeding squeaks, but when Mike turned off his motor to listen carefully, he heard only the distance social sounds of the rest of the group. It certainly looked and sounded like Vax was moping. His behavior was exactly like Snubby in 1987, when Sickle and Bibi excluded him from their consortship with Surprise.* Meanwhile, Vax's best friend Horton was still in the consortship, synching with Roleypole a lot. Poor Vax.

* See "Those Bizarre Boys"

§

The Prima Donnas Challenge Authority

A few days into the 1996 season we found Lucky with the Prima Donnas. We had known most of their members as juveniles in the 1980s. The juvenile period seems to be a time for males to explore their options, to try to find other young males with whom to form an alliance. They may have favorite buddies, like Lucky, Lodent and Pointer in the 1980s, but they mix and match with other juvenile males a lot. Through 1994, it seemed that Prima was considering an alliance with Captain Hook and his friend Bly, who lived more to the southeast of Red Cliff Bay. But by 1996–1997 it was clear that a new and formidable group of seven had formed. Other than Prima, it included Fred and Barney, who had been good friends as juveniles, Ridges, Big Midgie Bites, Wabbit and Natural Tag.

We choose names of dolphins and alliances to amuse ourselves as much as anything else. Big Midgie Bites was obviously named after the scourge that torments us during the cool months of June and July. Many times I have scratched myself bloody after being bitten by those tiny tormentors, sometimes called "no-see-ums." Natural Tag was named because of the tiny dorsal fin nicks that we used to identify him. One of our colleagues working on bottlenose dolphins at another site had published a paper on the three methods they used to identify individual dolphins: scars left from freeze branding, unfortunate encounters with motor boat propellers, or "natural tags" acquired from dolphins biting each other or other traumas suffered in their daily lives. This colleague illustrated the concept of a "natural tag" with a picture of a fin that was demolished, so we thought it would be amusing to bestow the name "Natural Tag" upon a dolphin with the tiniest of nicks. And the group name "Prima Donnas" signified nothing about the status of Prima within the group. The origin of his name, given when he was a juvenile, is murky, but his presence in the group offered a humorous alliance name.

The Prima Donnas had been maturing into an impressive alliance and were clearly a group to watch. Would they let Lucky join to become the eighth member? I didn't think so. They had known Lucky their whole lives; Prima, Fred & Barney especially had often played with Lucky and Pointer as Red Cliff Bay juveniles in the 1980s. So while Lucky was welcome to visit with the Prima Donnas, he would not be able to join their group.

As we had clearly seen in 1995, The Wow Crowd was clearly The Authority in the area between Red Cliff Bay and Guichenault. However, just like male humans, chimpanzees and a host of other mammals, as young males mature they want to challenge authority. Male alliance friendships and strategies are ultimately about trying to reproduce more than others. Dominant alliances can take females from other groups, so it makes sense for up-and-coming groups, as they grow older and stronger, to start challenging dominant alliances.

In late July we witnessed the Primas act up with some of the Wow Crowd, but there would be consequences. We found eight of the Wowsers on the 28th, including a new trio of Latch, Gripe and Pik, with a female. I had become so used to seeing Latch and Gripe with Hobo that I took them for granted. Hobo was not among the eight, so I wondered if he was herding a female somewhere with another trio.

We found Wow, Hobo and Veetop on the 31st. They were acting like a good trio but didn't have a female. We ducked in close to shore to avoid a squally shower and when we returned offshore we found Latch, Gripe and Pik. They still had the female from the other day, so Hobo would have to wait until their consortship was over to rejoin his regular buddies.

Latch, Gripe, Pik and their female were alone, so we started a follow. We saw a large group of Wowsers approaching, but as they drew close we saw it was not more Wowsers but all seven Prima Donnas! Gripe turned and swam back to the Prima Donnas and appeared to mount one. Gripe then returned and the Primas joined our Wowser trio. The level of excitement in the group now increased; the Primas seemed very interested in the Wowser's female. Gripe mounted Prima but the Primas didn't leave; they were excited. Suddenly the Latch trio swam rapidly away, leaving the female with the Primas! I was astonished; the Primas had apparently taken the female from a Wow Crowd trio!

Not so fast. The Latch trio wasn't running away from the Primas, they had captured another female! Regardless, the Prima Donnas were clearly happy to have the female the Latch trio had abandoned; they were incredibly excited around her. We stayed with them but kept an eye on the Latch trio with their new female. They turned back toward us, approached and rejoined the Primas with an escalation of rowdy behavior. Then, out of nowhere, Wow, Hobo and Veetop slammed into the Primas at full speed, there was intense splashing and the Primas fled. The Wowser trio did not let up and continued to pursue the Primas. The female was gone. This wasn't about her; the Wow trio were putting the upstart Primas in their place. They charged into the Primas again and aggressively mounted them. The Latch group, with their new female, were simply following and watching as their friends laid it on the Primas. It was total domination of seven by three, but of course the other Wowsers were around.

After that episode, we stayed with the Wowsers a while, then left them to look for other males. Later in the day we relocated the Prima Donnas and watched them chase and capture another female. The chase lasted for 15 minutes, which is a long time. Apparently, the female was just about as determined to avoid capture as the Primas were to capture her.

We saw another revealing interaction between the Prima Donnas and the Wowsers the following year. The wind dropped sharply around noon on the first of July. We headed up to Guichenault and found Sharky, Crackle and Sylvester spread out doing their usual tail-out dives as they fished in deeper water. Then we found the Prima Donnas. They were socializing when suddenly three blasted off from the group and captured Dent, who was with her calf Duchess. Then the rest of the Primas came flying in and all were terribly excited around Dent, chasing her around. We joked that we should watch for the Wow Crowd to come in and steal her. Not long after, we saw a trio approaching; it was Latch, Hobo and Gripe! They cruised into the group, and the hydrophone erupted immediately with aggressive sounds, intense long whistles and growling accompanied by chasing and a head-to-head faceoff between Gripe and one of the Primas. The three Wowsers moved right in and took up station behind Dent. She was now their female, but the Primas were not going to go away. They pressed in from all sides, bumping and pushing. During the kerfuffle, we heard continuous intense whistling and aggressive sounds including hits. There were a few episodes of pops, which we assume were directed at Dent. We filmed for 45 minutes and, after a time, things seemed to gel into a kind of stalemate. The sun was sinking low on the horizon and I was worried that we would not see the resolution of this conflict. But then Latch, Hobo and Gripe, still behind Dent, casually traveled away from the Primas. Well that was anticlimactic, I thought, until I turned and saw a group of seven more Wowsers, just as casually, moving in from the other direction. They met up with the Latch trio as the Primas had retreated some 80 meters. The Primas didn't back down for Latch, Hobo and Gripe, but they knew well enough to get out of the way when the reinforcements came in.

I came away with two impressions. The fact that the Primas contested the Latch trio showed that they were willing now to challenge the Wow Crowd, at least if they had the numbers on their side. On the other hand, the relaxed manner of the approaching Wowsers evinced a lack of respect for the Primas. The Primas might be willing to challenge the Wowsers, but that didn't mean the Wow Crowd would take them seriously. The Primas had a little more growing up to do before that would happen.

Late in July of 1997 we watched Prima, Fred and Ridges herding Bad Ghost after seeing them traveling together as a trio, but without a female, a couple of days before. The other consistent alliance seemed to be Natural Tag and Wabbit with either Big Midgie Bites or Barney. Those particular trios were different from the pattern we documented in later years (2001–2012), so the "little more growing up" they had to do would entail changes within the group.

§

Terra Becomes a Troll

During the mid-1990s we watched Lucky's slow, agonizing eviction from the Real Notch Crew. In the hyper-competitive Shark Bay dolphin society, males clearly want and need to be part of an alliance. What options are available to a male that suddenly finds himself forsaken by his friends? In 1997 we discovered a surprising possibility.

The Kroker Spaniels were not as far along as the Prima Donnas; I doubted they would even talk back to the Wow Crowd. The Krokers had not tightened up their group membership like the Primas, and were a big messy mob of older juveniles and young maturing males around 10–14 years old. We knew that Ceebie, a real scamp, was 10 in 1996 and Skini, whom we had known from infancy, was two years older. In 1996 and 1997 the Kroker Spaniels did not strike fear into the hearts of any other alliances in the area.

We had seen the Wowsers put the Krokers in their place before and we would see it again. The Wow Crowd were in an especially rowdy mood on 21 July 1996, with a lot of crazy pre-mating season shenanigans.[*] Anvil, Pik and Krill had caught and let go one female already and we thought they were after another when they bee-lined away from the group and began chasing in the distance. I radioed Mike to run up there to see which female they had captured. Instead of a female, Mike found them giving the Kroker Spaniels a hard time. There were about as many Kroker Spaniels as Wow Crowd members, so it was easy to imagine that a few years on, as they matured and grew a little larger and tougher, the Krokers might become a formidable group and even challenge the Wow Crowd. But right now they were just maturing and the three Wowsers dominated the whole group. I was reminded of how Real Notch and Hi had dominated the young Crunch Bunch back in 1989.[†] As Ceebie, Anvil and others surfaced excitedly around Mike's boat, he recorded what sounded like a dolphin in distress, even whimpering. Later that day the Anvil trio returned to the rest of the group with

---

[*] *Including a case of male bonding herding: see "Poor Vax"*
[†] *See "The End of the 80s"*

the second female they caught and, as the weather deteriorated, the level of excitement and aggression in the Wow Crowd escalated. At one point, just before a bunch of them charged and hit somebody, we heard what sounded like a tribal chant. It was amusing and more than a little creepy.

The B-boys and Sharkies were the two groups of older males in Whale Bight that we had known from the 1980s. Each had six members then. In the 1980s the B-boys were two very stable trios; BJ, Bam-Bam & Bumpus and Biff, Bo & Biddle. Biddle was no longer around in the 1990s and Bo and Biff were not seen much. I suspect they were just getting on in years and needed to fish alone most of the time. Old males can't afford to socialize and travel around together as much as younger males. BJ, Bam-Bam and Bumpus were still a good-looking trio and sometimes were found with Sharkies; the two groups seemed to get along quite well. They probably needed a friendship with the Sharkies since their mates weren't available as much anymore.

We didn't see the Sharkies consistently enough over the years to have a good sense of their internal organization. They lived further offshore in Whale Bight and were the ultimate deep-diving specialists. They would spread out all over the place and dive for a long time, which made them very difficult to find and follow. There had also been turnover in the group since 1991. Snap and Pop were gone. Now Sharky and Crackle were mostly with Sylvester and occasionally Sly. Terra's best buddy in the Sharkies was Fang, and they may have joined together in the early 1990s, possibly as "replacements" for Snap and Pop.

We had seen the Wowsers chasing the entire Sharky group in 1995.* In 1997 we watched interactions that were almost comical. On 22 July we found Anvil, Pik and Krill with a female they had been with for a while. No other Wowsers were around, but they weren't alone; they were with Sharky, Crackle and Sylvester! There was no sign of aggression, just a little excitement, and they even rode the bow together. I remembered how Snubby, Sickle and Bibi could get along with TBC or CBL when Real Notch and Hi were not around.† Maybe this was a similar situation; the two trios from different alliances could spend some quality time together as long as the rest of the Wow Crowd were not present.

---

* See *"The Rulers of Whale Bight"*
† See Male Dolphins: *The Politics Emerge"* and *"More Fun Than Baboons!"*

Before we found the Wowsers with the three Sharkies, we saw the Kroker Spaniels. To our great surprise, Terra was with them. What was a big tough Sharky doing with these little punks? He was so out of context that I started to doubt it was really Terra, but it was. The Sharky trio with the Wowsers was not far away, so maybe Terra was just messing around with the youngsters.

On the 25th we found Anvil, Pik and Krill with their female, and Wow, Myrtle and Veetop, who did not have a female. Roleypole, Horton and Wannabee, a new Wow Crowd trio, were there as well. It was clear that Roleypole was the most "flexible" of the Wowsers; he had displaced Myrtle as the male with more alliance partners than anyone else in the group. We didn't know if that was because he was popular or simply more often tolerated when two males needed a third. The Roleypole trio left the others to travel south a good distance to near Cape Rose where they captured Goblin, with minimal fuss. To our great surprise, Sharky joined them during the post-capture excitement. He stayed with them or nearby for the next two hours, clearly interested in Goblin. At one point he was petting with Roleypole. Sharky left but returned later with his buddy Crackle. They approached the Wow trio and we heard aggressive sounds when they were all underwater. Of course, the aggression may have been directed at the female. The Roleypole trio still had the female when they returned to the surface. Crackle seemed completely disinterested and left to resume fishing, but Sharky remained excited, several times swimming straight into the Roleypole group and brushing past Goblin. The Wowsers showed almost no reaction, the exception being Roleypole, who returned from fishing a couple times when Sharky entered the group. Roleypole lay on his side when Sharky approached him. What was that about? Maybe Sharky was dominant to Roleypole in a one-on-one encounter and Roleypole was just politely acknowledging his status, while backing up his mates in case Sharky tried something. Later Sharky returned with his other buddy Sylvester, but he seemed as unenthusiastic as Crackle had been. It was an amazing interaction, due as much to the nonchalance of the Wowsers as to Sharky's funny antics.

Perhaps frustrated by his inability to get Goblin, Sharky led his buddies Crackle and Sylvester in delivering a spanking to the Kroker Spaniels, whom they found harassing a female. The female traveled with the Sharkies for 15 minutes before leaving. I was reminded of TBC's rescue of UHF from Wave and Shave in the 1980s.*

The next day we found Wow, Myrtle and Veetop with Goblin. I wondered how that transfer happened.

On the 27th we found no Wowsers, but saw other alliances, including the Prima Donnas, who were herding a female, the B-boys, and the same three Sharkies. I wondered why I had not seen Fang this year. He was Terra's main buddy in the Sharkies. Was he gone; is that why we saw Terra with the Krokers? We had also seen quite a bit of BJ, Bam-Bam and Bumpus but not their mates. However, on the 30th we saw Biff and Bo with the other three B-boys.

We found Terra with the Kroker Spaniels again on 7 August and then again on the 12th. I could no longer dismiss the observation as Terra just messing around with punks. We had still not seen Terra's main buddy in the Sharkies, Fang, and neither had we seen Terra with the other Sharkies. We had not seen Sly this year either. Something had happened to the Sharkies. It appeared that Terra was now a Troll, the term we use for older mature males that join groups of juvenile/maturing males. Like Lucky, Terra may have been evicted from his group once his buddy Fang was gone. These days, we mostly saw Lucky with groups of non-cycling females. A lone male may join up with another old male that has lost his buddies or join a younger group. If neither option works out then they remain alone, and lone males usually don't last long in Shark Bay.

Without Fang or Sly, Sharky, Crackle and Sylvester would be a lone trio, without a second-order alliance partner. Perhaps the B-Boy trio filled that role. After what happened with RH, TBC and CBL in the 1980s, one had to wonder if that B-Boy-Sharky friendship played a role in the changes involving Terra, Sly and Fang.

* *See "Wave's Bud Spud" and see also "An Alliance Triangle" for another possible case.*

§

Anvil's New Old Friends

We had started the 1997 field season in late June and found our first Wowsers, Latch, Hobo and Gripe, on the 24th. They were boring. The trio remained alone, resting during the three-hour follow, but we were rusty so boring was good. The next day, 25 June, we found Pik, who was joined shortly by Krill and Ajax. Vax was in the area hanging out with some females and juveniles. The following day we found the first Wow Crowd consortship of the year: Pik, Myrtle and Roleypole had Goblin. Mostly they fished but they threatened Goblin with pops a couple times. Pik shouldered the load guarding her, but switched off with the others occasionally. That was another new trio, lifting our total to 30 different trio combinations in the Wow Crowd. I felt good about the study; we already had a nice amount of data on these guys showing how different they were from the other alliances.

1 July was that amazing day when we watched Latch, Hobo, and Gripe, eventually backed up by seven more of their group, take Dent from the Prima Donnas.[*] When we next found the Wowsers, three days later, Latch, Hobo and Gripe had traded Dent in for Mini. Wow, Pik and Veetop had a female consort, and so did Myrtle and Roleypole, who seemed to round out their trio with Horton, but we weren't able to watch them enough to be sure.

After the relatively stable trio of Latch, Hobo and Gripe, we had come to understand that the Wowsers had a group of "players" who were regularly in trios herding females: Wow, Veetop, Myrtle, Pik, Anvil, and Roleypole. Krill, Horton, Ajax and Wannabee might be on a rung or two below the core group, and Vax was at the bottom of the ladder. Vax and Wannabee seemed to bookend the group age-wise, with Wannabee the youngster and Vax the more lethargic older male. Vax was always with Horton when herding a female, but Horton participated in trios without Vax.

I was already noticing something different about this year. Anvil had been a clear core member of the group in 1995 and 1996, but we had

[*] *See "The Prima Donnas Challange Authority."*

yet to see him this year. I wondered if he was still alive.

When we found the Wow Crowd on the 7th, Wow, Pik and Veetop had the same female as last time, and Ajax, Krill and Wannabee had a new female. Latch, Hobo & Gripe had Dent again, but only briefly, later racing off to capture Bad Ghost, who had been with the group initially.

Roleypole, Myrtle and Horton showed up later, as before, without a female, but Anvil stole the show with his first appearance of the year. There were also two dolphins we didn't recognize in the group.

We got busy with our follows of consortships while Anvil remained in the vicinity, but not with our sub-groups. Later the Wow Crowd coalesced into a large group and Anvil returned, with those same two strangers. Anvil was swimming side by side with the new individuals, and they started surfacing synchronously. These were males! Who were these guys? This was totally bizarre; I thought we knew the males they might associate with up here, the Sharkies, B-boys, Primas and young Kroker Spaniels. How could Anvil show up with total strangers like this?

The Anvil group left. Just before the parting they moved slightly apart from the others, snagging at the surface. We heard aggressive sounds and the two groups moved off in different directions. Were the Wowsers telling Anvil and his friends to get lost or were they threatening one of the females? Most likely the latter, but we could not be sure.

Lynne followed the Anvil group for the next one and a half hours. Shortly after the split from the Wowsers, Anvil seemed indecisive, turning back and forth between the strangers and his Wowser friends two or three times, but he stayed with his new friends.

When we reviewed the pictures later, we realized that Anvil's new friends were in fact old friends. Anvil was originally sighted with Hammer and Drill several years earlier, hence their names. But Anvil had been a central member of the Wow Crowd since we first started watching them late in 1994. Was he maintaining old friendships and trying to introduce his old friends to his Wow Crowd buddies? Was he on the "outs" with the Wowsers now; could that explain why we hadn't seen him this year? I was fascinated and hoped the next few weeks would reveal something important.

As it turned out, we didn't solve the mystery in 1997. We saw Anvil continue his membership with the Wowsers, but a shift was underway;

one that may have begun in 1996. After 1995, Anvil was in trios with Pik and Krill almost exclusively, the exceptions being a trio with Vax and Horton, and another with Krill and Horton. Pik, by contrast, continued to herd females in trios with members of "central casting" such as Veetop, Myrtle and Wow.

§

Dolphins: The Wild Side

A crew filming for a National Geographic Society documentary, *Dolphins: The Wild Side* would be arriving in two weeks to film the alliances. Working with a film crew is a major imposition; it can be difficult to get good data while working on a film. However, we already had a good sample size on the Wow Crowd and informing the public about our fascinating discoveries is critically important. I also felt a strong obligation to the National Geographic Society, who had been our steadiest source of funding, right from the beginning. Other film companies often approach us, but they never offer any funding for our research.

Even though I felt good about what we had accomplished with the Wow Crowd so far, I was hoping to get in more observations before the film crew arrived.

On 13 July we found a new trio of Roleypole, Horton and Pik, with Goblin. Latch, Hobo and Gripe had a funny thing going with Dent, variously with her and not. They weren't herding her, but perhaps just keeping tabs. Males often stay close to cycling females, even when not herding them, and females may actively approach males. Vax was present but had no buddies today. Everybody else was present but Anvil; I wondered if he was with his new old friends.

Whatever the case, Anvil was back with the Wowsers the next day, herding a female with Pik and Krill. Horton was the only other Wow Crowd member present and all they did during the 2.5-hour follow was snooze. As the light was waning and we stopped the follow to head home, intense social activity drew us back to the group. The Primas were there, with Bad Ghost, probably trying to take the female from the Anvil group, but it was now too dark to make sense of it. Damn. We went back looking for them the next day. We first found the B-boys herding Goblin, but then we found the Anvil trio with the same female in the same place we had them the day before, sans Horton. Later we found the Primas with Bad Ghost again. Who knows what went on the day before. My greater concern now was the rest of the Wow Crowd; where were they?

Fighting males. © Whitney Friedman

The next day, the wind increased while we were up by the Grooves, so we pulled into the beach to climb to the top for the spectacular views. While we were up there we watched Real Notch & Hi and Bottomhook & Pointer enter the shallows with their females. We scampered down to follow them. The female with Pointer and Bottomhook wore a seagrass decoration; a strand was wedged in a narrow crack in the front of her fin.

We saw the same Anvil trio by themselves again on the 22nd and, to our relief, with other Wowsers on 23 July; both days featuring those interesting interactions with the Sharkies, described earlier.*

The National Geographic film crew had arrived. The filmmakers were a couple, the Atkins: laid-back chain-smoking Paul and hyperkinetic Gracie. When Flip Nicklin visited to photograph for the National

---

* See "Terra Becomes a Troll."

Geographic Society in 1991 he lived and ate with us and put a significant (to us) percentage of his expense money into our research. As a married couple, Paul and Gracie needed their own campsite. They ate well. I was not used to having bacon and eggs for breakfast, or sandwiches of smoked salmon with avocado and cream cheese for lunch. I visited their campsite often in the morning and looked forward to days when they came on my boat. The film they produced, on a range of dolphin species around the world and emphasizing the dolphin as a social predator, was a landmark documentary, vastly better than any of its predecessors.

But, as if playing a joke on us, the Wow Crowd chose the arrival of Paul and Gracie to go elsewhere. We looked anywhere and everywhere, even as far north as Peron, and in up to five boats, but did not find them again until 15 August. Well, Vax and Horton were still around. They had probably not received the memo announcing the trip. We continued to see other males, so Paul and Gracie filmed Real Notch and his friends herding females.

Then on the 15th we found the Wowsers, right where they "should have been," but were not for the last two weeks. We had 11 of the 14 males including three consortships. I was so used to finding new trio combinations in the Wow Crowd that I was surprised to find that all three of the trios on this day were ones we had seen previously. Unfortunately, Gracie, on our boat, was unable to hail Paul, with his camera, on the other. They didn't get the footage they needed of this huge second-order alliance.

Two more failed searches and a week of wind bought us down to our last chance before everybody left. It was 25 August; the wind vanished and the bay turned into a sheet of glass. We found 13 of the 14 Wowsers close enough to shore for Paul to film them against the stunning orange bluffs. We had seen dolphins chasing in the distance, and upon finding the Wowsers, we found the Krokers, with Terra, sulking nearby. The Wowsers had three females, one of which they had likely just taken from the Krokers. Latch, Veetop and Gripe were there with Mini; Hobo had shifted over to herd Bad Ghost with Wow and Myrtle, and Roleypole had joined buddies Horton and Vax to consort Dunce. Pik, Krill and Wannabee were acting like a trio, but with no female, and Ajax was "freelancing" around the group. Great film and great data made for a wonderful last day for 1997 and the Wow Crowd study.

The only Wowser missing that day was, not surprisingly, Anvil. We would discover what became of him when we next returned in 2001.

When we tallied up the data from the three years we found that we had recorded exactly 100 consortships by members of the Wow Crowd. It was a great data set that allowed us allowed us to demonstrate conclusively that the Wow Crowd, with 14 members, were both much larger than any other second-order alliance and much more labile in the composition of the trios they formed to herd females. Equally interesting, we showed that the Wow Crowd, embedded within the larger dolphin society, was itself a complex society with highly varied relationships. We found that males preferred to associate with some males in the group and avoided others. At one extreme we had poor Vax, who was in only 10 consortships with six different alliances that included a total of five Wowsers. Horton, who was in every Vax consortship, may have been the only reason Vax was allowed in the group. At the other extreme was Roleypole, with his 23 consortships in 12 different alliances that included a total of 11 Wowsers. But the real prize went to Latch, Hobo and Gripe because our data showed that males that had the most stable first-order alliances spent more time consorting females.

Our paper announcing the discovery of the Wow Crowd "super-alliance" made it into *Nature*, which, along with *Science*, is the Holy Grail of scientific journals. Getting into *Nature* is something of a crapshoot and depends on the whims of editors, reviewers, and what your competition from other submissions happens to be that week. Fortunately, this time the Gods smiled upon us.

Meanwhile, Michael Krützen was looking at the DNA of the Wow Crowd and made another startling discovery. While some males that formed stable pairs and trios and small second-order alliances, like Real Notch and Hi and the B-boys, were related, none of the Wowsers were related. This new genetic discovery, when combined with the differences in behavior, implied that there might be two distinct alliance strategies in Shark Bay. In one strategy, related males would form stable pairs and trios and small second-order alliances. In the other strategy, unrelated males would form large groups with labile first-order alliances.

If there were two distinct strategies, then we should find other large groups like the Wow Crowd in Shark Bay. We could also predict that there would not be groups of intermediate size. I didn't believe the dichotomy was real, but it was good stuff to put in grant proposals where reviewers like to see distinct hypotheses and nice clean predictions.

After making the initial observations on the Wow Crowd in 1994 I left with a queasy feeling that I didn't understand alliance formation in Shark Bay. In the three years since, we had clearly established that the Wow Crowd was a different beast from the alliances I studied in the 1980s. Our model of alliances from the 1980s was indeed incomplete but the unsettled feeling that followed the 1994 season was now one of excitement. We had fascinating new questions to pursue. Were there other large Wow Crowd-like groups? Were there ones of intermediate size? Would the stability of the first-order alliances correlate with the size of second-order alliances? Would the pattern of relatedness hold if we examined more groups? We had to greatly expand our study area. I now had a nice excuse to explore the same territory that I had in 1991 with Per, from Dubaut to the south, up to Cape Peron. I could not wait to return to Shark Bay, but it would take several years to raise the needed funds.

Part III

The Alliance Network

2001-2006

The Cast

The Alliances, from North to South:

Peron Posse (?? males) a name given to a large number of males around the top of Peron Peninsula. We never saw them enough to get a good handle on membership. **Marcel** is mentioned in one story.

The Skipjacks (11 males), named after the lighthouse point near the top of the peninsula that seemed to be their home base, they wintered in Herald Bight but moved south of Guichenault during the mating season. They were often found in shallow water. I had photographed one member, **Viking,** in the late 1980s.

The Grand Poobahs (12 males) also wintered in Herald Bight and moved south during the Austral spring. The first **Poohbahs** that we encountered in 2001 included **Dominic, Monkey** and **Mulligan,** who proved to be quite a stable trio.

The Hammers (6 males), close associates of the **Poobahs**, included **Kermit, Rasty, Spoof, Hammer, Drill** and, incredibly, **Anvil** from the 1990s **Wow Crowd**. As juveniles, Kermit and Rasty had visited Red Cliff Bay in the mid-1980s.

The Jacques (3 males), a lone trio observed in Herald Bight and Whale Bight.

The Wow Crowd (10 males) had dropped from 14 to 10 males by late 2001. Gone were **Hobo, Roleypole, Vax** and **Anvil**.

The **B-boys** and **Sharkies** still roamed the deeper waters of Whale Bight, venturing into Red Cliff Bay during the mating season. **Biff** was the only survivor of his trio and we only saw him fishing alone. He was gone after 2003. The other trio, **Bjay, Bam-Bam** & **Bumpus** was intact and spending more time with the remaining Sharky trio, **Sharky, Crackle & Sylvester.**

The **Kroker Spaniels** (14 males) had matured into our second group of 14 males by 2001. **Skini & Bolt** formed trios with several others in the group, including **Deet, Moggy, & Pong**. **Krok** was a key friend to old male **Terra. Ceebie, Dangit, Imp, Midgie, Pasta, Quasi** and the oddball **Noggin** were members.

The **Prima Donnas** (7 males) began to associate more with the **Kroker Spaniels** during this time. The Primas held steady with the same seven members since their origin in the mid-1990s: **Prima, Natural Tag, Wabbit, Fred, Big Midgie-Bites, Ridges & Barney.**

Real Notch, Hi and **Pointer** were still an alliance to be reckoned with and they maintained good relations with the **Prima Donnas**. Hi was gone after the 2005 field season, leaving **Real Notch** and **Pointer** as a pair.

The **Rascals** (7 males), juveniles during the 1990s, matured during our 2001-2006 study and started consorting adult females. **Lucky** joined **Cookie, Jessie, Hedges, Lando, Smokey** and **Urchin** and the gang to form a group of seven males.

Pirate's Crew were a trio of males, **Pirate** and two buddies that favored the Outer Banks and seemed to have other friends in La-La Land.

The **Crunch Bunch** (6 males), by 2001, were a group of two stable trios, **Jimbo, Comb & Typit** and **Debe, Twirp & Smudge.**

Antoine, Wart & Worries spent considerable time with the **Crunch Bunch** and so were known as the "Friends of the Crunch Bunch." They were old males we had photographed out east during the 1980s. Antoine sometimes fished with sponges.

The Blues Brothers (8 to 11 males) named after members **Jake & Elwood,** matured into a group of eight by 2004, including **Czar, Grub, Rickets, Seven, Smelt & Toque.** They associated with young, adult males **Poodle, Hosehead** and **Tool** in 2005-2006. Several members were sponge-carriers.

The Exfins (8 males) were named after an old male **Exfin,** who had been part of a different group in the 1980s. The other males probably matured prior to our study; we had observed the group consorting a female in 1994. They roamed the main channel out east.

The Gas Gang (6 males) was a tough group of **Frans, Octane, Mangle** and **Klaus & Slider,** with **Argon** as the infrequently seen oddball of the group. Their main range seemed to be further east and southeast toward Faure Island.

Hook's Crew (7 males), named after **Captain Hook,** included Captain Hook's friend **Bly** and **Dweeb, Dagwood** and **Link.** Their core area, southeast of Monkey Mia, featured extensive banks. They were seen kerplunking.

Other second-order alliances in the southeast, such as the **Sweepers, Ghengis Khans** and **The Usual Suspects**, we saw only occasionally.

The Females:

Bad Ghost (Banshee), Blip, Fuf, Joy's Friend, Little (Tryky's daughter), **Mini (Skini's** mom), **Nook, Phantom, Scallop (Mussels), Shock** (daughter of **Surprise**), **Spongemom, Talladega, Tuck (Nip's** oldest daughter).

§

Expanded Horizons

Returning in 2001, after four years, there had of course been a bit more attrition among our alliances. Most significantly, Bottomhook was last seen in 1999. At least one dolphin was happy about that development: Lucky! He was back in the big-time, herding females with Pointer in a second-order alliance with Real Notch and Hi. Until, that is, Real Notch, Hi and Pointer decided that they were better off as a trio than in two pairs with Lucky as a member. By the time we started our new project in 2001, Lucky was, again, out of the group. Poor Lucky.

Looking at things from Pointer's perspective, I could not help remembering all those days in the 1980s when he was "it" and subjected to what seemed like sexual assaults from the older males in Red Cliff Bay. In reality, such mounting was probably the equivalent of the punch in the arm one received from older boys on the playground, letting you know your position in the hierarchy. We speculated then that by being subjected to such behavior, Pointer was able to spend more time and develop relationships with the "big boys" and that might serve him well in the future.[*] Our speculation may have been correct, because by 2001, Pointer was in a trio with Real Notch & Hi.

Spud was the remaining survivor from the Snubby, Sickle, Bibi gang, but only a month into our 2001 season we found his body washed ashore just to the southeast of Monkey Mia. Since Wave had vanished, he had taken up with a group of males, "Hook's Crew," that resided down there. Spud passed before we could watch him in action with his new friends.

Of all the males we watched in Red Cliff Bay in the 1980s, we were left with only Real Notch, Hi, Lucky and Pointer and the old geezers Codon and Judas, and Judas would be gone after 2001.

The mighty Wow Crowd had suffered losses as well. Anvil, Hobo and Roleypole were gone and Vax was last seen during 2001, so the Wow Crowd dropped from 14 to a group of 10 for the new study. It wasn't surprising to lose Vax; we always thought he was the oldest of the group. I wondered if Anvil was dead or with those new/old friends we saw him

---

[*] *e.g., "Wave's Bud Spud"*

with in 1997.* I was most disappointed about Roleypole; he was fun to watch as the most "versatile" member of the group, having herded females with 11 of the 14 Wowsers in our 1990s study.

While our discovery of the Wow Crowd "super-alliance" in 1994 had upset our understanding of male alliances, our detailed study of the group from 1995–1997 only exacerbated the problem. We had accrued a magnificent dataset on the Wowsers that showed, in no uncertain terms, just what a different beast they were from the TBCs and CBLs of the 1980s.

The new questions that we had to answer were obvious. Were there any other big groups like the Wow Crowd? If so, would they also be composed of unrelated males that were happy to consort females with a variety of males in their group? Conversely, would other small groups outside of Red Cliff Bay fit the pattern from the 1980s, with stable pairs and trios?

Perhaps most importantly, did alliances really fall into two distinct classes, small ones of four to six males with stable pairs and trios of kin, versus the "super-alliance" pattern involving non-kin forming more labile pairs and trios? I thought that was unlikely, as I saw no reason why there could not be alliances of intermediate size. In fact, we already knew of one: the seven-member Prima Donnas. They had grown up during our Wow Crowd study and we had seen their members consorting females. But that was just one group and we needed many more to learn about overall patterns.

To answer these questions would require a massive effort. We had to greatly expand our study area to learn about a lot of new alliances. We also had to get enough data on each new group to be sure of their memberships and to learn about their relationships with each other; did males consort females in stable or labile pairs and trios? And of course we wanted to get DNA from all the new males, so Michael, who joined me on the new effort, would need to do a lot of darting.†

It seemed to me that the area I had explored in 1991 with Per

---

* See "Anvils' New Old Friends"

† Michael worked with the company Paxarms from New Zealand to develop a small dart that would get a good sample but cause minimum harm to our relatively small dolphins. The dart they developed would go on to be used around the world on cetaceans as large as humpback whales!

Berggren, from the top of Peron Peninsula to Dubaut Point, south of Monkey Mia, would be just about right. We could race up to the top of the Guichenault shallows in less than an hour (in good conditions!) and look around in Herald Bight, up to Peron, for new groups. The area to the southeast was similarly accessible.

This was going to be fun; I had really enjoyed my time on Per's project, exploring the different areas along the Peninsula. Now I was going to be able to do that while watching male dolphins! It was the best of both worlds.

Real Notch and Hi (nearest) surface synchronously.
© Dolphin Alliance Project

Michael, Bill Sherwin and I started writing grants. Now, nobody will fund you for more than a two or three-year project. You are expected to write grants that clearly present the questions you are going to address, the methods that you will use, and provide evidence that you can acquire enough data to answer the questions in the time frame of the grant. Well, that might work for people studying insects, birds and such, but we were working on a long-lived, complex mammal in an incredible study site, but also a weather-limited one, where we could only get data on about half the days. I knew damn well we were not going to get enough data in two to three years.

So yes, our grant proposals were a tad fanciful in terms of our projected timelines, but I had no qualms about that. There is something amiss in a system where the rigid requirements of science funding agencies would deny us the peanuts (relative to the cost of most scientific research) required to learn about the social system of the animal with the largest brain, relative to body size, after our own.

Clearly, the key for us was going to be not only getting the initial grants, but continued funding to keep it going.

We succeeded. The project rolled on for six years, from 2001 to 2006. For most of the study we ran two boats, which was essential to get the number of observations we needed. On a good day we could have two boats documenting consortships in different alliances simultaneously. Michael not only darted dolphins from his boat, Gene Machine, but he also documented consortships. And I could call him over to dart dolphins he needed to sample when I was finished recording behavior. We were fortunate also to have a Ph.D. student from Georgetown University, Jana Watson-Capps, overlap with us for three years as she studied the behavior of females during consortships.

We ran the project during July–November most years, training teams of assistants to keep going when I went back to teach and Michael could not be there. Old assistants and colleagues came to the rescue when we fell short on help.

At the end of the project we had documented over 500 consortships and had good data on the alliance membership and behavior of 120 adult male dolphins! Gene Machine obtained samples from almost all of them, as well as a huge number of mothers and offspring, so that we could better understand who was fathering the infants. We also learned a bit about another 75+ males, although we didn't get enough data to include them in analyses.

I still had my hydrophones from the Wow Crowd study, so we kept them in the water as much as possible when watching males. We also pulled out the video camera when things got exciting, although that often seemed to signal to the males to stop doing whatever it was that prompted us to film them.

Michael and I also decided that it would be a good idea to use Nortrek again. We could sail her up to Herald Bight with Gene Machine and Bony Herring in tow, and use her as our floating hotel just as Per had done in the 1990s. It was interesting how that changed the psychology of being up there. If you went to Herald Bight from Monkey Mia and the wind came up, you knew you were in for a long and unpleasant trip home. But when home was Herald Bight, we were quite happy to stay out later in more challenging conditions.

The drawback, of course, was that if the weather was lousy we were stuck in the cramped quarters of Nortrek with a crew of five to six people. We had to pick our trips well, pouring over forecast charts to try to get a workable window of four to five days (which was determined by the amount of fuel we could carry for dolphin work). Our first trip was a huge success, but our ability to guess the weather in Western Australia was, well, no better than anyone else's.

On one trip, we were out late the first day getting good data and having a great time. The forecast for the following day could not have been better. The strength of the wind was forecast by the spacing between isobars on the weather charts, and the weather chart for the following day showed no isobars anywhere near Shark Bay. It was going to be one of those glassy calm days we lived for, so never mind the high, thin overcast that spread over the sky late that afternoon.

Given the calm conditions, we didn't tie up the boats too carefully that evening. Then at 2 a.m. the sound of boats banging against each other disturbed our peaceful slumber. Ok, so there was a little breeze, no big deal, we'll just secure the boats and fall back to sleep. But glancing up toward the top of Peron, I was startled by a huge forked bolt of lightning. What the hell? This was August. Winter. We almost never had lighting and thunder at this time of year, and there was nothing on the weather map for a thousand miles!

That, as it turned out, may have been the problem. Perhaps nature does abhor a vacuum. An unforecast low-pressure system was forming right at the top of Shark Bay. The next day it moved slowly down the peninsula. So instead of watching Herald Bight alliances in splendid glassy conditions, we huddled in Nortrek as 40-knot winds raged outside. The wind direction rotated though the course of the day, but mostly came from shore toward our boat, anchored in the shallows. I was amazed at the size of the waves generated in shallow water over such a short distance.

That was the worst weather misadventure on our Nortrek trips, but a couple more disappointing ventures made the idea less enticing. It seemed better to just pick a good day and run up there in Gene Machine and Bony Herring.

We ended up getting the answers to the questions we posed, but as in each of our previous major efforts, the most important discoveries were unexpected. Serendipity plays a huge role in science and it always has in our study. Along the way, we gained much more insight into the richly variable and sometimes quirky nature of these male dolphins and the alliances they form.

§

A New "Wow Crowd"

27 July 2001 was the first day we launched the boat in our new study. And to my delight, the first group we found had Real Notch, Hi & Pointer in a consortship with the original Spongemom, whom I had followed for six hours in 1986.[*] With them were seven members of the Kroker Spaniels, that juvenile male group that the Wow Crowd used to slap around in the mid-1990s.[†] Well, they weren't juveniles anymore; in my absence they had been busy growing up. Today, the Krokers were consorting a female.

I recognized Skini among the Krokers. It was his mother Mini that they were herding! I couldn't sort out which of the seven males had Mini, but later in August we saw Skini, Bolt and Deet herding Skini's mom again. Our geneticists have indeed detected inbreeding in the bay.

Skini had been born in the early 1980s, so he was turning 19 this year. We knew the mothers of a few other members. Ceebie was born in 1986, so he was turning 15, and Quasi was turning 13. Midgie may have been a year younger than Quasi, which could explain why he wasn't involved in any consortships until the start of the prime mating season in 2002. By then all members were consorting females and we had our second super-alliance of 14 males.

---

* See "Female Dolphins: Different Personalities and Lifestyles"
† See "The Rulers of Whale Bight" and "Terra Becomes a Troll"

One of the Kroker Spaniels was much older than the rest. It was Terra the Troll, who had surprised us so much in 1997 when he showed up with the then-juvenile Krokers after losing his place in the Sharky group.* I guess his patience had paid off.

A trio of Kroker Spaniels dive synchronously © Dolphin Alliance

Unlike the Wow Crowd before them, the Kroker Spaniels spent much time in Red Cliff Bay. That was terrific; they were going to be easy to find. For the next six years we found them often. We recorded over 100 consortships in the group, which made for an interesting comparison with the Wow Crowd we had known in the 1990s. There were fascinating similarities and differences. The Wow Crowd had one trio, Latch, Hobo and Gripe, who were stable compared to the rest of the group, and they were found with females a lot more. There was no such trio in the Kroker Spaniels, but there was a pair, Skini and Bolt. Now, like the Wowsers, the Krokers strongly preferred to herd females in trios instead of pairs. That means that Skini and Bolt needed a third and they always had one. They would cycle through runs of herding with Deet, Pong or Ceebie, occasionally letting Pasta or Moggy have a turn. I would give anything to know the social mechanics of being the odd-male-out with Skini and Bolt. Did the third leave after becoming

* *See "Terra Becomes a Troll"*

exasperated with not getting enough chances to copulate? Or did Skini and Bolt grow tired of partners who perhaps didn't guard the female enough while Skini and Bolt were fishing? Probably some of the "selection" had to do with who was not already in another consortship and thus available to join Skini and Bolt.

Deet enjoyed the first run with Skini and Bolt in 2001. But he matched their total consortship numbers by swinging with Krock and a third much of the time. Sometimes that third was Terra. It seemed that Terra's place in the group depended on Krock. I was reminded of old Vax in the Wow Crowd; he could only get into a consortship if Horton was present, but Horton didn't need Vax.* Likewise, Krock was almost always there for Terra's consortships, but after Terra disappeared after 2004, Krock didn't miss a beat. He didn't seem to need Terra at all.

Pong had his run with Skini and Bolt from the mating season in 2002, through winter 2003. But by the start of the mating season in September that year, Pong had formed a trio with Midgie and Quasi that would last through the study, with few interruptions. They became that stable trio that Skini and Bolt never formed. Unlike Latch, Hobo and Gripe of the Wow Crowd, they didn't excel in the consortship department. In fact, I often remember seeing Quasi, Pong and Midgie traveling along, synching side by side, looking really impressive, but without a female. They were too young to match the success of older adult trios like Latch, Hobo and Gripe. An oddball of the group was Noggin, whom we would often see fishing alone in the first channel to the east and north, at times quite far from the rest of the Krokers. Researchers found that when male chimpanzees are not hanging with other males they often go to forage in their mother's range, where they originally learned to look for food. I wonder if that was what Noggin was doing.

§

The Prima Donnas

When we first saw the Prima Donnas in 2001 they were with the Wow Crowd. All 10 remaining Wowsers and seven Prima Donnas was an

---

* See *"Anvil's New Old Friends"*

imposing sight. They also had three female consorts; one trio of Prima Donnas had a female, as did two Wowser trios. Veetop had replaced the missing Hobo in the top trio with Latch and Gripe. Latch and Gripe had Pik as their third member a couple of times in 2001, but they jelled with Veetop after that.

I didn't recall seeing the Wowsers and Primas just hanging out together like that in the 1990s. Obviously the relationship had changed, probably reflecting a shift in their relative power. After all, the Wowsers, while still a formidable group of 10, were no longer the dominant force of 14 they were in the mid-90s. And the Prima Donnas, just young upstarts in the 90s, were now moving into their 20-something prime.

The Prima trio with us that first day was Fred, Ridges and Big Midgie Bites. Shortly after, we saw another trio of Prima Donnas, Natural Tag, Wabbit & Prima, herd a female. That was pretty much the story of the internal affairs of the Prima Donnas. We saw them as much as the Kroker Spaniels and recorded lots of consortships, and it was always those two trios, which were different from the few we observed in the 1990s.* Well, those two trios and Barney. We scored 27 consortships for Fred, Ridges and Big Midgie Bites ("Big" for short); 29 consortships for Prima, Wabbit and Natural Tag, and only ONE consortship for Barney. We found him herding Tuck with Big on 23 August 2002. We were happy for Barney, and cheered him from the boat, but his opportunity would be short-lived. Wow, Pik and Myrtle joined. They wanted Tuck. Big and Barney must have protested because Ajax, Krill and Horton came flying in from the north, with their own female in tow, and Latch, Gripe and Veetop came blasting from the south. They gave the two Primas a drubbing and chased them off. Wow, Pik and Myrtle left with Tuck. The Wow trio may have called for help, but most likely their mates simply heard the commotion and came running over to give unneeded help. The theft was yet another demonstration that interactions within and between alliances can vary with context. The Wowsers and Primas had friendly relations at times, but that did not preclude the Wowsers from taking a female from the Primas. So much for Barney's chance to pretend he was "one of the boys."

Barney clearly had a closer relationship to the Fred, Ridges & Big

* *See "The Prima Donnas Challenge Authority"*

trio. When the trios were not together we would see Barney with those three but almost never with Wabbit, Prima and Natural Tag. You wonder why he stayed. It might make sense if he were related to one of them; perhaps his juvie playmate Fred, but we can't yet examine relatedness on such a precise level. Once, Barney consorted a female with two Krokers. Maybe Barney simply didn't have a better option than to wait for a vacancy to open in his own group, the Krokers, or some other group. But a vacancy never opened in the Primas, and Barney didn't join the Krokers when members disappeared. Maybe they didn't want him.

If the Prima Donnas had a relatively simple internal structure, their relationships with other groups were anything but simple.

§

A Third Level of Alliance

The winds were light on the morning of 2 August 2001, so I decided to work out east. We had a productive time, finding several mature alliances and younger ones to keep an eye on in the future. We worked north through the main channel and ended up north of the Outer Banks. The bay was glassing out to the northwest. I made what turned out to be a very good decision: we blasted off to the Grooves to enjoy the glass up there. We ran into the B-boys pretty far offshore, then headed a bit closer inshore just north of the Grooves, where the fun began. I spotted a huge group; it was all seven Prima Donnas and four Krokers, Pong, Ceebie, Pasta and Quasi.

Prima, Wabbit and Natural Tag were herding the female Fuf, and Big, Fred and Ridges had the female Bad Ghost with her infant Banshee tucked under her side. Each trio was lined up behind their female. Barney was, as usual, just being Barney. The female Little was there, not being herded by anybody.

The four Krokers were soon joined by a fifth, Midgie. They had the female Mini but there seemed to be some commotion going on as we went over to see which males had her. Suddenly Ceebie and Pasta were chasing each other all over the place, racing from group to group. They turned and faced each other; it was a tiff! They sat there jawing, head to head, squawking what must have been the equivalent of dolphin profanity as they told each other off. Like kids in the schoolyard, other dolphins came around to watch. Unable to resolve their difference of opinion verbally, Ceebie and Pasta started fighting. The fight gave way to a chase, but it was now two dolphins chasing one, almost certainly Ceebie.

In the distance we saw a trio of dolphins, spread out, moving steadily our way. The tussling continued in our group; one chased another away from the group. The approaching trio were closing in, tall fins slicing the surface; the chasing pair retreated to our group, who were popping relentlessly as if to herd their females close. A burst of growling and screaming erupted as the trio cruised into the group. It was Wow, Myrtle and Veetop!

The arrival of Wowsers did not provide a reprieve for Ceebie. He was still getting it; everybody seemed to be after him. Twice other males chased him, each chase preceded by a deep, creepy sound that I don't think I had ever heard before.* In the second chase Ceebie wheeled around to face his tormentors; they surrounded him, paused for just a second, and charged.

I wondered what Ceebie had done to provoke this abuse. There were four Krokers with Mini when we arrived and there was clearly aggression among the males before Ceebie and Pasta got into their fight. Four is a crowd when it comes to herding females, so maybe Ceebie had stepped over some social boundary regarding his place with Mini and the consortship. While that might explain why the other Krokers got after Ceebie, it doesn't help us understand why males from the other groups joined in against him. Even Veetop got into the act, giving Ceebie a good thump. We had seen this kind of "everybody-on-one" a few times before. It sure seems like the whole group responds when a dolphin commits a serious faux pas.

We would not be able to verify which three Krokers had Mini, because Wow, Pik and Veetop had not joined the group only to help bash Ceebie; they wanted Mini too.

The focus was no longer on Ceebie, but the rowdy behavior and

* *The descending frequency of the vocalization was like the even creepier sound that Rachel and I heared in 1994; listen to "A New Project"*

blizzard of aggressive sounds continued. There were only three Wowsers against five Krokers, but there were also the seven Primas present, and they were involved in the action, but on whose side? We couldn't tell; we had a jumbled mess of 20 dolphins surfacing and chasing this way and that.

Minutes went by. Nothing changed. Neither the Wowsers nor the Krokers were yielding control of Mini. They seemed to be in a stalemate. The constant chasing and fighting among the males must have been very disconcerting to Mini, who found solace with Little, bonding to her during much of the turmoil.

Thirty minutes after Wow, Pik and Veetop joined, I looked to the east and saw a trio of dolphins leaping our way from 200 meters off. Another trio was 100 meters behind them. Here comes the cavalry!

As they drew closer we braced for the attack. Seconds ticked off. Nothing happened. We checked our group. Where have Wow, Pik and Veetop gone? They were no longer here. The hydrophone was still bursting with aggressive sounds; the Primas and Krokers had not gone quiet.

Suddenly a massive phalanx of dolphins surged past our boat and into the Krokers and Primas. It was all 10 Wowsers. A bit of growling, a few smacks and this fight was over. We knew it, even though the Kroker Spaniels didn't leave right away. The vocal chaos resumed as the group porpoised westward, building to a crescendo and then sudden, synchronous, silence. It was startling. The noise level slowly rose again and continued, even after the Kroker Spaniels, without Mini, retreated some 80 meters away where they sat at the surface, defeated.

The Primas and Wowsers remained excited for some time, splitting up and coming together in various combinations, as they gradually settled down. The bouts of aggressive vocalizations may have signaled continued disputes among the males, but no more females changed places.

As we continued to watch, the various Wowser and Prima Donna trios peeled off with their females, or just dispersed to fish. Wow, Pik and Veetop had Mini.

I think that as the other Wowsers drew near, Wow, Pik and Veetop left the Krokers to join their mates for the big charge. The other Wowsers had clearly come a considerable distance to help their friends take Mini, but once they had done so they simply left to go about their business.

In the 1980s we had been puzzled about the friendly associations between pairs and trios, why CBL and TBC spent so much time together. If they were simply competing for estrus females we shouldn't see such friendly relations. The discovery of second-order alliances on 19 August 1987, still the greatest day in our project's history, explained those friendships.* Since then, as we extended our study area and observations to include a larger number of second-order alliances, we had noticed that some second-order alliances also had special friendships with one or two other groups. The same logic applied; if second-order alliances were only competing with each other, we should not see such friendships.

The Kroker-Wowser-Prima fight was the first time we saw three second-order alliances involved in a fight, at least when we had some idea of what was going on. I recalled that chaotic event during the NOVA filming in 1991, and that unsettled feeling that I had missed something important.†

The Primas were active in the group during the entire skirmish so it was hard not to think that they may have helped one side or the other just a little bit. If so, we had a third level of alliance formation. But since we couldn't tell if the Primas took sides, we didn't have our "smoking gun" evidence.

Incredibly, we would have our second third-order alliance interaction only 10 days later, and involving the same groups and the same females. This time there were nine Kroker Spaniels, seven Wowsers and the seven Prima Donnas. We had arrived before the Wow Crowd the first time, so we saw that the Krokers had Mini before the Wowsers came and took her. We would not be so lucky today.

Again, it was glassy calm. We saw a big group and headed toward it, but I could see another large group moving toward them also. I had a strong hunch that another fight was about to erupt, so we raced toward the groups to get there first. Cameras were popping out of cases as everybody scrambled to get ready, but it was a race we were going to lose. The two groups collided just before we arrived. We would not see

* See "This is Like Science Fiction!"
† See "Nova: Filming the Boys"

who had which female before the fighting started, and start it did; one dolphin was heaved out of the water right by our boat; then several were chasing one. It was chaos. In her excitement an assistant had forgotten to remove the cap from the camera lens. Oh well, that sort of thing happens.

The groups separated. We ran over to look at the nine Krokers. They had Fuf who had been with Wabbit, Prima & Natural Tag on the 2nd. Those three now had Mini and Fred; Ridges and Big still had Bad Ghost. Now that doesn't imply that Bad Ghost had been in one continuous consortship since the 2nd. During the Austral winter, consortships are typically brief affairs and Bad Ghost may have been consorted several times since the 2nd. She may have been taken from the Krokers during this fight. As in the previous fight, after this one the Wowsers and Primas remained together peacefully for a time and we even saw Wow and Prima petting.

In the 1980s, we learned that first-order alliances that support each other in a fight remain together for a time afterwards. If the same pattern extends to third level interactions, then the Primas and Wow Crowd were allies in these two fights. The seven Wowsers didn't have a female after the second fight, but if the Primas had helped them in the first, maybe they had returned the favor. By the end of the 2001-06 we would see the relationships among the Primas, Wowsers and Krokers undergo a major realignment in favor of the Primas and Krokers.

§

Real Notch & the Prima Donnas

By the latter part of the 2001-2006 study, a third-order alliance friendship between the Prima Donnas and Kroker Spaniels had developed to the point where we took it completely for granted. We often saw them together or near each other. However, the Prima Donnas were also good friends with another alliance: Real Notch, Hi and Pointer.

On the afternoon of 3 August 2006 we had a big leap-feeding melee in Red Cliff Bay with a lot of Primas and Krokers involved. After they finished feeding and settled down we started following them around to see who was consorting whom. Gene Machine found Fred, Ridges and Big with Blip. My team found a large group of nine Krokers with a female.

Four Krokers left our group to go over to theirs. Aggression broke out and rapidly escalated. The Krokers were trying to steal Blip from the Primas! Immediately our group blasted off toward theirs and other dolphins came leaping in from different directions; it was the rest of the Primas and seven more Krokers. As we headed to the fight I saw a dolphin get knocked into the air. I radioed the other crew to get their video going and we did the same. The aggression continued. It wasn't as violent as the fights that we had seen with the Wow Crowd but it was intense and my ears were filled with a cacophony of growling and screaming. Neither group would back down. Then, a half-hour after the fight started, other dolphins entered the fray, a few young Rascals and Real Notch and Pointer, who were herding Joy's Friend. The aggression immediately escalated. Six minutes later the Krokers left the Primas. Real Notch and Pointer remained with the Prima Donnas. The Krokers were clearly still agitated; some chased Ceebie and mounted Pasta. The Krokers vacillated, turning back toward the Primas, then away, then back again. We thought they might have another go at the Primas but they settled down and left to the north.

I was surprised! The Prima Donnas and Kroker Spaniels had been having such a good relationship over the last few years. Now they had fractured that relationship in a fight over Blip. I wondered if they would now become rivals or if they would try to rebuild their friendship.

We received our answer the next day. We found a big resting group of Fred, Ridges and Big, who still had Blip, and eight of the same Krokers they had been fighting with the day before. Earlier we had seen the other Prima trio fishing in the area. I think I was even more astonished at the sight of this resting group than I had been by the fight. This really showed me the complexity of their relationships. These two second-order alliances, numbering 7 and 13 individuals (since Terra vanished after 2004), were friends; friends that had a spat and made up, as friends do. We see that sort of thing between individuals of many species, but to see that between two large male alliances was simply stunning. The only other species that does this sort of thing is the one we see in the mirror.

The other interesting aspect of the fight was what happened after Real Notch and Pointer entered. The aggression escalated and the fight ended shortly after. Real Notch and Pointer had continued to travel with the Primas after the fight ended. It seems likely that they played a role in ending the stalemate and causing the Krokers to give up.

Later that month, we witnessed more funny goings-on with the Prima-Kroker-Real Notch triangle.

On 14 August 2006, we had round three of the Prima-Kroker-Wow Crowd battles. Things had changed a lot since the first two fights in 2001. We had seen the Prima Donnas associate amicably with the Wow Crowd that year, but didn't know if the Wowsers and Primas had enjoyed the kind of enduring relationship that existed now between the Primas

Watching the Wow Crowd. I am driving and recording observations into a head-mounted microphone while David Wrangham films the action and visiting scientist Lindsey Porter watches another group nearby. An underwater microphone (hydrophone), fed through the PVC pipe in front of the boat, picks up the dolphins' vocalizations. © Dolphin Alliance Project

and Krokers.

In many ways, the day's events unfolded like the first fight in 2001. We decided to work out east and were having a productive day out there but gradually worked our way to just north of the Outer Banks. The crew on Gene Machine were itching to head over to Whale Bight, so I encouraged them to go for it while I continued to poke around the Outer Banks. But then I changed my mind and decided I wanted to top the day off with Krokers and Wowsers, so I headed out there as well. Just as we got underway we received an excited radio call from Gene Machine. They had a big leaping group of dolphins and needed help. They thought the dolphins were leap-feeding* but they weren't sure, so they started filming. I floored it. Just as we arrived I saw a dolphin get knocked over a meter into the air. A huge pack of dolphins was surging through the water. This was a war! Both research teams were now videotaping and blasting away with cameras. I called out names as I saw them; there were Krokers and Wowsers and Primas here. Then the huge mob split into two groups, one behind the other; then another split and there were three groups. The trailing group slowed down and started to leave to the west. I sent Gene Machine to check them out. It was seven Wowsers with the female Fuf. They seemed very subdued as they moved away. Our group was still excited; they were still moving fast with lots of petting. We had 12 Kroker Spaniels and one trio of Prima Donnas: Wabbit, Natural Tag and Prima. Blip was in the group as was one other female we weren't familiar with. The new one was clearly getting a lot of attention. We stayed with them as they slowly settled down. Eventually we got a nice separation for Blip; Skini, Bolt and Ceebie had her. The Primas drifted away, but the remaining nine Krokers remained close to the new female until we had to leave, so we didn't see which three had her. Now we don't know who stole from whom as both groups had females after the Wow Crowd split from the Krokers and Primas. But, given that the males were so excited around her, my guess is that the Krokers stole the new female from the Wow Crowd. The Primas remained with the Krokers after the fight ended, when the activity dwindled from rowdy excited behavior to petting to just traveling. As in the 2001 fights, that was a pretty good indication of whose side the Primas were on. Someone suggested that maybe the Primas weren't helping the Krokers but simply joined the fracas to try to get the female for themselves. The odds would not seem good for three Primas trying to wrest a female away from seven Wowsers or 12 Krokers but maybe in the chaos of the fight, with other females present, such a tactic might work occasionally. To my way of thinking, the idea that each alliance was acting on its own doesn't jibe with the Primas continuing to travel amicably with the Krokers after the fight,

---

* In leap-feeding, dolphin orientation with respect to each other is not consistent and they are more widely spaced. Closely packed "surging" dolphins is typical of fights.

or the fact that the Primas and Krokers had friendly relations in general, resting, traveling and feeding together.

We next saw the Primas three days later on 17 August and then on the 18th. The Prima trios now had Blip and the new female, and they were with Real Notch and Pointer, who were still herding Joy's Friend. Thinking about their history,[*] I wondered if Real Notch and Pointer had played a role in the transfer of the two females from the Krokers to the Primas.

I don't think the Real Notch–Prima Donna relationship was a one-way street. After they evicted Lucky, Real Notch, Hi and Pointer needed friends. They were a lone trio, and once Hi vanished after 2005, a lone pair. That didn't bode well for their ability to keep a female. Sure, they were tough guys, but numbers do matter.

Real Notch, Hi and Pointer had formed a friendship with a group that was basically two stable trios. Hmmm. This had a familiar ring to it.[†] We noticed that we would see the Real Notch crew with the Wabbit, Natural Tag, Prima trio when the other Primas were not around, but we rarely saw them alone with Big Midgie Bites, Ridges and Fred. Were Real Notch, Hi and Pointer trying to split the Prima Donnas like Real Notch and Hi had split up TBC and CBL in the 1980s? Were they trying to form a new second-order alliance with Prima, Wabbit and Natural Tag? Well, if that is what they had in mind it never worked because the Prima Donnas remained a strong, cohesive group.

The Real Notch crew probably benefited from the size and strength of an intact Prima Donna group. On sabbatical in 2004, I spent the mating season months of September to November in Shark Bay. We would find the Prima Donnas in a tight group herding one or two females, and not with them, but not far away would be the Real Notch crew, with a female. It was a defensive formation. Second-order alliance members with females stay close to their group during the mating season. The Real Notch-Prima Donna association was more of a third-order alliance relationship, not between two second-order alliances, like the Prima Donnas and Kroker Spaniels, but between a lone trio and a second-order alliance.

See "This is Like Science Fiction!"
† See "An Alliance Triangle"

§

A Theft Among Friends

In the latter half of September 2006, we ran out on a glassy calm day, but conditions deteriorated rapidly as the wind rose. With all those whitecaps about we were unlikely to find anybody, but sometimes you get lucky. The Wowsers had been mostly missing in action so far this year, but we found Wow, Pik and Krill herding Blip. Shortly, a second Wowser trio, Myrtle, Horton and Wannabee with Scallop and her little one, Mussels, joined them. We settled in to try to get one hour with them so we could score the two consortships. It is too easy to lose dolphins in that sort of chop, so we really had to be on our game. Dolphins typically breathe four or five times then dive, for a minute and a half. I had developed a kind of internal sensor that goes off before they are due to surface, and I alerted the team to double down on their searching efforts when my "alarm" went off. Dolphins can lull you into overconfidence by going a particular direction for a while. Then they change direction underwater, and when they come up going away from you, their fins are but slivers and are easy to miss. If you miss a couple of surfacing bouts they are gone.

So we were all on full alert to avoid losing the dolphins when events took a very surprising turn. Latch, Gripe and Veetop cruised into the group and all hell broke loose. Leaping, splashing and hitting; it was a fight! But who else was here? Nobody. It was Wowser against Wowser and when it settled down, Myrtle, Horton and Wannabee were gone and Latch, Gripe and Veetop had Scallop. One trio had taken a female from another trio in the same alliance! Finally, we had seen what we had suspected for years. How many times had we found a female with one trio in an alliance, then the next time she was with a different trio (or pair in the case of the Beach Boys in the 1980s)?* Of course I remembered the strange cases from the 1980s when Real Notch and Hi were in the thick of their triangle with TBC and CBL.† We found TBC with a female together with Real Notch and Hi, who didn't have female.

---

* See "Snubby, Sickle & Bibi"
† See "This is Like Science Fiction!"

The next day Real Notch and Hi, still without a female, were with CBL, who had the same female that TBC had the day before. The next time we saw them, Real Notch and Hi were with TBC, who had the same female again. So there had been plenty of strong hints that friends would steal from friends.

Now I don't think all, or even most, of the cases where we found that a female had moved between trios or pairs in the same group were due to thefts. Most of the time the female probably got away or was let go, then recaptured by the second trio. We may have seen just such a case involving the Gas Gang, a group of six tough males that lived more to the southeast. In August 2004 we came across the Gas Gang trio of Mangle, Frans and Octane with a female. They were on a shallow bank, fishing. Another member, Klaus, was in the area and his usual buddy, Slider, was off fishing in the distance. Not long after we had settled in to document the Mangle, Frans and Octane consortship, screams on the hydrophone alerted us to a big chase. The female was on the fly, but our guys were just sitting there watching. They could not have cared less. But Klaus and Slider did care and were chasing the female in a large arc that stretched out over a kilometer before they finally subdued her. We have seen consortships end when the males just lose interest in the female. The males don't respond when the female swims or bolts away, and the consortship is over.[*] Although we had not been with them long enough to score the consortship for Mangle, Octane and Frans, the female was clearly with them. When they let her go, or she bolted, Klaus and Slider decided that they wanted to keep her for a while.

Latch, Gripe and Veetop had shown us that thefts do occur within groups, and I found it especially interesting that they were the most stable trio in the Wow Crowd. We had shown that the 1990s edition of the trio, Latch, Gripe and Hobo, consorted females more than other males in the group. We have not yet been able to measure dominance relationships between males within groups, but differences in the amount of time males spend with females suggests that dominance is important. And we had always thought that two of the males that were victimized by the Latch trio, Wannabee and Horton, were at the low end of the Wow Crowd pecking order.

* For example, "Reliving Old Glories"

§

Lucky & the Rascals

After being gradually dismissed from the Real Notch crew in the mid-1990s, Lucky started spending a fair bit of time with some young, 5–7-year-old males in Red Cliff Bay, mostly Cookie, Jessie and Smokey. Like Terra with the Krokers, Lucky was a troll. But really, Lucky was the original troll. Based on his belly speckles, we think Lucky was in his mid-late teens in the 1980s when he was best mates with the juveniles Lodent and Pointer. To a degree, the troll life worked for Lucky. When Pointer grew up in the early 1990s, Lucky got to consort females with him. Obviously, being a troll isn't ideal, because you have to suffer through several years of hanging out with juveniles when you would obviously rather be consorting females with other adult males. I remember an episode in October 1988, when 10 or so juvenile males and females, including Lodent and Pointer, were "play herding" with different individuals, male and female, trading off being "it."* The one who was "it" at any moment would be goosed and mounted by others acting in pairs and trios, all good practice for what they would be doing as adults in a few years. Lucky participated to some degree, but much of the time, while the juveniles were piling all over each other, erections flying, clearly having a blast, Lucky was just sitting off to the side of the group, snagging. He looked bored. Being a troll must require considerable patience.

When Lucky was given a temporary reprieve with Pointer in 1996, he stopped trolling, but he was back at it as soon as that ended. Lucky's final shot with Pointer came in 2000, after Bottomhook vanished,† but that too was short-lived and Lucky was back to spending time with females and Rascals.

But the Rascals were starting to grow up. By the mating season of 2002, we saw Lucky with the Rascals consistently. Most of the Rascals were now 12–14, the age when males start trying to herd mature estrus females. With Lucky they were a group of seven; I was excited to see

---

* See "Play Herding"
† See "Keeping Up With Old Friends" & "Expanded Horizons"

a new alliance form right in the heart of Red Cliff Bay and happy for Lucky that he could participate.

From 2001 to 2003 we had been busy looking at adult alliances up and down the peninsula. Because we often drove to other locations through Red Cliff Bay, we could keep tabs on developments with Lucky and the Rascals. By 2004, with most of the males now 14–16 and their group a solid seven, I decided that it was time to bring the Rascals into the study. It was in September of that year that I watched my first consortship with a trio of Rascals, including Lucky! Good for him, because Lucky was now in his 30s, and might not have that many more years left to try to squirt his genes into the next generation.

It was great to see Lucky get back into the swing of things. He was a member of an adult alliance again, and consorting females. Well, that was the good news. The bad news was that Lucky didn't get to consort females very often. Whatever it was about Lucky, his small size or some other attribute, that led to his being a troll in the first place, and that led to him being dumped by Pointer, must have become evident now to the other Rascals. If they had indeed been impressed by Lucky when they were youngsters, they probably saw him now as nothing more than a rather weak old male. Lucky's status in the Rascals fell rapidly. Lucky was in one more consortship in 2004 and only one of the 10 Rascal consortships we recorded in 2005. Mostly he was just there; or not, as on 19 July when there seemed to be a bit of conflict between two trios over Shock, the recently matured daughter of Surprise. Smokey, Jessie and Hedges were herding Shock, but Urchin, Cookie and Lando seemed to want to take over. There was a lot of socializing, some aggression, mounting and displays, but none of it included Lucky. Mostly he just fished away from the group.

Lucky was not in any of the Rascal consortships in 2006 for the simple reason that he was no longer a Rascal. Lucky had been kicked out of an alliance yet again. It was back to being alone and hanging out with non-reproductive females. We wondered if Lucky would look around for some more juvenile males.

§

East Meets West

We were poking around out northeast one nice July afternoon in 2002 and happened upon the Crunch Bunch. I thought back to the first year I came here to work on my Ph.D. research in 1986. A crowd of young, rowdy Crunch Bunchers was in Red Cliff Bay, harassing the female Square, when suddenly she ducked under the bow of our boat and floored it.* We hadn't discovered herding yet, so at the time I just thought she had had enough of the brats. By my last thesis season, in 1989, the Crunch Bunch had matured as we recorded their members herding several females. There were 10 members of the Crunch Bunch back in those days, but several of their members had since vanished. By the time we started our new study in 2001, they were a dignified alliance of six males, now in their mid- to late 20s.

Unlike all the other alliances out east, the Crunch Bunch disdained herding in pairs. They formed two completely stable trios, and unlike the Prima Donna trios, life was not equal in the Crunch Bunch. Although we only recorded 20-some herding events by the Crunch Bunch, Jimbo, Comb and Typit enjoyed the majority. Smudge was clearly the odd-ball in the other trio, as he was often fishing away from the other two.

On this day they were herding the sponger Gumby, who Sickle, Snubby and Bibi had introduced to us in the 1980s. But the two trios would not give us a decent separation before dusk, so when the next day's sunrise revealed a glassy calm bay, we shot out northeast to document the consortship. We found them, and Gumby was there, but the Crunch Bunch didn't have her. Their friends did. The "Friends of the Crunch Bunch" were a trio of elderly males, Antoine, Wart and Worries, whose glory days were long past them. They were fully mature, tough males back in the mid-1980s, but all their mates from those days were gone and they were now a lone trio. Their friendship with the Crunch Bunch may have filled that void, perhaps like the Primas did for Real Notch, Hi & Pointer.† We often found Antoine, Wart and Worries with their

---

* *See "Female Dolphins: Different Personalities and Lifestyles"*
† *See "Real Notch & the Prima Donnas"*

pals, snoozing.

We set about watching the "Friends" snooze with Gumby for the requisite hour to get the consortship. It was easy for one's attention to wander when your subjects are doing nothing, and in such glassy conditions interesting distractions might be detected at a considerable distance. I saw a small group way out east of us moving north, quite rapidly. As I watched them through my binoculars, I saw another group moving in the same direction. The two groups coalesced and were now blasting along to the northwest, about 2 kilometers from us. I knew that a group moving like that was up to no good but we still had 10 minutes to go to get the consortship. Surely, I thought, we could just mosey over that way and use our binoculars to keep an eye on our sleepyheads. So off we went, and as we approached the leaping group they slowed down, which allowed us to get a look at their fins. It was the Gas Gang! We could never find the Gas Gang enough, so we were always thrilled to see them, and the way they were moving along meant that we were going to get to see them cause trouble!

The Gas Gang picked up speed again. I looked north in the direction they were heading and sure enough, there was a rowdy group up there! We raced alongside the Gas Gang, snapping photographs to make sure we documented their group before the you-know-what hit the fan. As they drew close to the target, the Gas Gang slowed down. They seemed to hesitate, but then, minds made up, they attacked. An explosion of splashing, charging around and chasing, and it was over; the Gas Gang had taken the female Phantom from the Prima Donnas! Wow. Only it wasn't all of the Prima Donnas; only Fred, Ridges and Big with tag-along Barney. Then I saw the reinforcements racing in to join them. It would be interesting to see what happened now, with all the Prima Donnas together! But the group joining Fred and friends wasn't the other Prima trio; it was six Kroker Spaniels! Skinny was here with Bolt and Deet, also Noggin, Moggy and Dangit. Now they had the numbers on the Gas Gang; it was going to be ten versus six. The Primas and Krokers approached the Gas Gang; they were now only 20 meters away. Our adrenaline was pumping; we were ready to film and photograph an epic fight. But nothing happened. For 30 minutes they followed the Gas Gang, and then fell back, trailing 150 meters behind, but they didn't leave. Finally, over an hour after the theft, with renewed fortitude, they again sped up toward the males that had dared to take their female. Surely they would call the Gas Gang to account this time! But the courage they had worked up from a safe distance drained away as they again moved to within 20 meters of the Gas Gang. They would approach no closer. The Primas and Krokers gave up and left the area.

I had always wondered what would happen if our alliances from the Red Cliff Bay area and just north were to meet up with the east side toughs. In this case they lost, but I'm not sure that would have been the case if the other Primas had shown up instead of the somewhat younger Kroker Spaniels. Where were the other Primas anyway? Were they too far to hear what was going on, or did they hear but not want to help? And for that matter, I wondered about the other Krokers. I imagine the outcome would have been different if the full complement of 14 Krokers and 7 Primas were present.

Although the Krokers and Primas didn't re-engage the Gas Gang, the day's events did shed light on why second-order alliances might want to maintain friendly relations with another group or two; that is, why we find third-order alliances in the bay. Males are often spread out over quite large distances from their allies. If you are attacked and your main second-order allies are not around to help, maybe other friends will be there to join with you in battle.

I also want to caution that there is no real east–west divide; there is no Maginot line separating groups of alliances. Most of these guys know each other, and the Primas and Krokers certainly know the eastern males well. In some years they spend a lot of time out east. In 2004, during the peak mating season, we consistently found the Primas and Krokers in the channel just south of the Outer Banks. Now, we don't know why they spend a bit more time here and there in different mating seasons; most likely it has to do with the numbers of receptive females in the area and movements of rival alliances. At any rate, it is fun to think about what would happen if this and that alliance met; and in the case of the Primas and Gas Gang, we had a little taste of it. And although the Gas Gang won that battle, as we will see later, they may have lost the war, by virtue of where they lived.

Within any area, there will be variation in the ferocity of the alliances.

The Gas Gang clearly demanded respect, but there was one eastern alliance that nobody worried about.

§

Captain Hook's Not-So-Tough Crew

Around 1990–1991, a juvenile male with a spectacular hooked fin began to poke around in Red Cliff Bay once and a while. We named him "Captain Hook" and his best friend "Bly." Their core area turned out to be "around the corner" to the southeast of Monkey Mia, in an area that was covered by shallow seagrass banks with a few deeper channels. Not surprisingly, with all those seagrass beds, members of Hook's Crew were

Captain Hook © Dolphin Alliance Project

often seen kerplunking. They did venture further afield, often into the main channel out east and northeast of Red Cliff Bay. For the first years of our study there were six males in Hook's Crew, then a seventh joined by 2003.*

They liked to watch. Sometimes while following a group of males

---

* *And Spud appears to have been a member during the early 1990s before he died. See "Expanded Horizons"*

that were getting rowdy around a consorted female, we would look up and see two or three or five Hooks, snagging tens of meters away, just sitting there watching the action. Once we saw four members of Hook's Crew take a young, probably immature, female from three maturing males, but that was the extent of their bravery in battle.

One day in 2003 we were past Cape Rose in Whale Bight watching some aggression among the Prima Donnas. Real Notch and Hi joined the group and seemed to be adding their opinion to the discussion, but we could not figure out what the argument was about. I looked up and saw Captain Hook and Bly sitting there 20 meters from the action, just watching. We had never seen them so far northwest.

We also caught them watching on 21 August 2001. We were with some Exfins,[*] a group of eight males who herded in both pairs and trios. The Exfins were in the main channel out east, their core area, herding a female. I glanced up to see four dolphins snagging in our direction. We popped over for a quick peek and saw that it was Captain Hook, Bly, Dagwood and Link. We returned to the Exfins, but I did look back to see the Hooks leaving to the southeast toward their core range. A short time later we saw a splashing, leaping rowdy group in the direction they traveled, so we sped over to catch them in the act of catching two females. The chase was fast and long, with spectacular synchronous leaps. Once they had sequestered the females, they continued moving south, going with the flow of the incoming tide. I was intensely following their every move, hoping to get the required 10-meter separation that would tell us which pair of males had which female. We had a brief separation at one point showing that the female with a nasty looking shark-bite scar was with Hook and Bly. I wasn't satisfied, so we kept on it until suddenly the shark-bite female was gone. Evidently, they had just let her go. Fortunately, a bit after that Hook and Bly moved ahead of the others, so we got our confirmation that Dag & Link had the other female. I relaxed and looked around to the northeast toward Faure Island. Wait a minute, that's not Faure, where in the hell are we? I looked all around at the unfamiliar coast, and back northeast, when it dawned on me that the land I first thought was Faure Island was in fact Petit Point. We had

---

[*] See "A New Project," for the time in 1994 when Rachel and I recorded creepy sounds from the Exfins.

traveled all the way down into L'Haridon Bight!

We had never followed any of our males that far south. L'Haridon Bight was super-salty so there wasn't much of anything down there, but it was beautiful as the water was as clear as a swimming pool.

We watched to see what the Hooks were going to do in such a barren place. After a time the answer became clear: absolutely nothing. Well, it occurred to me, they were doing something; they were hiding. I remembered how Snubby, Sickle and Bibi used to retreat to the southeast around the corner as soon as they had filled their bellies at Monkey Mia.* In that case it was clear that they wanted to avoid Real Notch's crew, but as we would come to realize, the Hooks probably wanted to avoid just about any other alliance of adult males. They had caught a prized female, probably within earshot of a number of other groups, and so they beat a path down here where nobody would look for them.

The Hooks also had great places to hide right in their core area. The extensive shallows and banks hid small, hard-to-find channels. We found four Hooks one day in 2004 with two females in a little isolated channel buried way down in the shallows near Dubaut. Sound would not carry at all well from that channel, across the seagrass-covered banks, to points beyond. Their rivals out in the deeper channels would not hear them if they made any of the usual vocal racket that accompanies herding.

The Hooks were not so well concealed on an August day in 2006. We were just completing a survey of a group of females in the channel north of the Monkey Mia banks, near Which Bank, when Captain Hook, Bly and Link charged in and captured Nook. After the capture, Bly kept leaping around while Link rubbed against Captain Hook. Bly seemed to be having a temper tantrum, as he was not included in the herding, which was unusual; Captain Hook always had Bly as his first mate. Bly settled down and left the group but then returned with another member of the crew, Dweeb. Bly and Dweeb stayed tight together, swimming side by side for a while, before leaving together.

At one point, while we watched Captain Hook and Link with Nook, I remarked that Nook seemed to be kind of far off to the side instead of in the female's usual spot in front of the males. Evidently, the same thought occurred to Hook and Link as they turned suddenly and charged at

See "Dolphins Burning"

Nook, chasing her in a large circle, ending in shallow water over Which Bank. We looked up and saw three males blasting in; it was Skini, Bolt and Ceebie! The Kroker trio slowed as they entered the group, then snagged, as did Hook and Link. We had the hydrophone in the water. There was nothing but a long, pregnant silence. Skini, Bolt and Ceebie slowly moved away-- with Nook! Once they were clear of the Hooks by 20 meters or so they sped up and began excitedly leaping. Hook and Link just sat there, not making a move, a whimper or a peep of protest.

Never had I seen such total acquiescence by males. I have seen a lot of thefts and fights over females, and losers always make a fuss when their female is taken. And it wasn't as though Hook and Link weren't excited about having Nook; the charge and long chase showed that. We were astonished and amused, and it's a good thing Hook and Link could not understand our jokes as we mocked them without mercy.

When we looked back over our data, two things about the Hook's Crew stood out. They were the only group that herded females exclusively in pairs and, unlike other groups, the Hooks didn't seem to have close ties with any other second-order alliances. I suspect they tried; the only time we ever filmed a tango,* an intense male- bonding display of back and forth synchronous movements that evokes (at least to me!) the dance, was when Link and Dagwood joined the Blues Brothers pair Jake and Elwood. Jake and Link tangoed right behind our boat. But the Hooks never developed a special relationship like that between the Primas and Krokers, the Poohbahs and Hammers, RHP with the Primas or the Crunch Bunch and the Friends of the Crunch Bunch. That lack of a friendship with another group may have either exacerbated their lowly status or been the reason for it. Maybe other groups just didn't value their company. The Hooks were probably of little use in a fight.

If the Hooks were so low ranking, you had to think about why they lived where they lived. Maybe it wasn't the most ideal habitat for a male dolphin.

---

* *Tango displays were mentioned previously in "An Alliance Triangle," "Starving Dolphinas," "This is Like Science Fiction!," "Wave, Shave & Spud on Their Own" and "Resolution."*

§

Pirate & Fargo Look for a Home

A week into exploring our new, expanded study area in 2001, I decided to go out to the Outer Banks and beyond, into La-La Land, to see if we could find some good alliances for our project. We found some familiar males, but not surprisingly, just into La-La Land we came across a group that wanted nothing to do with us.* There was a mother with her infant in the group and she was unperturbed to the point of riding our bow, but the rest were afraid and kept moving away. I had a hunch they were males and one had a fin that was bent right over, so I gave him the obvious name: Bent-fin. You could tell it was Bent-fin from a kilometer away.

A week later we saw a trio in the distance that would not let us anywhere near them. Identifying the other two was impossible, but there was no mistaking Bent-fin.

A month later I found Bent-fin and his buddies again. There were four in the group, and as I watched, I could tell that they were a trio of males with a female consort. One of the males came right over, but not Bent-fin; he was evasive again, but he seemed less scared than before. As we lingered he seemed to settle down, although not to the point of allowing us to approach him. They were a good-looking trio and I decided that I would put some effort into making Bent-fin more comfortable with us so they could be part of the study.

We next saw the Bent-fin trio in mid-August 2002. I set out to habituate them; but how do you habituate a dolphin? I had enough experience trying to photograph the scared dolphins in La-La Land to know that the first pass is often the closest you will get. After that, they realize that you are not just a boat passing through but that you are actually (gasp!) following them! Paranoia sets in and they start making evasive maneuvers, and further attempts to approach only serve to reinforce their fears. The key is to avoid approaching the dolphins directly, travel a course that is close to parallel with theirs, and slowly try to shave off some of the distance between you and the dolphins. Later

---

* See *"Beyond Red Cliff Bay"* for our discovery of skittish dolphins in the area.

I would learn to use an additional technique that I think helps. After a while, the dolphins you are paralleling will turn towards you and maybe even approach a few meters as if investigating this persistent nuisance. When they make such approaches I turn away from them, hopefully conveying the idea that I am a little bit afraid of them also. I think this builds their confidence, and at any rate, it seems to work.

Our efforts were producing results and we were starting to get close enough for decent pictures of Bent-fin and his mates. I could see that Bent-fin had tangled with a shark since we last saw him; he had new damage to his fin and scars on his body. Then, fortuitously, three familiar dolphins joined them. It was Antoine, Wart and Worries, the old friends of the Crunch Bunch, who were completely comfortable around our boat. They were with the most popular female of the year, Phantom. The Bent-fin trio immediately took over consorting Phantom, and if that bothered Antoine, Wart and Worries, it didn't show. The two groups stayed together, mostly resting, with the Antoine trio behind the Bent-fin trio, who had Phantom in the "consort position" in front of them. The presence of such tame dolphins seemed to put Bent-fin further at ease, and we were allowed much closer. With that I considered them to be part of the study.

That was the last I saw of Bent-fin. Suddenly, in 2003, his two buddies were everywhere. It was amazing; with timid Bent-fin out of the way, we sighted them time and time again. It made me wonder if there are other dolphins I didn't see because they, or their friends, were so afraid of boats. I was reminded of how Wave and Shave acted evasively in 1987 when Spud first joined them.*

Bent-fin's friends were two peas in a pod, the best of mates and the tightest of pairs. But quickly a third male filled the vacancy left by Bent-fin. It was Pirate. Now this was fascinating. We had been seeing Pirate out east since the start of the study in 2001. The impression was of a happy-go-lucky male who was friends with everybody. We saw Pirate with the Exfins, the Gas Gang, the Sweepers, but the reality was that Pirate was an adult male without a home. Even back in the mid-1990s he was a well-speckled adult male. Here, nearly 10 years later, he was still bopping around out east, spending time with this group and that group

---

* See ""Wave's Bud Spud"

but belonging nowhere, until Bent-fin died. Pirate had found a home at last and he was going to stick to his new mates like glue. From that point on Pirate was always with his new friends.

With Pirate onboard, maybe it was time for this now ubiquitous trio to revisit some relationships with other alliances. After all, second and third-order alliance relationships are important in Shark Bay and it wasn't clear to us if the Pirate trio had such friendships with other males. Something was clearly percolating with the Crunch Bunch. The two groups had some intense and puzzling interactions; not fighting but not mellow petting and rubbing sessions either. Perhaps they were testing out a possible relationship. I suspected that would be complicated, as all the individual and group dominance relationships would have to be clarified. That may be why their interactions typically included aggression, inter-alliance petting and synchrony, and behavior and vocalizations that were just plain weird. One such interaction during August 2003 suggested that Pirate's novitiate status was not entirely without friction. While with the Crunch Bunch, Pirate was chased around and harassed by the Crunch Bunch and his own buddies. I had seen this movie before!* But such was life in the dolphins' system of nested alliances and it didn't seem to impact Pirate's place in his new trio.

Things didn't work out so well for Fargo, at least we don't think they did. His situation was different from Pirate's; Fargo was a maturing male in his early teens, the age where he would normally be forming alliances with other age-mates. But Fargo seemed to have loftier goals. In 2004 we found him consorting a female with an established mature group, the Exfins.

The Exfins lived and hunted almost exclusively in the main channel out east. We had known their namesake, Exfin, since the late 1980s when he was a member of a stable trio, Exfin, Unfin and Nonfin. Those names derived from Non-Fin, whose fin looked like Nicky's. When we saw him the first time we responded in mock horror, "not another Nicky!" and the initials for that exclamation, NAN, morphed into Non and he became Nonfin. The other names in his trio were assigned to fit the theme.

* See "Male Dolphins: The Politics Emerge" and "A Third Level of Alliance"

Anyway, by the early 1990s his mates were gone and Exfin had to find a new home. He might have joined the Exfins as a troll, when they were still maturing, or perhaps after they had already begun to herd females. Regardless, when we started watching them closely in 2001 they were a group of eight mature males that herded in pairs and trios. We didn't see much of Exfin in July and August. While the others were herding females he mostly stayed by himself, diving for fish in the channel, but when the mating season came around and it really counted, he was there, consorting females. As a much older male, Exfin had to put in more effort to maintain his condition; he had to focus on feeding all winter so he could consort females in the spring.

The Exfins were also a royal pain in the you-know-what. Probably because they mixed pair and trio herding, it was often difficult to get good separations for them. The situation was totally different for the nearby Hooks, who only herded in pairs, or the Crunch Bunch, who were two stable trios. Separations were frequent and obvious for those groups, but there often seemed to be a "hanger-on" with Exfin pairs. I think that of all the groups, the most errors in the data are found in the Exfin consortships, where some listed trios were probably, in reality, pairs. They were easier if we found them in the mating season and everyone was in a consortship. Then the consorting groups would come together and split up nicely, with no males left out and hanging around someone else's consortship.

We had Fargo in a few more consortships with the Exfins, but we also found him with younger maturing males and the Blues Brothers, who had matured and started herding females midway through our study. Fargo consorted females with the Blues Brothers twice. Cases like Fargo lead me to think that males are sometimes given "tryouts" with alliances. Fargo was given an opportunity with the mature Exfins and the newly formed Blues Brothers. Ultimately, it didn't work out for Fargo with either group.

We don't see Fargo anymore. Maybe he found a home outside of our study area. I hope so, but I doubt it.

§

The Blues Brothers Have a Bad Day

Simon Allen had joined our team in late August 2005. An east coast Australian who had fallen in love with the west after visiting us in Shark Bay a few years earlier, Simon was a great field worker and natural comedian, so we loved having him visit and help us on the project. In 2005, we had lost two assistants and were going to be understaffed, so Simon kindly came on the project to take the reins after I left at the end of the month to return to my teaching duties. He came out with us on the 26th.

We weren't having much luck finding dolphins; then we struck it rich between two of the Outer Banks. We found the Crunch Bunch and their friends, the old geezers Antoine, Wart and Worries, spread out in the channel between This Bank and That Bank, diving for fish. At one point Jimbo did some extremely intense tail-slaps. They weren't at all like kerplunks or normal social tail-slapping. He would arch his body up, then slap his flukes down violently, and while fishing alone in 20 feet of water. Was he trying to scare fish at that depth? Was that the reason for the intensity of the slaps? We didn't know. It was just another of those observations that you tuck away for the future.

Around the top of one of the banks we ran into a bunch of the Blues Brothers who were herding one of the sponging females. The boys were greatly excited around her, so we geared up for a longish follow in hopes of determining which two or three of the six males present actually had the consortship. Sometimes it can take a good while to find out. As we knew well, when males are excited and flying all around a female, the males not consorting with her get side by side and synch with those that are. Such inter-alliance synchs probably reinforce bonds in tense situations, and once they have finished socializing they often start to snooze, all packed together, and you must wait for them to wake up. Unfortunately, such snoozing bouts can last for up to three hours. When they wake up and spread out to fish we can finally see which males stay with the female. Frustratingly, sometimes before we can sort it out, we run out of daylight or calm weather. I was known to stay to the bitter end, trying to get that 10-meter separation between first-order alliances to see who had the female. Even if the sun had vanished, as long as there was a bit of a glow left on the western horizon, I would maneuver the boat to keep the dolphins in the fading light reflecting from that glow. Of course, if we failed, we would run out the next day and try to find the same group.

Fortunately, on this occasion, some dolphins back in the channels hit on a bonanza of fish, and most of the Blues Brothers tore off in that direction to join in the leap-feeding melee. Grub and Seven stayed behind with the female. Okay, we knew which males had her; now we just had to stay with them for an hour. But we lost them for the commonest of reasons: they moved into an area with other dolphins and started diving for fish. With all those other dolphins in the area it was easy to get confused and approach the wrong ones, which we did promptly. Damn.

We kept looking, and spotting a rowdy group, we ran over to see Grub and Seven sulking near an excited social mob of three Crunch Bunch members and Antoine, Wart and Worries with the same female! They had evidently just taken the female from Grub and Seven and now they were enjoying the same excitement over having her that the Blues Brothers had shown earlier. The Crunch Bunch and friends settled down and traveled together a while before Antoine, Wart and Worries left with the female. Not surprising, I thought; the Crunch Bunch and their friends are much older than the teenagers Seven and Grub, and they had the numbers in their favor.

A short time later we saw the Blues Brothers in another tangle, and this time they would not be able to complain that they were outnumbered.

After a bit more looking around, we were attracted to yet another rowdy group, and found seven Blues Brothers with the female Talladega. There was evidently some disagreement among the Blues Brothers, as we saw a couple of tiffs indicating that the aggressive sounds we heard on the hydrophone were not all directed toward the female. A few of the males left the group but shortly returned. Thus, the Blues Brothers were seven strong when Pirate's trio cruised unhurriedly into their midst.

The innocent way that the Pirate trio sauntered into the group didn't arouse our suspicions, and they may well have not been intending to cause trouble when they first arrived. After a short time in the group they started to leave as casually as they entered, but after traveling a short distance Pirate stopped, paused and turned around, then headed back into the group. His two friends followed. The theft was on.

Our hydrophone erupted in growling, hitting and pops as the water boiled and the dolphins porpoised around in tight masses, which continued until a lone stranger came blasting into the group. He was here to help the Pirate trio and that seemed to be enough. Shortly they blasted away from the Blues Brothers with Talladega in tow. As they leaped and porpoised along at high speed, the Blues Brothers gave chase, leaping along in hot pursuit. We raced alongside the Blues Brothers, filming the chase as I called out the names of dolphins I saw, "There's Rickets, there's Seven and Poodle," "there's Czar;" on and on the chase went. The Blues Brothers seemed to be gaining ground on the thieves; we expected to see another fight. Then the Pirate group abruptly turned around; the Blues Brothers slammed on the breaks and fled in the opposite direction. The Blues had turned to flee the instant the Pirate group turned toward them; on the video there was no more than a half a second between the two groups turning.

The Blues Brothers really had me fooled! Sure, I had seen the losers in a theft "pursue" the victors enough that I should have known better, but the Blues Brothers seemed really convincing. I thought they were serious about wanting to get Talladega back from the Pirate group, but it was all show.

The Pirate trio turned back and started swimming again in the direction they had been traveling. They were swimming fast, but not nearly as fast as before. Then to our surprise, the Blues Brothers came charging up again, chasing the "fleeing" males who stole their prized Talladega. As I watched the Pirate group up ahead I swear I could see what they were thinking; in fact, what I was probably detecting was subtle hesitation as they tensed just before their next dramatic move. They didn't just turn around this time; they turned and charged back full speed at the Blues Brothers, who retreated quickly to a safe distance.

The Pirate group surfaced a few times, then resumed traveling at a normal pace. We looked around for the Blues Brothers. They were nowhere in sight. It was calm and we could see a long distance, so we kept watching. Finally, the Blues surfaced, several hundred meters away and still going.

The episode had been, in equal parts, amazing and funny. The jokes flew, as Simon and I amused ourselves at the Blues Brothers' expense, but our observations were not finished, so we became serious again. One learns to switch quickly between "comedian" and "serious scientist" modes during fieldwork.

Two big tough-looking dolphins came in to join ours. They swam abreast, forming a nice trio with the stranger that had come to help the Pirate trio take the female. Wait, I had seen one of the new ones before! I was thrilled! This trio were obviously friends and quite possibly second-order alliance partners of Pirate's crew. The two trios sure looked like a second-order alliance as they swam along separated by a few meters, with Talladega in front of Pirate's Crew. Probably their ranges overlapped extensively north of the outer banks, in La-La Land, where we seldom ventured. While we saw much of Pirate's crew in our northeastern study area, their friends were strangers to us. It was an important lesson for us; dolphins we think we know well may have good friends that we have never or rarely seen. I recalled the day in 1997 when Anvil bought his new old friends to see the Wow Crowd.*

The Blues Brothers-Pirate Crew affair illustrated again that numbers are not everything when it comes to conflicts between male dolphins. Age plays a big role, as males in their 20s and 30s are likely a bit larger and stronger and may have an established track record of being dominant. We know from studies of chimpanzees and other mammals that an established reputation means something. Dominant individuals are not always challenged and defeated as soon as younger ones become physically capable of doing so.

26 August 2005 was not a great day for the Blues Brothers. They had two females taken from them and they had been trounced by a group half their size. The Blues Brothers would have to wait a few years, but their time would come as they would grow not only older, but larger.

Poodle had been a pain. In 2001, when we were out looking for new alliances, I ran into him a lot, often messing around with his friend

---

* See *"Anvil's New Old Friends"*

Hosehead off the northeast edge of the Monkey Mia Banks. They looked large enough to be consorting females. They were definitely males to watch. Well, watch we did, year after year, but there was not much to see; like dolphin Peter Pans, they seemed to never grow up.

Given their disappointing history, we were surprised by Poodle and Tool (another enigmatic young male from the east) on the 26th. They had seemed quite enthusiastic joining the Blues Brothers in their pursuit of Pirate and his fellow thieves, even seeming to lead the chase. Perhaps they were applying for membership and impressing the others with a show of bravery would help their cause. Of course, any such pretense was exposed the moment the Pirate Crew turned to face them.

The Blues Brothers, named after Jake and Elwood, a fairly stable pair in the group, had solidified their membership of eight by 2004. Following the example of the Prima Donnas, who crystallized into a group of seven in the mid-1990s and had remained stable since, we figured the Blues Brothers were pretty well set.

Poodle and his friends didn't care much for our expectations. Their affiliation with the Blues Brothers solidified the following year. On 30 July 2006, we found four Blues off the south end of That Bank, with a herded female. With them were Poodle and Hosehead, who also had a female consort.

More interesting to us was how the males swam together like members of the same second-order alliance. Were Poodle and Hosehead now officially members of the Blues Brothers? Obviously, we would have to see them together a lot more than this one day and, after all, they hadn't yet consorted a female with any of the core eight members. They countered that objection a few weeks later.

On 13 August we found Poodle and Tool herding with Rickets, and the female they had was none other than Talladega! Celebrating the initiation party with them was Czar, in a pair with Hosehead, herding a female that seemed quite young; she was a bit small, had a clean fin and was frisky like a younger female — indeed, it may have been another case of "male bonding herding."* That would make sense if Hosehead was being initiated into the Blues Brothers. In fact, much of the males' behavior, even some of the displays, seemed to be addressed

---

* See "Any Female Will Do," "A New Bond," "Terra Becomes a Troll"

to each other rather than to the females. There was a lot of petting and some aggression between the males. In one especially bizarre display, Poodle and Czar performed a side-by-side rooster strut with a twist; synchronously turning their snouts in toward each other. Was it a competitive or bonding display? I couldn't tell! It may have been another one of those weird displays that they seem to make up as they go.

I also heard a weird vocalization during the consortships that sounded as if more than one male was producing it. Hmmm, I thought, maybe they are doing vocally what we suspect them of doing with physical displays--being creative. Certainly we have "regular" displays that we see performed in tandem, like the rooster strut or tango. But there are quite a few synchronous displays that we have only seen once, so we suspect the males sometimes create displays in the moment; perhaps one male closely follows the lead of the other. Might the same be true for vocalizations? We hear common vocalizations, such as pops, performed synchronously, but there are also cases of strange sounds produced in tandem that I haven't heard before or since. Maybe we simply haven't listened enough and each tandem vocalization has a distinct meaning or evinces a specific emotional state or level of excitement, but it also seems possible that they might display with sound in the same creative way that I think they do with their astonishing variety of synchronous leaps and turns.

Whatever the significance of the unusual displays and vocalizations on that day, Poodle's prospects were undiminished. He was seen in several more consortships with the Blues Brothers in 2006. Poodle had finally grown up!

§

Invaders from the North

At the start of the study in 2001, I was excited about finding new alliances in Herald Bight, between Guichenault and Cape Peron. Of course, part of the draw was simply the spectacular beauty of Peron, which I had come to know in 1991 when working with Per. It is one thing to drive up to the top (4-wheel drive required) and look out over the bay from the bluff, but it is entirely another matter to take in the view of Peron from a boat; the striking bright orange bluff set against blue sky and water is wondrous.

Outside of the dedicated trips on Nortrek, if we were going to do a "Peron day" we had to resolutely drive to the top of the shallows at Guichenault; if you stopped at every group along the way, you would never get there. Of course we could never be that disciplined, so we did occasionally stop for an interesting-looking group. If we didn't get too distracted, we could reach the top of the shallows in under an hour and start looking for dolphins between there and Peron. And the faster we got to Herald Bight, the less my assistants had to listen to my modified version of a Pet Shop Boys tune, "Peron, life is peaceful there...."

Sometimes we encountered lots of dolphins as soon as we arrived at the top of Guichenault shallows. The tops of the peninsulas, Guichenault and especially Peron, seemed to be places of biological rock-and-roll, with drop-offs and colliding currents creating the conditions for an abundance of marine life, and hence food for dolphins.

Our first Peron Day was on 3 August 2001. After reaching the top of the shallows I pointed the boat toward Peron and started looking for dolphins. Partway there, in nearly 40 feet of water, we found a group of four dolphins that were spread out fishing, doing tail-out dives. But they kept converging at the surface after dives. As we watched we realized that they seemed to be converging each time on one particular dolphin. This looked like a consortship, so we stayed an hour with these strangers, noting the subject of the convergence as the "putative female." The males didn't just dive and spread out underwater, they would dive, going down in different directions from the female. Rather than leaving one male to guard the female, they were keeping her in the middle of their fishing triangle.

On occasion, we just ended up at the top of Guichenault or in Herald Bight, almost by accident. That is how I got my first good look at the Grand Poobahs. We found Real Notch, Hi and Pointer in Red Cliff Bay, then a bit further along we ran into the Prima Donnas and Kroker Spaniels. We stayed around to document three consortships from those groups and kept going north. We found the Wow Crowd and stayed to get another consortship with Latch, Gripe and Veetop. The day was still young, so we kept going.

Moving up to the deeper waters off the Guichenault shallows, we found a trio of strange males, side by side, then another, then another. Two of the groups had females. As we watched, the groups would come together and separate again. Incredible; here was a new second-order alliance of at least nine males! And these were clearly not young, recently matured punks. Wait a minute; one of these trios was familiar! It was the same trio we had watched converging on the female during our trip on the 3rd. They would become known as Dominic, Monkey and Mulligan, one of the most stable trios in the Grand Poobahs.

Over the next few sightings we found that the Grand Poobahs were a group of 12. Now we had our third "super-alliance," which is the term we give to any group that reaches double digits in size. The behavior we had seen on that first day with Dominic, Monkey and Mulligan was typical for the group, so common that we had to create a new behavioral category for them, "converging on the female." The Poohbahs, like the Wow Crowd before them, were deep-water fishers. By spreading out from the female and from each other, they were likely avoiding feeding competition as they dove toward the bottom seeking single fish.

The Poohbahs also liked to feed on schools of fish. Sometimes we would find them with lots of other dolphins, and tons of birds, leap-feeding in Herald Bight. There seemed to be more large schools of fish up there.

Later we discovered that the Poohbahs had friends and those friends brought another wonderful surprise, Anvil! Anvil, and the same buddies that had accompanied him for that awkward meeting with the Wow Crowd in 1997. Anvil, Hammer, Drill and Rasty, were part of a group of six, rounded out by Kermit and Spoof.* Anvil had indeed left the Wow Crowd to join another group!

Over the course of the study, we came to appreciate that the Hammers and Poobahs didn't just associate occasionally; they often shadowed each other. I learned that the Hammers were often inshore of the Poohbahs, as though they preferred to fish in water a bit shallower than that favored by the Poohbahs.

In 2002 we discovered another Herald Bight super-alliance that was

---

* See "Anvil's New Old Friends"

to figure prominently in our study. The Skipjacks were a group of 11 males named after the lighthouse point, "Skipjack," just south of Point Peron, because they seemed to use that area as a home base. The first day I realized I was dealing with another large alliance was in late July. We had just crossed over the top of the Guichenault shallows when we encountered nine Skipjacks. Some were familiar; indeed, I had first photographed Viking in the 1980s. As we followed them for the next five and a half hours, they engaged in what I came to realize later was classic Skipjack feeding behavior. They moved rapidly, feeding and hunting, across the shallows, then down along the east side, just off the edge of the shallows in 4–5 meters all the way to Guichenault Bluff. Then they turned around, moved a bit farther offshore, and moved back north doing the same thing. When the Skipjacks fished along the shallows, they really moved. If it was a bit choppy, you could lose them in a heartbeat. They did fish in deeper water, and would join the Poohbahs and Hammers in leap-feeding melees, but we never saw Poohbahs fishing in such shallow water. We knew that if we wanted to find Skipjacks, the best place to look was in the shallows up to 7 meters, and for the Hammers, it was in the 7–8 meter range, and for the Poohbahs, it was in waters deeper than 8 meters. Again, these were just tendencies.

When we don't know groups well, it can be hard to decipher social interactions in real time. That was the case on 19 August 2002, when we found the Skipjacks, who were still a novelty for us, with others we didn't know. They had females and there was conflict between the male subgroups, including some very intense aggression. One especially intense bout of growling and hitting was announced with a shrill vocalization that sounded as pleasing as a dentist's drill. In such chaos, while trying to sort out what is going on, we keep taking pictures of each subgroup as they join and split in hopes of being able to piece together a more complete story later. In this fashion we reconstructed events on an August day in 2003, when the Skipjacks, some Peron males and a lone trio called the "Jacques"* were all setting upon one poor individual, Marcel, of the Peron Posse. I was reminded of how Ceebie, Patches and Pirate were tormented by males from their own and other

---

I had learned, from reading Barbara Tuchman's "Through a Distant Mirror" that Jacques was a 14th century term for French peasants.

alliances.* The day also featured another of those remarkable creative displays, this time with both males flipping their flukes up with each surfacing. I would have named it the "dandy display" if I thought we would ever see it again, but we did not.

As each winter season drew to a close and the heart of the mating season approached, the Herald Bight alliances did not confine themselves to the north. Down they came, past the Grooves, as far as Cape Rose. They maintained the same pattern with respect to depth; we would find the Skipjacks in shallower water than the other two groups, and the Hammers inshore of the Poohbahs.

Now, we had known since the 1980s that dolphins that lived to the north of Red Cliff Bay moved into the bay during the mating season. Then we would see the Sharkies and B-boys in Red Cliff Bay. Later in the 1990s I noticed that the Wow Crowd moved a bit further south during the mating season. We saw females doing the same thing; I remembered the fascinating case of the northern female Couch coming right into the Monkey Mia shallows to visit her friend Holey-fin during consecutive Octobers.†

I had been thinking that females were probably moving south after some seasonal change in the distribution of their food and/or sharks and that the male movements were following the females' range shifts. But seeing these huge super-alliances move south gave me a new perspective. These were male armadas moving south in the mating season. If the Hammers and Poohbahs supported each other in conflicts, rivals could be dealing with a force of up to 18 males! The Kroker-Prima combination was larger, but the Krokers were still a bit young. Clearly, there was pushing going on in Shark Bay. If a rival super-alliance moves into your area, and you want to hang onto your female consorts, you had better shift ahead of them.

Now that raises another question. If the Herald Bight alliances were pushing formidable groups like the Wow Crowd, were there even larger forces pushing them in turn? We had seen phenomenal fights between groups of males around the top of Peron in winter. We were never able to see those males often enough to bring them into the study. I wondered

* See "A Third Level of Alliance," "Male Dolphins: The Politics Emerge" and "Pirate and Look for a Home"
† See "Beyond Red Cliff Bay"

if the Skipjacks and Poohbahs were being pushed by some huge alliance or alliances. I lumped some Peron males into a group called the "Peron Posse" that I thought was more fantasy than anything else.

Later, I had my one and only indication that a Peron Posse super-alliance was real. It was on 16 November 2004, in the peak of the mating season. We had traveled up past the Grooves when we came upon five subgroups of four dolphins each, spread out from each other but moving south in what seemed to be a coordinated fashion. This was exactly the behavior of a super-alliance. We ran from group to group, snapping pictures. Some were familiar to me from Peron while others were complete strangers. We figured that each group was a trio with a female. But it was a race against time that we lost. The spring "sea-breeze" was coming up — it should be called a "sea-gale" — and once it hit we wouldn't be able to find anyone. We were working on the fourth group when the wind engulfed us, and we had no hope of finding the fifth group in the ensuing whitecaps. That would have made an alliance of 15 males, the biggest yet recorded, and, of course, the group may have been even larger.

§

An Open Society

Sometimes when I talk about the alliances I think people envision a bunch of billiard balls, rolling around in the bay, bouncing off each other in conflicts over females. Sure, the alliances are very real entities and it is impressive to see a large second-order alliance traveling around with their females, but alliance members are often spread out over a wide area. As individuals and in groups, males have numerous chances to interact with other males, and the vast majority of those interactions are not hostile. The range of each male overlaps with a large number of other males, and they know those individuals.

Noggin, a Kroker Spaniel, had one of the more dramatic fins in the bay. You could spot him a long way off. When he was not with his Kroker friends, you might find him with males from other groups. We had seen Noggin with Exfins, Hooks, the Gas Gang, Blues Brothers,

Rascals and the old guys, Antoine, Wart & Worries.

The relationships that males have with their first, second and third-order alliance partners are anything but simple. Males in a group may have a tiff or they may favor certain group members over others for herding females, and they vary in how stable their herding partnerships are. They may have to leave their group and try to find another. Relations between groups vary from predictably hostile to mostly friendly, as we saw with Primas and Krokers.* And second-order alliances can have more than one friendship at a time with other groups.

There are males in our study that probably don't know each other at all. Or maybe they have heard the signature whistles of males they have never seen. The northern alliances may probe as far as the top of Red Cliff Bay in the spring, but they do not go to the southeast. They probably do not know the eastern Gas Gang or Exfins or alliances down to the southeast that we don't see often enough, like the Ghengis Khans and the Usual Suspects.

Then there are alliances that might know each other just a little bit. Maybe their ranges overlap a tad and they see or hear each other only when in that area of mutual overlap, once every year or two.

It is really an amazing thing. These dolphins live in an open social network, a society without a social boundary. I know of no other mammal that lives in a comparable society, that has the combination of complex social relationships among individuals that travel around in a seemingly endless mosaic of overlapping home ranges.

Chimpanzees live in a "community," a defined territory patrolled by males. Baboons live in troops. Wolves live in packs. Each of these societies contains reproductive females and has a social boundary; either you are in it, or you are not. Perhaps not surprisingly, the only other mammal that comes close to the dolphins is the brainy African elephant, which lives in nested female-based groups that seem to extend into a huge open social network like the dolphins. The only thing missing from the elephants are descriptions of the kind of complex alliance interactions we find in Shark Bay.

Living in an open society has to complicate the social lives of our dolphins, beyond all the shenanigans that go on in their alliances, and

* See "A Third Alliance Level" and "Real Notch & The Prima Donnas"

especially considering the fission-fusion nature of their society.

Imagine that you are an alliance-forming dolphin. You want and need to know what other males are up to, who is forming an alliance with whom. But members of your own group may be strengthening their bonds, at your expense, when you are not present. You and your friends may encounter a male group that you easily defeated two years earlier, but you may not know if they have since gained powerful new allies.

The Shark Bay dolphins not only have to negotiate a multi-level alliance network, they have to operate in the dark to a degree, about what their friends and foes are up to. You have to wonder how this kind of uncertainty affects their social lives, their interactions and relationships with those they know well or hardly at all. Perhaps it favors a kind of social caution, an ability to discern changes in the attitude of others and certainly a good memory for past encounters. But in general, it must be a factor in the evolution of their large social brains.

Part IV

A Shifting Alliance Landscape

2009 - 2012

The Cast

The Alliances:

The Fruit Loops (about 8 males, now somewhat larger) were an alliance of young mature males in Herald Bight in 2005-2006. They have been observed sporadically in recent years with a significantly changed group composition. The Rascal member **Hedges** was observed with them once in 2006 but not since.

B-boys & Sharkies: by 2009 **Sylvester** was the lone survivor of these two groups.

The Wow Crowd (8 males) had eight surviving members but the group effectively operated as two trios. **Latch, Gripe & Veetop** were one trio and **Wow & Pik** were steady members of the second trio. **Myrtle** and **Krill** alternated years in the third position in Wow's trio. **Ajax** was always fishing alone.

The Hooligans (9 males) were a newly formed group of nine males in their mid-teens that roamed in Red Cliff Bay and Whale Bight.

The Prima Donnas (7 males) were still going strong with their original group intact, albeit Barney was with them less often.

The Kroker Spaniels (10 males) had dropped from 14 to 13 with the loss of **Terra** after 2004, then to 10 individuals by 2009, with the loss of key members **Skini, Bolt, & Midgie.**

The Rascals (four males) had lost three members when we returned in 2009. Still present were **Cookie, Urchin, Smokey & Lando**. Missing were **Lucky, Hedges** and **Jessie**. In 2006 Hedges had been observed once with the Fruit loops and Jessie was associating with another young male named **Squibeau**.

The Lost Boys (about 12 males) were a super-alliance of about a dozen mature males from La-La Land.

The Blues Brothers (14 males) not only retained their 2001-2006 members (**Czar, Elwood, Grub, Jake, Rickets, Seven, Smelt, Toque**) but they added six new members (**Picante, Poodle, Sloopy, Shitzu, Tool & Wham**) to become the third second-order alliance to reach 14 members.

The Gas Gang had only two members remaining, **Frans & Octane**.

The Dead Rockers (about 12 males) were a fearsome looking super-alliance of about a dozen mature males that moved into the area just north of Red Cliff Bay, including **Allman, Buddy, Cash, Garcia, Hendrix, Winehouse & Zandt**.

Arnie's Mates a large but poorly known group that lived in a deeper water north of Which Bank and the Outerbanks, partly in La-La Land.

The Females:

Blip, Clam (**Scallop's** daughter), **Cyrano** (Bergerac), **Flint, Joy, Phantom, Piccolo** (**Puck's** daughter), **Scallop, Whine**.

§

Keeping Track of the Boys

We had a lot of analysis and writing to do after we finished the 2001-2006 project, so we took a break for two years. But we had also come to realize just how important it was to keep track of the alliances. We were planning to do more focused projects on the males, and obviously needed to maintain a working knowledge of alliance membership and find new groups that formed from males that had been juveniles in the 2001–2006 study. Beyond that, some of the strongest evidence that males form alliances in a strategic, intelligent way, are the occasional changes in membership that we see; when Lucky was kicked out of the Real Notch Crew, then the Rascals; when Terra was evicted from the Sharkies and then joined the Krokers; when Anvil left his central position in the Wow Crowd to join the Hammers. Each one of those observations is worth its weight in gold, but they are infrequent. To catch more cases, we need to keep track of a large number of alliances. If we can do this over another 10- to 20-year period, we will have an even more amazing story to tell.

Another important reason to consistently monitor the alliances is to see which males are having success consorting females. As we had seen in the Wow Crowd study in the 1990s, and in our study on 12 second-order alliances from 2001-2006, some males consort females a lot and some, well, not so often! Poor Vax rarely consorted females while Latch, Hobo and Gripe were consorting most of the time. They were also the most stable trio in the Wow Crowd. Amazingly, we found that result held for all 12 second-order alliances in our 2001-2006 study: males with more stable first-order alliances consorted females more often!

We returned in 2009, to check on the membership of the groups we studied from 2001–2006, observe consortships, and look for new groups. Whitney Friedman, a Cognitive Science student at UCSD, came on board as an assistant in 2010. A teacher at UCSD, Christine Johnson, an old friend and fellow Ken Norris groupie from our days at UCSC, had approached me about giving Whitney some experience watching wild dolphins while she sorted out what kind of research she wanted to do. Well, a season in Shark Bay convinced Whitney that she wanted to work on our alliances for her Ph.D., so she helped lead the project from 2011.

§

Real Notch and the Rascals

We didn't see much of Real Notch in 2009; just a few times with females, but it was enough to know that Pointer was gone. Real Notch had lost Hi after 2005 and now Pointer as well. Real Notch had to be approaching 40 so I thought he might be done. I remembered how the old male Steps seemed to go downhill once he lost his buddy Kodoff.* Once males like Real Notch became old loners they usually don't last very long.

Count out Real Notch? I should have known better. Two days after we started the 2010 season we found him with the Rascals. Real Notch and Cookie were interested in the young female Piccolo (Puck was her mom) while Urchin, Lando and Smokey were pursuing Blip. Now this was interesting; Cookie was born in early October 1988† and so was nearly 20 years younger than Real Notch.

Maybe the Rascals needed Real Notch as they had lost two more members after kicking Lucky out of their group. Hedges and Jessie were no longer Rascals and we have not seen them or Lucky since. Lucky was older so we think he probably died, but I still wonder about Hedges and Jessie. They seemed to be laying the groundwork for a new future in 2006. Hedges' mother Wedges had a unique feeding strategy; she had somehow learned to subdue a large kind of fish, Golden Trevally, which were nearly half as long as she was. She would swim into the shallows with one of the huge fish and spend over half an hour breaking it up to eat, sometimes with a large tiger shark nearby. Her diet was likely related to her unusual range, along the shore from near Monkey Mia to the top of the peninsula! Hedges would have traveled up and down the peninsula with his mom during the first few years of his life. Perhaps that helps us understand the otherwise startling observation in 2006 of

---

* See "The End of the 80s"
† See "The Triangle in 1988" for the first mention of Cookie as a new infant.

Hedges in Herald Bight with a maturing alliance called the Fruit Loops! We also saw Jessie southeast of Red Cliff Bay in 2006, associating with other young males including Squibeau, an oddball male who showed up Red Cliff Bay associating with the mature resident female Square. Squibeau's behavior was like that of male Bonobos, the "other" chimpanzee, whose social organization differs markedly from that of common chimpanzees. Females are the powerbrokers in bonobos, and a young male entering a new group seeks out the protection of a female and her network of female friends. Coming from who knows where, Squibeau seemed to employ that same bonobo tactic to gain entry into the Red Cliff Bay social scene. If Hedges and Jessie were still around and looked the same we would know it, but maybe they are out there somewhere with new fins and friends. That is why I always encourage our team to compare new fins to missing ones; recognizing a changed fin is relatively easy if the dolphin has not changed social companions, but much more difficult if it has!

When we found Real Notch with the Rascals again a week later my interest was really piqued, so we decided to follow them. They were up in Whale Bight close to shore, fishing in 4–5 meters of water. Real Notch was paired off with Cookie again. The whole group was actively feeding as they surfaced rapidly and porpoised around, chasing fish. They passed a group with Blip, Joy and her young infant. I thought they might try to capture Blip since she was so popular this year, but they were clearly focused on food, at least for the moment. Suddenly they turned and swam rapidly back south, and it was shortly clear why. A large leap-feeding group had erupted down there. This time however, Real Notch and Cookie took a break from leap-feeding long enough to capture Blip. I was amazed; this old guy had apparently joined an alliance of males just reaching their prime. I recalled the interaction from 1997 when Real Notch was mounting a juvenile Cookie;* back then I could not have imagined the two as future partners.

The capture of Blip was not dramatic; there was no long chase or overt aggression. As I watched Real Notch with Blip, I thought about how well they must know each other. They were about the same age. In 1984 Rachel had found Blip with her infant Flip. We watched Blip

---

* See "Keeping Up With Old Friends"

in a consortship with Real Notch in 1987[*] and here he was consorting her again 23 years later. Most males and females continue to use their mother's home range as part of their own, long after they mature. So it seems a good bet that Blip and Real Notch had played together as Red Cliff Bay toddlers in the 1970s. I can't help thinking that the herding relationship is different for males and females with that sort of long history, compared to ones less familiar.

A week earlier, we had been startled by Blip's behavior during a consortship with the Prima Donnas. She was very frisky, leaping all over the place, rubbing against other dolphins and bonding[†] for several minutes with a female friend. It was clearly what biologists call "proceptive" behavior: when females take the initiative and show interest in sexual behavior.[‡] Mostly, we see proceptive behavior when females first come into estrus, then afterwards it is likely masked by the males'

Three Rascals, (l to r) Urchin, Smokey & Cookie, synchronously charge into a female who is just under water in front of them. © Stephanie King

behavior. Once they are really "on," the females don't need to encourage the males as much. I had often seen such behavior by females over the years, but mostly in younger ones. Seeing 40-year-old Blip act like an 11-year-old dolphin debutante was a real surprise.

[*] *See "An Alliance Triangle"*
[†] *See "This Bonding Business"*
[‡] *See examples in "Sex at Monkey Mia."*

We continued to find Real Notch with Cookie and the Rascals. One day, Urchin, Lando and Smokey had a female and Real Notch and Cookie did not, but they were still acting like a tight pair.

As we moved into the mating season, Real Notch was seen alone again or with non-reproductive females, and the Rascals were found a few times without him. I wondered if they had kicked him out or if he had simply grown tired due to his age. Exfin seemed to have learned to pace himself by not joining the consortships in the winter months while he fished in the channel out east. He was then ready for the mating season.* I wondered if Real Notch was having trouble maintaining his condition.

It was hard for me to think of Real Notch as an old "Gerry" now. I was so used to seeing him dominate the show in Red Cliff Bay. Real Notch had been a male in his prime for a very long time, stretching at least from 1987 to 2006—20 years!

Once again, my concerns were premature. When we returned in 2011 Real Notch was right in the thick of the action with the Rascals. But we got the impression that things were still unsettled in the group. In the mating season of 2010, while Urchin, Smokey and Cookie were together for a long consortship, it would have made sense for Lando and Real Notch to pair up, but except for possibly herding together one day, they did not. Some individuals in the same second-order alliance just don't care much for each other. Maybe that was the case with Real Notch and Lando.

In 2011, Real Notch, Cookie and Urchin teamed up to herd a female, then another, named "Whine," starting on 18 July. Smokey and Lando consorted a female as well.

10 August was not a research day. Lily Samuels was visiting with her guardians, Deb and Jeff Kaufmann. Lily's mother, Amy Samuels, had been studying juvenile dolphins in Red Cliff Bay for some years.† Lily had spent a good part of her childhood in Shark Bay, going out with her mother to watch dolphins and going to school in nearby Denham. After we lost Amy to melanoma in late 2008, plans were made for Lily to return to Shark Bay to spread some of her mother's ashes on the waters

* See "Pirate & Fargo Look for a Home"
† See "Keeping Up With Old Friends" for the first mention of Amy's research and the Rascals.

Amy loved so much. Amy had been a dear friend of mine so it was an emotional day for all of us.

It was windy, so we would not go far. I was hoping against hope to find dolphins that Amy had studied, but it would not be easy in these conditions. Then I looked toward Red Bluff and saw dolphins; we drove down there to find the Rascals. This was perfect; Amy had studied the Rascals extensively when they were juveniles romping around the place and had given the group their name. Lily knew these guys. The Rascals were socializing and leaping all around the boat; it was the perfect show for Lily, and Deb and Jeff, who had never been to Shark Bay. And it was a nice way to celebrate Amy's life.

Whine was the last female that Real Notch would consort in 2011, but that was fine because Cookie and Real Notch were with her through the end of our field season in early October, 2.5 months! Urchin was with them for the first month only. Urchin left the trio about the same time that we sensed that Lando might be in trouble with the group.

The day out with Lily was the last time we saw the Real Notch, Cookie and Urchin trio with Whine. Smokey and Lando were acting like a good pair that day. When we next saw them on the 18th, Lando was absent and Urchin and Smokey were side-by-side, synching. Urchin was no longer part of the Whine consortship with Real Notch and Cookie. Two days later we found Lando to the southeast in an odd mixed social group of younger males and a couple of mature ones. This was unusual and we wondered if Lando had been kicked out of the group. But from mid-September, when they were next seen, through early October, Lando was back in a trio with Smokey and Urchin herding females and traveling with Real Notch, Cookie and Whine.

It would not have diminished my estimation of Real Notch had he not been able to mount a comeback with the Rascals. After all, in 2011, Real Notch was at least 40 and they were in their early 20s. It was not that long ago that we thought males always died before age 40, and here Real Notch was still in an alliance consorting females. His 2.5-month consortship with Whine occurred 24 years after he revealed second-order alliances to us on that magical day in 1987.*

---

* See *"This is Like Science Fiction!"*

§

The Super Blues Brothers

When we returned in 2009 we were anxious to find the Blues Brothers. Poodle, Tool and Hosehead appeared to join the Blues in 2006, which would have increased their membership to 11 males, our first eastern super-alliance! Or perhaps Poodle and his friends, like Fargo with the Exfins,* had failed their "tryout" and we would find our original group of eight.

On only our second day out in 2009 we found the Blues Brothers. In the main channel we first encountered Rickets and Czar. Then a bit later we found them in a larger group, including Jake & Elwood, Tool, sporting a mangled new fin, and Poodle. But there was no Hosehead. Seemingly in his place, swimming side by side with Poodle, was an unfamiliar little triangular fin that we would later dub "Shitzu." Picante and Sloopy were also in the group. We had known Picante and Sloopy for years, first as juveniles, then as "maturing" males. I don't know what happened to Hosehead. I heard from others that he was still around in 2009, but we never saw him again.

I wondered if Poodle and the other recently matured males were forming a new group rather than becoming members of the Blues Brothers. Perhaps they would be friends with the Blues Brothers, sort of like the relationship between the Prima Donnas and Kroker Spaniels. Indeed, a few days later we found six core members of the Blues and a seventh fishing nearby. Two pairs in the group had females and Poodle and his friends were nowhere to be seen.

But on two days in August† we found groups that were a mixture of the old guard and new boys, including a mixed group of 10 that featured Poodle, Shitzu, Tool and Picante with six members of the original eight. I was starting to think that maybe we had a new super-alliance of at least 12 members.

On our first day out in July 2010 we found seven of the original Blues plus Poodle. The missing "original" Blues Brother was Smelt, who had

* See "Pirate & Fargo Look for a Home"
† The first day was during the conflict described in "Unwitting Allies."

always been the oddball of the group. A male sponger, he probably had to work longer hours to feed himself than the others in the group, so he wasn't around to socialize as much. It seemed like each year we would wonder if Smelt was still around and a member of the Blues; then he would show up again. As the Blues Brothers' group grew larger, we kept thinking that he would be the first to go, but it never happened. Smelt remained an oddball Blues Brother.

We had further confirmation of our new super-alliance two days later. Nine members were present; Jake and Elwood had a female consort and Czar, Rickets and Picante were herding Talladega! Poodle, Tool and original member Grub were there as well. Later another pair of original Blues came in with a herded female so we had 11 males and three consortships. Five days later we had another group of 10 Blues with two new consortships (after all, it was July, when consortships are usually short). This time Sloopy was one of the 10 boys. It was like watching the Kroker Spaniels or the old Wow Crowd again. These guys were going to be a lot of fun!

That proved to be an understatement. On 5 August we found Poodle, Tool and Grub herding a female in the channel between This Bank and That Bank. Czar, Rickets and Picante were hanging around looking for something to do. Suddenly a big chase broke out, with intense splashing and rowdy behavior signaling a capture. They had Talladega again. Everybody was terribly excited, with lots of side and belly-slapping displays. The party got the attention of other Blues Brothers in the area, who came flying into the group. Even Smelt was there. We now had all eight of the original Blues plus Poodle, Tool and Picante. The joining Blues also had a herded female but we were not destined to sort out which males had her. Everybody was too excited and they were not going to settle down before sunset. There were beautiful synchronous leaps including one triple leap with two males going one way and another going the opposite direction. Picante erupted into one of the more exaggerated rooster struts that I have ever seen; bobbing up and down and zigzagging to and fro as if possessed. He capped off his display with a leap, perhaps a final flourish or exclamation point to his presentation. I can't speak for the dolphins present, but we were certainly impressed. At one point Czar sat at the surface emitting long, intense whistles. I think that he was being "uninvited" from his trio of the day and he was understandably upset about it. Some of the brief separations we saw during all the chaos suggested as much.

The Blues Brothers had more surprises in store for us. We had not seen Shitzu with the Blues yet this year, and we were still unsure about Sloopy's membership. Just before sunset on 19 August we found a group of 10 males with two females. Shitzu and Sloopy were both there, but with a new male, Wham. Were they introducing yet another member? As we found out later, the answer was a resounding "yes!"

On the 22nd we were approaching This Bank from the west and saw a rowdy group on the other side. As we arrived we saw Rickets, Picante and Czar with Blip and the last vestige of the Gas Gang, Frans and Octane. Another large rowdy group was closing quickly. At least seven lined up and came crashing into ours. We thought it would be a rival group but it was a large mob of Blues Brothers. Then more arrived and we ended up with 13, including Sloopy and Wham. Not surprisingly, only Smelt was absent. He was probably off in a channel somewhere, groveling on the bottom with a sponge glued to his nose. It was our biggest mob of Blues yet and indicated a total membership of 14. The Blues Brothers were only the third group in our study to reach 14 members. The Wow

A rowdy group of the Blues Brothers on 22 August.
© Dolphin Alliance Project

Crowd in the 1990s had numbered 14, as had the Kroker Spaniels until Terra vanished after 2004.

The group was racing and chasing and leaping all over; everybody was very excited and clearly, Blip was the center of attention. Finally, they separated and we saw that Picante, Czar and Rickets had her.

As was often the case, we found the group because we saw their rowdy splashing from afar, so we can't be sure of what happened. A likely scenario is that either Frans and Octane or the Picante trio had Blip initially, and the others challenged them for possession, bringing the rest of the Blues into the action. But Frans and Octane stayed quite a while, unlike a rival that has been defeated. They were much older than the Blues so maybe they were much tougher and wouldn't give up easily in spite of an overwhelming numerical difference. Or perhaps Frans and Octane were, in general, friends with the Blues Brothers but just happened to have a spat with them over a female, much like the Primas and Krokers.

During this period we saw Frans and Octane acting rather like social butterflies; they were also seen with the Exfins, the remnants of Hook's Crew and the Sweepers, a group we saw infrequently that visited from the northeast. They were the last members of the Gas Gang, a lone pair now, so they may have been searching for new allies or just trying to maintain good relations with other eastern groups.

In the thick of the mating season, after I had returned to teach for the fall term, Whitney encountered the Blues Brothers in the midst a big confusing fight with Arnie's Mates, a group that lived north of the banks. Arnie's Mates were a large group, but it had been difficult for us to determine how large because some of them were quite friendly while others seemed afraid of us. We suspected that was because their range extended into La-La Land* and some of their members grew up there.

All 14 Blues Brothers were in the area, with at least a dozen involved in the fighting at one point. Even several Krokers joined and appeared to engage the Blues after their battle with Arnie's Mates, perhaps trying to take a female from the now tired Blues Brothers. Whether the Blues lost or gained females in their fight with Arnie's Mates we can't say, but they lost no more to the Krokers on that day.

* *See "Beyond Red Cliff Bay"*

Whitney found the Blues the day after the big fight. They had four females, including two that had been with them at the end of the fight. Elwood and Jake were taking a break from each other as each was paired with another member. Notably, we recorded the first Blues Brothers consortships by Sloopy and Wham. Sloopy was paired with Grub and Wham was in a trio with Picante and Shitzu. Wham even popped at the female and became aggressive with her.

Doubt persisted that this huge new group could keep everybody together, but when we returned in July 2011, we saw a group of 10 blues on one day and 11 Blues two days later. Between the two days, all 14 members were present and accounted for.

Then in September, we found all 14 Blues Brothers consorting five females! I think that is a record for one group, a record never attained by the Wow Crowd or Kroker Spaniels because of their insistence on herding females in trios. The Blues were herding in three pairs and two trios; only Jake and Elwood were without a female, preventing the Blues Brothers from achieving a "full house."

All our previous super-alliances had used the open water area north of the banks and Red Cliff Bay for at least part of the year. That was also true of the Blues Brothers; they ranged up and down the length of the main channel out east but also roamed north of the banks. Once we followed them as they traveled north of the Outer Banks. When we finally turned back to look for other groups, they were a mile north of the banks and still going north. I would love to know if their overall range, and use of open water, increased as they grew from eight to 14 members. I suspect so as larger groups do have larger ranges.

The Blues Brothers showed us a very different kind of second-order alliance formation than we had seen with the Prima Donnas, who formed a group of seven and never added more members. The initial group of eight Blues Brothers continued to add members over a five-year period. Most of them had probably known each other as tiny tots playing out east. A core group formed, and more members were added as they matured. We only know the mothers of a few Blues Brothers, but original member Grub was born in 1989, so was around 14–15 when we noticed the group acting like adults and consorting females in 2003 and 2004. Wham, the last member to come on board in 2010, was six years younger than Grub.

I thought back to 2005 when Pirate and three friends took Talladega from the Blues Brothers.* I mused that it would not be so easy to take a female from the 2011 version of the group.

While the Blues Brothers gave us an example of a group that keeps growing, we have, of course, seen the reverse, a group that initially forms at a certain size, then shrinks. The Rascals had started as a group of seven but eventually spat out three members before adding Real Notch, making a group of five.

§

Unwitting Allies

There had to be super-alliances out in La-La Land.† The areas of open water seemed to support such large groups and there was a big expanse of open water north of the Outer Banks. I had seen great looking males up there, at a distance of course. Some of them had such nice messed-up fins that it had been worthwhile taking long-range photographs.

The first clear hint of a super-alliance in La-La Land came in 2004. On 10 October we found the Poohbahs in Whale Bight engaging in leap-feeding behavior on smallish brown schooling fish. All 12 Poobahs were consorting females; the four trios were dispersed about the area, then someone would find a school of fish and they would all rapidly converge on it. They would leap and porpoise-feed in the area for a few minutes, but as soon as the feeding died down the four groups would leave in different directions. Then the process would be repeated. I hadn't seen them engage in this variant of leap-feeding before, so I assume it was based on the kind of schools formed by a fish species that visited Shark Bay in the austral spring. The repeated episodes of converging consortships was quite convenient, as it allowed us to keep track of everybody while giving us nice separations between the groups.

The next day we went out to the area just south of the Outer Banks where the Krokers and Primas had been lounging lately. Lounging is the

* See "The Blues Brothers Have a Bad Day"
† See "Beyond Red Cliff Bay"

operative word as they seemed to be doing nothing but lying low with their females.

We found the Primas with two females and a bit further on the Krokers, who had three females. The other Kroker trio, Quasi, Midgie and Pong were, as was so often the case, moving around side by side, looking good, but without a female. While waiting for the hour to score the snoozy Kroker consortships, I looked north past the outer banks and saw exactly the kind of converging leap-feeding groups that I had watched the day before. It sure looked like a Poohbah-sized group in La-La Land. As soon as we finished with the Krokers, we sped up there, but the feeding had ceased. Nonetheless, we found and photographed one group of eight that I suspect was probably two trios with two females. Of course, it was La-La Land and they didn't favor our company.

On 11 August 2009, we went out east and found two Hooks: Bly and Link. We were hoping that they would lead us to the rest of the Hooks, but after an hour or so that no longer looked promising so we gave up and went north into the main channel. It was calm, so we stopped to scan around. I didn't see much as I panned around from the north to the west, then southwest, just a large boat in the distance, sending up spray as it moved rapidly in our direction. Kathrin, one of the Swiss assistants working with us, was scanning in the same area and saw the boat as well. But something didn't look right to her and Kathrin did a double take. "What is that?" she asked. I said it was a boat heading our way. "I don't think so," she replied. I looked again. Holy smokes! Kathrin was right; it was a huge mob of leaping dolphins! We raced over and alongside what was the biggest group of surging dolphins I have ever seen, rumbling along like a freight train! Two assistants were firing their cameras like automatic weapons and another was on video. I started to call out names, but I was confused. Some I knew; there was Prima, I kept calling Barney's name, and some Krokers, but the rest ... Edge? What was he doing here? Edge was probably a "Lucky," someone with no home who had lately latched onto some maturing males. But other hacked-up fins riding atop big tough-looking dolphins were strange to me. Who the hell was this? Minutes after we joined, groups started peeling off from the mob, one after another, every two minutes or so. I assigned people to watch each group. We would be able to go from group to group and take pictures of everybody. We were left with a mixed group of Krokers and Primas, who remained excited for a time and then settled down.

Quickly we ran from group to group, snapping pictures. Here was a trio of Prima Donnas with a female, here was Edge and his young friends, there were 7–8 Blues Brothers and finally the huge mob of gnarly looking strangers. We made a reasonable pass by them and got a round of pictures, but they were evasive and kept moving away from us. They wanted to head north to La-La land. I was determined to get good pictures and we had already photographed the other groups, so I settled into the maneuvers I had learned while habituating Bent-fin and his mates.* We drove parallel to them and, when they turned toward us, we moved away. It worked, and a half-hour later we were getting great pictures. They still weren't friendly, mind you, so once we had multiple shots of each dolphin, we left them to continue their way home to La-La land.

After leaving the strangers, we went looking for the Primas and Krokers. I had a hunch where we would find them, hunkering down in the first channel just east of Monkey Mia. The two Prima trios each had a female consort. The Krokers, who also had a female, soon joined them.

Back onshore, pouring over our pictures, we sorted out what was going on. We had all seven Prima Donnas, seven Kroker Spaniels, Edge and six of his young friends, and that group of 14 strangers. We never found evidence that the Blues were in the surging mob; they may have simply come around to watch the fight. The Primas and Krokers had been at the front of the surging mob with the strangers behind them. Edge and friends may have thought they were supporting one group or another, but their efforts would have been of little consequence.† Even if the Blues Brothers were never in the group, when female consorts are counted, we were looking at a mob of nearly 40 dolphins! No wonder I thought it was a big boat! And given that the strangers were hard on the heels of the Primas and Krokers, it was clear that they were down in our study area to steal a female or two.

Our photographs revealed one well-known female in the stranger group that were chasing the Primas and Krokers, which we later named

---

* See "Pirate & Fargo Look for a Home"
† Much like when Lucky and Pointer were along for the ride in "The Battle for Flo-Jo."

the "Lost Boys." I suspect the Lost Boys had another female as well. That would leave a dozen males; we finally had our La-La Land super-alliance.

Now I understood why we were often finding the Primas and Krokers way down in the first channel. They were hiding from big, fearsome open-water groups like the Lost Boys and Dead Rockers.* The Primas and Krokers often used open-water areas; when we first came to know them in 1990s they were often in Whale Bight, but here they were, cowering deep in the channel. Although the Kroker Spaniels were still as large as the Wow Crowd of the 2000s, they were no Wow Crowd!

I remembered how Snubby, Sickle and Bibi used to head southeast into the channels immediately after stuffing their faces at the beach, to avoid Real Notch's Crew in Red Cliff Bay and how the Hook's Crew would hide in little channels and even L'Haridon Bight when they had females.† To some extent, hiding seems to be an important tactic for all but the biggest and toughest groups, at least if your range affords you a place to hide. Hiding might be more difficult for alliances that don't have banks and channels in their ranges.

I don't think the Lost Boys had succeeded in stealing a female from the Primas and Krokers and I think the reason was us. The Lost Boys gave up the chase only two minutes after we arrived, and they were clearly afraid of us.

When we discovered the evasive Bent-fin in 2002‡ I thought that we might be missing some alliances in La-La Land because they were afraid of us. But it hadn't occurred to me that, by following our study alliances to record consortships, we were offering them de facto protection from groups that were afraid of boats.§

We think that our presence is a mild irritant to the dolphins, but they enjoy occasional bow rides. Maybe they are also aware of the effect we have on some groups that would threaten them.

On 2 October 2011, Whitney surveyed a group of six dolphins. They had been moving toward a resting group of Krokers and Primas with female consorts, but they were evasive and left the area. It was six Lost Boys.

* See "The New Boys in Town"
† See "Burning Dolphins" and "Captain Hook's Not-So-Tough Crew"
‡ See "Pirate & Fargo Look for a Home"
§ See "Kerplunk" for a case where our presence protected a female from a male alliance.

§

New Life for an Old Crowd

Our first survey in 2009 was of the Wow Crowd member Horton, fishing alone in Red Cliff Bay. I didn't recognize him at the time, partly because I was rusty and partly because his fin had changed. We never saw Horton again. Later, when I was reviewing pictures from that day, I recognized him and saw that Horton was badly emaciated. He probably didn't live much longer.

Another Wowser we never saw again was Wannabee. He was a younger member so I still wonder if he is out there somewhere. Maybe he lost his position in the Wow Crowd and had to move on, perhaps to a new group with a new fin that we have not yet matched to his old one.

A short time after our Horton encounter we found two trios of Wowsers, each with a female. Latch, Gripe and Veetop had Clam, and Wow, Pik and Krill had Clam's mother Scallop. We stayed not only to get the consortships, but hoping to see other Wowsers. Our patience went unrewarded.

We saw the same two trios five days later. The end of my journal entry for the day asks, "Where are Myrtle, Wannabee, Horton and Ajax?" I still didn't know that we had seen Horton.

I wasn't really that surprised. After all, it was now 15 years after we discovered the Wowsers in 1994. They had diminished in the last study from their 1990s peak of 14 members, so it was expected that they would have lost more members since 2006.

As it turned out, Myrtle wasn't gone; he just wasn't with the Wow Crowd much. We saw him on 22 August. There was a huge mob of dolphins fishing as though they were pursuing one or more fish schools moving along the bottom. There were occasional leaps and rapid surfacing, with dolphins coming together and splitting up often. There were adult males, adult females, juveniles and maturing males. And there was Myrtle. Since it was our first Myrtle sighting of the year, we followed him. I wanted to see what he would do when the feeding died down. Among the maturing males was one trio that was swimming around in very tight formation, although whom they were trying to impress wasn't clear.

After the feeding, six to seven young males formed a tight group with Myrtle, and together they traveled to the east. We knew the mothers, and hence the ages, of some of the younger males, and they were turning 12–13 in 2009. I thought that Myrtle might have become a troll, but that really wasn't a fair charge since males that age are either consorting females already, or close to it. Still, they were a lot younger than Myrtle.

Hope for Myrtle was rekindled later in September, when he was found with Pik, Wow and Krill. At least they were still friends. A few days later we found Ajax, fishing alone. At least he was still alive.

The same two trios, Latch, Gripe & Veetop and Wow, Pik & Krill, were seen consorting females on the last day of the season. No other Wowsers were around. It was starting to look like the Wow Crowd was, for all practical purposes, down from 10 males in 2006 to 6 in 2009.

Things didn't improve for the Wow Crowd in 2010, but they did for Myrtle. Now he was herding females with Wow and Pik and traveling around with Latch, Gripe and Veetop. The move came at Krill's expense, and we saw little of him during the season. And poor Ajax reminded us of Lucky: we found him in groups of non-reproductive females or fishing alone.

On 23 September, Whitney was following the two Wowser trios, which included Myrtle with Wow and Pik of course, when she looked up to see 11 dolphins charging into the group. They were members of two other second-order alliances, so the old Wowsers were greatly outnumbered and lost a female in the fight. But as soon as the attack started, Krill came flying in to help his mates. Krill was around, and still willing to fight on behalf of his old friends in a losing cause.

The problem was simply that the Wowsers, like so many open water groups, were really addicted to trios. Presumably Krill could have gone over and rounded up Ajax in his favorite fishing area off Cape Rose, and herded a female with him, but he didn't. With eight remaining members, there could be only two trios, and Krill and Ajax would remain alone.

Two weeks into our 2011 season, we found the two Wowser trios again and, incredibly, Krill and Myrtle had flipped roles again. Krill was back in the trio with Wow and Pik. I saw Ajax for the first time that season on my last day, unsurprisingly fishing alone off Cape Rose.

Whitney continued to lead the team through October. She next encountered the two Wow Crowd trios, both in consortships, on 11 September. Then on 16 September, she was startled to find a nice-looking trio of Myrtle, Ajax and a stranger with a really hacked-up fin. Back at camp, pouring over photographs, she came to a stunning conclusion; the stranger was not a stranger at all, but the Sharky Sylvester!

Sylvester was the last remaining Sharky. Crackle had vanished after 2005, and in 2006 we had a few amazing sightings of Sharky, Sylvester and Bumpus, who seemed to have left his mates of 20 years, BJ and Bam-Bam, to fill Crackle's spot in the Sharkies. But we never got any observations of Bumpus herding with them, and I didn't expect them to still be around by 2009. Indeed, all the B-boys and Sharkies were gone when we returned, all except for Sylvester.

When I saw the trashed fin that Whitney was claiming belonged to Sylvester, I was skeptical to say the least. We had to be very sure of ourselves, since such radical shifts to new groups are so important and rare. When the nicks and tears along the fin's edge are no longer reliable, you can look at other scars. And indeed there were complex patterns of scars on both sides of his fin that matched perfectly between the old 2010 version of Sylvester and the new one. I wondered if his fin had been shredded so badly before or after he joined the Wowsers.

Sylvester's new Wow Crowd membership made all the difference in the world. Myrtle and Ajax were now in a trio with Sylvester and were really and truly Wowsers again. On her last day out, on 15 October, Whitney was greeted by a group of all three Wowser trios, and each was consorting a female.

§

The New Boys in Town

The punks that we had seen with Myrtle in 2009 were seen now and again that year, but they didn't make much of an impression. The first time we saw a few of them in 2010, it appeared that three were consorting a female. That made sense; most of that crowd had been turning 12–13 the year before, so they would be turning 13–14 this year. Most males start trying to consort females in the 13–14 age range. Then on 1 September, we found nine males together. Most were still unfamiliar to us so we made up temporary names on the spot, "high-ding," "mid-ding," "so and so alike" if their fin reminded us of a familiar dolphin, so we could keep track of who was doing what with whom. We had no way of knowing it at the time, but that was our first sighting of the full membership of our newest group, the Hooligans. That's the way it works with a new maturing group that has been forming for a while; you don't know that you have seen them until you have seen them several times over a period of time. You watch them consorting females; you realize that their membership has become consistent and you welcome them into the adult male alliance study.

The Hooligans came into our study with an unusual amount of fanfare for such a young group. On 6 September, a few of the Hooligans were with a bunch of Arnie's Mates, who had joined them on the 1st as well. In fact, we had found members of the two groups together a few times before but again, not knowing them well, the observations held no significance for us. They would, however, soon become very significant.

The big day was 23 September, the day of the theft from the Wowsers. Whitney found the Wow, Pik & Myrtle trio herding a female. Fellow Wowsers, Latch, Gripe & Veetop, who had Phantom, soon joined them. They were relaxed, mostly resting; scoring these consortships was going to be easy. However, 20 minutes before the one-hour bell marking a scored consortship, the peaceful mood was shattered when nearly a dozen dolphins charged in and a huge fight broke out. The fighting did not seem that intense at first but it soon escalated with dolphins surging, charging, hitting and chasing all around. Krill, who had evidently been nearby, came blasting in to help his friends.

After five minutes the battling parties parted briefly. Phantom was still with the Wowsers. The groups clashed again but the Wow trio remained off to the side snagging. Wow then left his buddies to go help the Latch trio in their fight for Phantom. Loud whistles rang through the hull of the boat as the fighting continued, males surging in tight packs at the surface. Then 12 minutes after the initial attack, the groups again briefly parted. The Wowsers still had their females.

The surface churned with fighting dolphins on 23 September when the Hooligans helped Arnie's Mates take Phantom from the Wow Crowd.
© Whitney Friedman

Another group of dolphins rapidly approached the fight, but hesitated at a distance, then left.

The fighting continued, for six more minutes, with more surging, hitting and chasing. Six Kroker Spaniels approached closely but did not appear to join the battle. At about the same time, the attackers left, leaping away from the Wowsers.

The Wow Crowd swam along slowly. Wow, Pik & Myrtle still had their female, but Phantom was gone.

Speeding back over to the attacking group, Whitney saw Phantom. They were still excited, rushing around her. Slowly the group settled down. It became clear that a trio of Arnie's Mates had Phantom, and another trio of Arnie's Mates had another female they had brought along for the fight. The five males who had helped them departed after a while. They didn't have a female. It was five Hooligans.

It is always a huge adrenalin-churning experience to see groups of male dolphins go to war like that. The full significance of the observation wasn't immediately obvious to us as we were just beginning to learn about the Hooligans. As Whitney analyzed the piles of photographs and video, and as we came to realize that the Hooligans were a stable group of nine that associated occasionally with Arnie's Mates, the fight took on greater significance as one of our best examples of a third-level alliance interaction. The Hooligans and Arnie's Mates charged in together, fought together, and left together.

The Hooligans were so young; could they really have helped that much? Perhaps by force of numbers they tipped the balance in favor of Arnie's Mates. Alternatively, a vocal threat from the Krokers may have been decisive, even though they didn't join. Most likely, the Krokers were simply spectators; big fights often attract an audience of other male groups who come to watch. Important information is there to be gleaned about the fighting abilities of future rivals and allies, even if that future is a figment of their imagination (on this day Edge, the Lucky-like loser, was harmlessly hanging around the fight). But for the third-level alliance issue, the effect the Hooligans had on the outcome is moot. All that matters is that the Hooligans took a risk to help Arnie's Mates in a fight.

On 18 August 2011, we left Monkey Mia determined to go north. Trios of Primas and Krokers with female consorts kept throwing up road-blocks, but we resisted the temptation to do more than surveys and carried on north. We were still in Red Cliff Bay when we encountered a massive group. I did not know them. At least I did not know most of them; a few were vaguely familiar. These were no punk teenage Hooligans but some of the toughest, most battle-scarred males I had ever seen. As we watched and photographed them, we figured there were about a dozen males and a few were in consortships. They were in a tight formation and looked ready to take on all challenges from the locals.

We had a super-alliance of strange, fully mature, prime-age males in Red Cliff Bay in the middle of winter. I had never seen anything like it. By September, we expected to see the Herald Bight groups we knew coming around Guichenault and even pressing down close to Red Cliff Bay later in the mating season. But we did not expect an unfamiliar super-alliance so early in the season. Where did they come from?

The next day we charged up to Whale Bight. We found the group of strangers again, a bit further north from yesterday, and still in a menacing phalanx. When we poured over the photographs we realized we did know a few of them, from as far back as 2004. I remembered the occasion. My boat, Bony Herring, and Gene Machine, were up in

Herald Bight on 21 August 2004.

Anna Sellas was with us that year to cover darting duties when Michael wasn't in the field. She was a young American of Greek extraction born 30 years too late. Anna was a natural "Dead Head," the name for followers of the Grateful Dead, and for whom a rite of passage was to follow their beloved band around the country from concert to concert. She loved that sort of music and other southern "jam bands," but as a child of the 1990s and early 21st century, Anna had to make do with Phish, the latter-day version of the Grateful Dead.

The crew from Gene machine called me over to look at pictures from that day. They thought that they had a new male alliance, based on the behavior of the dolphins; a group of six or so with a female. One glance at those tall, wounded, triangular fins and I thought to myself, no doubt about it. Anna wanted to name one Garcia. That was all it took and we had the Dead Rockers, continuing the theme with Hendrix, Buddy, Allman and Zandt. We realized in 2011 that we had seen them in small groups a few times since that first sighting, but we had no idea that the Dead Rockers had been or would become a super-alliance. Whitney and the others were delighted to add names from their generation, like Winehouse, but I was able to get "Cash" in there (it wasn't hard; every generation seems to love Johnny Cash).

That first sighting of Dead Rockers in Herald Bight in 2004 happened on about the same date we encountered them as a super-alliance in Red Cliff Bay seven years later. I can only conclude that the Dead Rockers had shifted their range a bit. Now, we had been to Herald Bight many times but only saw the Dead Rockers there once. I suspect their normal range had been further offshore than we usually ventured. I had been way out there a few times, and there were lots of dolphins.

I knew that groups shifted sometimes. The Wow Crowd had moved their core area from the Grooves in the 1990s, further south to the waters just north of Red Cliff Bay during the 2001–2006 study. So maybe the Rockers had made a similar move, bringing them closer to us. I wondered if they were pushing or being pushed into the area, or both.

We were delighted to have the Dead Rockers nearby, whatever the reason for their presence. Another big alliance meant more chances for us to see male dolphin politics in action. They didn't disappoint. In

September 2011 they were caught in the act of stealing a female from Arnie's Mates. Arnie's Mates were vastly outnumbered, but they put on a brave face and chased the thieves for a while. At one point the several pursuing Arnie's Mates were sandwiched between the six Dead Rockers that had taken their female and six more right behind them! I hope they got out of that one with only their egos bruised.

The Hooligans and Dead Rockers illustrate two ways we can find new alliances in a particular area like Red Cliff Bay or Whale Bight. Males maturing in the area can form new alliances, or alliances that formed elsewhere can move in.

Thirty Years

November 2012*

---

* *I left this largely as I wrote it in 2012. See Epilogue for what has happened since 2012.*

I saw Real Notch today. He is alone now. I heard that he was still with the Rascals back in June and July of this year. But the Rascals evidently decided, with the onset of the new mating season, that they were better off in two pairs, Urchin with Lando and Smokey with Cookie. In fact we found the Rascals earlier in the day, on the Monkey Mia banks. They had been herding the beach females, Puck and Surprise, of late, but today Urchin and Lando had Puck but Smokey and Cookie didn't have a female. As I watched Cookie swimming side by side with Smokey, I wondered how the change had happened and if Cookie had a role in evicting Real Notch. After all, Cookie had been Real Notch's main ally in the Rascals. Or maybe the other three grew tired of being in a trio and forced the issue. Maybe Real Notch had dropped in rank or maybe they felt, with his advanced age, he couldn't keep up with them anymore.

We heard that Real Notch had been hanging around Cape Rose, on the opposite side of Red Cliff Bay from where we found the Rascals. He was there as advertised, at the edge of the shallows, mucking around with a couple other dolphins and chasing fish. I did my fake dolphin whistle (more of an ear-piercing shriek, and it is quite loud) when we found him and he did pop his eye up out of the water for a quick peek. I whistled again and he popped up again. It is quite possible that Real Notch knows that sound well since he has been hearing it for over 25 years, since I first started following him around in boats.

Real Notch photographed on hand-rolled black and white film in 1982 and 30 years later in 2012. © Dolphin Alliance Project

We watched as Real Notch caught a nice whiting then started to get excited around one of the others--Flint, a female. She paid him little mind so he moved into deeper water where he found the female Cyrano with her calf Bergerac. He became excited, raced in circles around her and arched his belly-up out of the water. Then, normal side up, he arched again, like a rooster strut, but without the bobbing. He stayed with them for the next hour, getting frisky every few minutes and racing in circles around Cyrano. During one of these frenzied episodes he crossed twice in front of her snout, arching his heavily speckled belly skyward. Cyrano didn't seem to mind all the attention.

It was wonderful to see Real Notch and to find him still so full of life. He was hardly the doddering old codger that one might expect of a dolphin his age. And I wouldn't count Real Notch out of the alliance picture yet either. He might yet find more opportunities to herd females with other males, perhaps even the Rascals. But even in the absence of alliance partners, Real Notch was still going to try to mate with females, and knowing how clever he had been in the world of male dolphin politics in Shark Bay, I think he still might find some success.

I am on sabbatical this fall term. It has been 30 years since Rachel and I first hitchhiked up from Perth to discover this amazing dolphin society in this magnificent bay. We already had a project running this year, so I had to come back, if just for a month, to celebrate my 30-year anniversary, to reflect on all that we have learned over the decades, to think about the future and especially to see Real Notch. After all, Real Notch has taught us more than any other dolphin about this incredibly complex system of male alliances. I hope this book makes him famous. He should be.

Real Notch was not the only dolphin I photographed in 1982 that is still alive. We also took a picture of Wow, and as luck would have it, after finishing our observations on Real Notch today, we started home only to run into Wow and some of his friends. He was with Pik and Krill, consorting Scallop, and nearby were Latch, Veetop and Gripe with their own female. The other day we had seen the third Wow trio, Myrtle, Ajax and Sylvester.

The heyday for the Wow Crowd is long past, and they now spend their mating season deep in Red Cliff Bay, likely hiding from the kind of huge formidable prime-age group that they used to be.

We don't know if Wow is as old as Real Notch. We didn't start watching the Wow Crowd until 1994, so it may well be that Real Notch has a few years on him. But Wow and Real Notch are bookends of a sort, as they represent the extremes of the continuum of Shark Bay alliances: Real Notch representing males that form small second-order alliances with stable pairs and trios, and Wow the large "super-alliance" whose males often switch partners between consortships.

I also got to see the Dead Rockers just past the banks north of Monkey Mia. The team had seen them earlier as well. So last year's appearance wasn't a temporary stopover.

I didn't get to see the Blues Brothers this month; the team saw them a few times earlier and all are present and accounted for. They saw 13 of the 14 together on one occasion and of course Smelt was the one missing. The Blues have maintained 14 members for three years, as did the Wow Crowd and Kroker Spaniels before them.

I came here to find out what dolphins were doing with those big brains and I feel like we have succeeded in a way that I never could have imagined when I was an undergraduate back in Santa Cruz, trying to raise funds for my first trip here. Big brains are about being social, about having to cooperate with the same individuals you are in competition with. It's about finding the right allies at the right time for the right reasons; it's about maintaining those alliances and repairing them after a conflict. It's about making new alliances or changing alliances to advance your interests.

Outside of humans, there is no other system of alliances that comes close to the complexity of those described in this book. Male dolphins in Shark Bay have to negotiate three nested levels of alliances. And they maneuver in an alliance landscape that exhibits remarkable variation, from whether males work in pairs or trios to consort females, to the stability of those pairs and trios, to the size of second-order alliances, and to the importance of third-order alliances.

The cases of Pirate and Fargo illustrate how hard it can be for males to find an alliance home.[*] The examples of Terra[†] and Lucky, who spent

See "Pirate & Fargo Look for a Home"
† See "Terra Becomes a Troll"

several years with maturing juveniles, show the lengths to which males will go to join an alliance.

We have so much more to learn about these amazing alliances. I am as excited about the future of The Dolphin Alliance Project as I have been at any point in the last three decades. We have a lot of exciting new projects on the burner.

A project currently running is Whitney Friedman's study on social coordination and interactions. Whitney employs "look down" video to better see the intricacies of dolphin behavior. This has been done before with small blimps but we are trying out a new system with a modified "kite-balloon."* Combined with side video, we should be better able to see who is doing what to whom. To date, we have been pretty much limited to behaviors that are visually striking when dolphins surface, like synchrony and bonding. Sure, we see lots of petting and other types of underwater interactions, but it's a hit-or-miss thing, and to really learn about behaviors like petting we need to be able to see it consistently. And that is important, since social interactions are the building blocks of social relationships. In many primates, for example, individuals tend to groom more dominant group members. Will we find that dolphins tend to initiate petting interactions with males that are more successful consorting females? And maybe we can learn more directly about dominance by peering at the dolphins from above. We also hope to see if particular individuals in alliances, perhaps those dominant or more successful ones, make the decisions about where to go and what to do. We may be able to see them initiate changes in the direction of travel.

We would like to better understand how males come to join a particular alliance and their role in it. We know that male dolphins start practicing alliance behaviors and making male friends probably even before they are weaned. But that late juvenile period, before they have clearly settled into a group, must be one of trying out partners and groups. How exactly do they do that? Dedicated behavioral observations on a set of 6 to 12-year-old males should teach us a lot.

An important question is why males that live in the banks and channels out east are happy to consort females in pairs while those that use the open water areas north of Red Cliff Bay and the banks are so

---

* In 2016 we entered the drone age.

stubborn about their trios. I think about the way Sylvester's joining the Wow Crowd gave the Wow Crowd a new life as a nine-member group, and how Pirate filled the void created by Bent-fin's disappearance. And I think about the Hammers. Once their namesake, Hammer, vanished after 2004 they were a group of five, and the Poohbah Skeet started filling that vacancy, switching back and forth between consorting in a trio with the Hammers and another with his Poohbah friends! Then the disappearance of Drill left the trio of Anvil, Rasty and Spoof with Kermit as an odd man out. We subsequently saw Kermit herding in a trio with Poohbahs. Incredibly, this month we found Kermit in a trio with Skipjacks! That was enough to suggest to us that a Skipjack member we have not seen this year is missing and that Kermit may have been recruited to fill his place in a trio.

Perhaps there are more sharks in the northern part of our study area, so the greater safety of being in a trio outweighs the reduced chance of fathering an offspring because you have to share with two males instead of one. Or maybe food is the issue. Being in a group is great if you are feeding on a school of fish, but if you must spread out to feed on single prey on the bottom, other dolphins are nothing but competition for lunch. If the open-water alliances feed more on schooling fish, or larger schools of fish, they can better afford to be in trios, making them safer from sharks and rival males. The schooling fish idea can also help us understand why we find such big second-order alliances up north; all the 'super-alliances' of 10 or more males seem to use open water at least part of the time.

The north-south difference in trios versus pairs may owe less to the abundance of sharks and schools of fish than to the overall abundance of fish in the area. Less food means fewer dolphins and if there are fewer dolphins you may not need as many allies. If you are likely to run into enemies, you had better be with your friends, but if you live in an area with fewer enemies, fewer friends will do. If males are less likely to encounter foes out east, then pairs may be favored for the simple reason that each male has a better chance of fathering the female's infant. But the chances of encountering rivals can be affected by many things, such as the number of estrus females, how much rival males move around, and even how well sound travels in the area. The racket dolphins make during consortships will travel much farther in the open habitats to the north compared to the east, where shallow banks will block much of the sound.

The density idea was bolstered by a major discovery that took me completely by surprise. Usually, when we analyze data on social phenomena that we have been watching for several years, we have a pretty good idea of what the results will look like. It was obvious to me, for example, that Latch, Hobo and Gripe were the most stable trio in Wow Crowd and spent more time consorting females.* Likewise, that result, I was not surprised to find, generalized to all 12 second-order alliances that we studied from 2001-2006: the most stable first-order alliances spent more time consorting females. Before the analysis I did not know if the result would be "statistically significant" but from my observations I could see that the trend was there.

But when we compared the rate that males in different second-order alliances consorted females, an astonishing result emerged that I did not see coming: the males out east, in the area of banks and channels, don't spend as much time in consortships as the males up north! It follows that if our eastern males are more often in pairs and spending less time consorting females, the area they live in does not have as many dolphins and it would have fewer dolphins because there is not as much food. This seems puzzling at first because there are lots of seagrass beds in that area, which should support a healthy fish population, but the salinity is higher there also. The southern part of our study area borders the very salty L'Haridon Bight, which is a biological desert compared to less salty parts of the bay.

I didn't see that result coming because I had always been impressed that some of the eastern alliances were real "tough guys." The Gas Gang and the Exfins were clearly capable of holding their own in battle with other alliances! I would not have guessed that they would be less successful consorting females than the northern alliances. Why did they remain in such a lousy area? Maybe it isn't easy for alliances to move to better areas; maybe males that learned from their mothers how to make a living among the banks and channels out east would be at a disadvantage catching fish up north compared to males that grew up

See "Dolphins: The Wild Side"

there. Of course, one alliance for which this exciting new result was not surprising was the not-so-tough Hooks Crew!*

Right now these are all interesting ideas. We need to get a bunch of Ph.D. students here to get the data and test the ideas.

The time is ripe also for studies on communication. Using multiple hydrophones, researchers can now locate dolphin sounds much better than we could in the 1990s, when Rachel and I cobbled together that system that proved so problematic. The way the alliances come together and split up, shadow each other at distance and come to the aid of each other in fights, provides a perfect opportunity for learning about dolphin communication. We also want to include dolphin sounds in our "lookdown" study of social interactions, to see if particular sounds accompany certain friendly (or not so friendly!) behaviors.

A question that nags at me constantly is what is going on with this southward movement from Herald Bight. In fact, we just had our best look yet at a new monster super-alliance, up near Guichenault, where we used to find the Wow Crowd. Some males in the group are familiar from 10 years ago but most are new to us. From what we saw of them, even the Poohbahs and the remaining Hammers might want to stay out of their way. Maybe that is why we are finding the Skipjacks and Poohbahs down near Cape Rose this month. And how revealing it was to leave the Poohbahs in Whale Bight, and travel home close to shore in the westerly chop, only to run into the three Wow Crowd trios hunkering down deep in the heart of Red Cliff Bay. That would have been unthinkable during their peak in the 1990s. It was amazing to watch Sylvester, having lost all his Sharky mates, swimming side by side with his new Wowser friends as though he had been with them all his life. A few days later we traveled the same route after leaving the Skipjacks just north of Cape Rose. This time we ran into the young Hooligans, still a group of nine, in the same area that we had found the Wow Crowd days before. The two groups of nine were in the same location, but they are on opposite sides of the life curve; the ascendant young Hooligans, now mostly 15 to 16-year-olds, are not yet competitive with older males, while the elderly Wow Crowd are on the way down.

If the biggest groups are pushing the smaller ones, why are they doing

---

* See "Captain Hook's Not-So-Tough Crew"

so? It can't be simply because there are more females as you go south, because the biggest male groups doing the pushing still end up on the northern end of the resulting compressed pile of alliances. And are those big groups coming around from Herald Bight, being pushed, in turn, by still larger ones from Peron? I would love to establish a camp in Herald Bight, to finally learn about the Peron alliances and to see what kind of alliances are in the Herald Bight area after the Poohbahs and Skipjacks have moved south.

The long-term changes fascinate me also. I think about the understanding of the alliances I had in the 1980s working in Red Cliff Bay; that the basic alliance "units" were stable pairs and trios that had friendships with each other, forming second-order alliances of four to six males. Once we came to understand that second-order alliances can last for two decades and that many males hop between different pairs and trios in those groups, we concluded that the second-order alliance is the "core" male social unit in Shark Bay. Had I started my thesis research in Red Cliff Bay in 2001 instead of 1986, I would have reached that

A dolphin with a just-captured yellowfin bream, a schooling fish.
© Dolphin Alliance Project

understanding much sooner. I would have run into the Kroker Spaniels and Prima Donnas in the same Red Cliff Bay waters where I had watched TBC and CBL 15 years earlier. But I would have thought the smallest second-order alliance numbered six males; we had no smaller groups during that study! Now of course, the 20-something-year-old Rascals are a group of four, patrolling the waters of Red Cliff Bay in two pairs.

Are these decade-long changes in the structure of alliances in a specific area like Red Cliff Bay just sort of random, due to the happenstance survival of a larger or smaller number of similarly aged-males in an area?

What role do longer-term ecological changes play, which might impact the amount of schooling and solitary fish in the area, and hence the cost of forming groups and the number of available females?

We have certainly witnessed some ecological changes. Back in the 1980s, a dominant and dramatic feeding behavior was "Bony bashing." Large numbers of dolphins in Red Cliff Bay would leap and porpoise as they drove schools of Bony Herring into the shallows, and then with their flukes they smacked the fish up to 3 meters in the air. The old folks who have camped at Monkey Mia for decades say they used to catch Bony Herring in their nets on a regular basis during the 1960s and 1970s. We watched Bony bashing a lot in the 1980s, but have not seen it since.

I have always thought that the Bony Herring, a temperate schooling fish, just barely made it up this far in the austral winter. Did they stop migrating this far because of long-term changes due to global warming? Bony Herring were a dolphin favorite because they are an oily, energy-rich fish. What effect did the loss of that huge pulse of energy in the winter do to our dolphins? Did they suffer from it? Did they compensate by eating other things or did they need less energy because it was now easier for them to stay warm in slightly warmer water?

Shark Bay sits on the border of temperate and tropical zones. One reason it has World Heritage Status is because of the mélange of temperate and tropical species, on land and in the water. Shark Bay should be an important barometer for the effect of climate change on habitats. The vanishing Bony Herring were only the first indication we had of changes afoot in the bay. I hear from fishermen that they are catching tropical species that they never used to catch. Since 2009 two humpback dolphins (genus *Sousa*) have been seen each year at the top of the peninsula. They are more of a warm water species and we never saw them during the 2001-2006 study, when we visited Cape Peron often.

On our last day out in the boat this month, we were shocked to find a humpback dolphin south-east of Monkey Mia.

More ominously, we recently had a huge die-off of one of the two dominant temperate seagrasses in Shark Bay (*Amphibolis antarctica*). The culprit was a combination of an unusual flood and a warm-temperature anomaly. Recovery from such a die-off can take years. If such temperature anomalies and floods increase in frequency due to global warming, Shark Bay may be in for big changes.

And obviously, basic changes in the ecology of plant and fish life in the bay will impact our dolphins as well. Will they be able to adapt? How will they adapt? What changes will we see in their society, in the alliances?

While the long-term health of the bay is a huge concern, in the next two decades we hope to reveal the Shark Bay bottlenose dolphin society, and hence the mind of the dolphin, in more detail than ever before. Based on my experience so far, I can make one clear prediction about our next exciting discoveries: they will be unexpected. In the mid-1980s we set out to learn about dolphin social relationships. We had no inkling that we would find males herding females and forming two levels of alliances. In the 1990s, after we came here to learn about whistle exchanges between alliances, we were completely caught off-guard by the discovery of the remarkable Wow Crowd "super-alliance." In the 2000s we wanted to find out if there was a continuum of second-order alliance sizes and if second-order alliance size was related to first-order alliance stability. We were again surprised to find a third level of alliance and that the size of first-order alliances (two or three males) and how much time males spend with females was related to habitat.

I can't predict what we will discover next, but I'm sure it will be fantastic!

§

Epilogue

Real Notch failed to show up for the 2015 field season. The loss of our most renowned and favorite male dolphin was not unexpected but still very sad. I am happy to report, however, that Real Notch did associate with the Rascals occasionally after 2012, and even herded a female with Cookie in November 2014! Digging through the earliest association data, I discovered that Real Notch was consorting females in 1985, so his consortship "career" spanned 30 years! It is a record that I suspect will stand for a long time. When it comes to Dolphin Politics in Shark Bay, Real Notch was a true master!

Wow "went missing" in 2016; he was last seen late in 2015 looking very elderly. His Wow Crowd is finally fading from the scene after an astonishing run that lasted over 20 years. We didn't see Sylvester anymore after 2012 but I'm still amazed that he was able to finish his life as a Wow Crowd member!

We also lost Prima and Barney from the Prima Donnas. Although we had named the group after Prima to amuse ourselves, and not because we thought he played any special role in the group, his loss had a devastating impact on his buddies Natural Tag and Wabbit, who almost gave up consorting females entirely. The other trio in the Prima Donnas, Fred, Ridges and Big, who had been friends and allies of Natural Tag and Wabbit for over 20 years, suddenly found their company less desirable. At the same time, to our surprise, a trio of Rascals began to associate with the remaining Prima Donna trio and the Kroker Spaniels (who were down to eight individuals). It was a shift in third-order alliance partners like we had seen between the Primas, Wow Crowd and Kroker Spaniels from 2001-2006.

We had not been able to document the Prima Donna-Wow Crowd-Kroker Spaniel shift well because we were working on so many alliances simultaneously. Fortuitously, the recent Prima/Kroker Spaniel/Rascal shifts happened during Whitney Friedman's detailed Ph.D. study of social interactions among the Krokers and Primas. Right in the middle of her study Prima vanished and the Rascals moved in, providing yet another remarkable case of serendipity! "Third order alliance dynamics" emerged as one of Whitney's most exciting discoveries. Whitney successfully defended her Ph.D. research in 2017.

As old alliances fade away, new ones have become the stars of our research program. The Hooligans and Alley Cats, a young group that matured in the past several years, have joined the Blues Brothers as researcher favorites. The Alley Cats roam the waters to the Northeast that used to be plied by the now extinct Crunch Bunch. Like the Hooligans, we know many of their mothers, which will greatly enrich our ability to interpret their behavior and relationships going forward.

We also achieved one of our key goals by recruiting one of the world's top dolphin communication researchers, Stephanie King. Stephanie had already made ground-breaking discoveries on dolphin whistle communication in Scotland. She studies dolphin communication using an array of four hydrophones, one for each corner of the boat, to localize dolphin vocalizations. Being able to tell who is talking is revolutionizing the study of dolphin communication. Now just imagine that new technology applied to our incredible alliances and you can understand how excited we are about Stephanie's project! I was thrilled to help Stephanie in 2016 with her inaugural research season at Monkey Mia. Stephanie confided that she had always wanted to work in Shark Bay so it was a dream come true for her. She has worked previously at other top bottlenose dolphin field sites around the globe but she was astonished by what she saw and heard from our dolphins.

Michael Krützen's students Livia Gerber and Sam Wittwer continue to work on dolphin genetics, with Livia examining the role relatedness plays in alliance development among juvenile males and Sam looking at where our population came from and how they relate to other populations of inshore bottlenose dolphins. Sam also designed and constructed a modern "relational" database that will allow us to ask questions --and get answers--about the dolphins of Shark Bay that would have been very difficult and time consuming in the past. With Sam's database and a great team in place, we are ready for an exciting future!

The Dolphin Alliance Project, Inc.

I am thrilled to close this book by announcing that we have established a non-profit 501c3 foundation in the U.S., The Dolphin Alliance Project, Inc., so people can make tax-deductible contributions to our research. Scientific grants are increasingly difficult to come by, especially for our kind of long-term study. We have to compete for grants with people who study insects and birds for which experiments are easier and answers come much more quickly. Of course it should not be that way, as what is more important than finding out about the largest non-human brain on the planet? To put things in perspective, tens of millions of dollars are spent in the quest to discover if there is other intelligent life in the universe, yet granting agencies contribute little to the study of intelligent life here on earth.

We are therefore turning to the public for help. The Dolphin Alliance Project needs your contribution. Every contribution counts! In fact, by purchasing this book you have already contributed to our effort as all proceeds go into the foundation. Thank you! We hope you will be inspired to contribute further.

Please visit www.dapinc.org to learn more.

We have larger scale financial plans ranging from the acquisition of a new boat that will be fully committed to collecting data on male alliance membership and consortship rates, to our dream project, a ten-year effort that will integrate the study of behavior, communication, genetics and ecology! Such a study would be unprecedented, truly groundbreaking and produce incredible new discoveries!

The future is exciting; we hope you will participate!

Although not quite synchronous, two leaping male dolphins impress with the height they achieve © Dolphin Alliance Project

GLOSSARY

Apeshit display A male arches high out of the water, falling forward or on its side, careening around, sometimes with mouth open and tail-flailing.

Bolt A female accelerates rapidly away from a pair or trio of males, seen directly or as a trail of "fluke-prints" caused by upwelled water.

Bonding One dolphin (actor) lays her flipper against the side of another, just behind her dorsal fin. The two dolphins appear to be "stuck together" with the actor positioned slightly behind the dolphin she is bonding to.

Breach A dolphin leaps out of the water coming back down on their belly, side or back.

Butterfly display Males perform synchronous turns and loops, sometimes a "figure eight," around a female. Name derived from the appearance of figure eight (wings) on either side of the female (body of butterfly).

Chin slap and chin slap-tail slap A male brings his rostrum out of the water and slaps it down, often followed quickly by a tail slap.

Circle swim 2-3 dolphins swim right next to each other, in tight circles.

Consortship An association between 2-3 males and a single estrus female, lasting from minutes to weeks and, in most cases, established and maintained by aggression. The female with the males is their "consort."

Displays A male or males perform exaggerated movements, typically around a female. The variety of coordinated and synchronous displays suggests that some may be "created" spontaneously. More common displays are listed here by name.

Double roll-out Two males approach the female from behind, tilt bellies in toward female and brush past her as they arch up and away from her. The males may have erections.

Fight Males try to bite and hit each other with their peduncles (tail stocks) and flukes. Biting can result in tooth-rake marks but typically not severe injury. Hitting has much greater potential to inflict damage and fighting dolphins often twist, turn and maneuver rapidly to avoid and deliver blows.

First-order alliances Males that cooperate in pairs or trios to herd individual females.

Fissions and fusions A fission occurs when individuals leave a group or the group splits and fusions are events where individuals or groups come together.

Focal follows Following an individual or alliance for an hour or more to record systematically behavior and vocalizations, as well as changes in group composition (see fission and fusion).

Genital inspection A male or males angle with rostrums close to the female genital area. Accompanied by a high-pitched whining sound which represents a very rapid click rate.

Goosing A dolphin probes the genital slit of another with its rostrum. May be performed gently or roughly.

Head-jerk A sharp vertical or lateral movement of the head. Accompanied by a "crack" vocalization.

Head-to-head Dolphins lined up head-to-head (see Tiff). Several dolphins may line up head-to-head against one.

Herding A term for consortships that are maintained by aggression. Pops, other vocal threats, charging and hitting are used to keep the female close.

Hit One dolphin strikes another with its peduncle (tail-stock) or flukes.

July thing The name we gave to wintertime consortships which are typically of short duration. Many females that conceived during the peak breeding season (September-December) were herded during the previous winter months of July and August

Kerplunking A dolphin fishing over shallow seagrass beds lifts its flukes high, then drives them into the water producing a large vertical splash.

Leaping The dolphin emerges entirely from the water, remains right-side up and re-enters head first. Distinguished from a breach in which the dolphin lands on its side, belly or back.

Leap & Porpoise feeding Dolphins spread out in an area, leaping and porpoising in different directions. Indicative of feeding on schooling fish.

Milling Dolphins surfacing and diving in an area with different orientations with respect to each other. Usually indicative of fishing.

Mount One dolphins slides up over the back or side of another.

Petting A dolphin strokes another with its flipper (pectoral fin).

Pops A vocal threat males use to keep consorted females close. Composed of low frequency clicks produced at a relatively slow rate, mostly underwater but sometimes in air.

Porpoising The dolphin emerges rapidly with part of its ventral side emerging from the water but the dolphin does not leave the water completely as in a leap.

Rapid surface The dolphin surfaces rapidly, as in a porpoise or leap, but their belly does not emerge.

Rooster-strut A display in which a male arches his head out of the water and bobs his head up and down. Sometimes performed by two males synchronously.

Rubbing A dolphin rubs part of its body against the body of another dolphin.

Second-order alliances Teams of 4-14 males that cooperate to take females from other groups and defend against such theft attempts.

Snagging Dolphins resting at the surface, often with flukes drooping into the water so their dorsal fins are submerged or nearly so. Dolphins often snag side-by-side, resembling sausages. Snag is an Australian slang term for sausage. Similar behavior in other species of cetaceans is sometimes called "logging."

Snacking Chasing small fish belly-up near the surface.

Sponging A dolphin fishing with a sponge on its snout.

Synch Two or three dolphins surfacing side by side in unison. If two dolphins are performing multiple synchs, we describe them as "synching."

Tail-flailing Rapid, short up and down movements of the flukes, much more rapid and shorter then in swimming. Often accompanied by other elements such as a chin slap.

Tail-slap A rapid slap of the fluke on the water surface, sometimes as a component of other displays (e.g. chin slap-tail slap).

Tango A display in which two dolphins, swimming side by side, make synchronous short turns to the left and right while maintaining the same overall direction. Occurs in intense male-bonding contexts.

Third-order alliances Relationships between two second-order alliances or a lone trio and a second order alliance based on competition with other alliances for females.

Tiff Two dolphins line up head-to-head, sometimes shaking their heads up and down and vocalizing. May precede a fight.

Acknowledgments

My parents, Martha and Robert Tresnak, encouraged my academic interests and, while they might have preferred that I attend medical school than take on such a risky career move, they have greatly enjoyed my success in dolphin watching. I grew up with wonderful siblings, Lynn and Bill. A special debt is owed to my late brother Bill, who not only turned me on to so much music, but whose fascination with snakes helped inspire my childhood interest in animals. Three partners, Gerry, John and Don, (the male dolphin Dominic, of the Grand Poohbahs, was named after him) played a huge role in my life.

Another special thanks to my cousins, Jim Connor and Elizabeth Barrett-Connor, for letting me spend the summer of 1976 with them in San Diego. That summer, taking a course in marine biology at Scripps Aquarium, was transformative.

I am grateful to my academic mentors at UCSC for their support and advice over the years. As an undergraduate, Ken Norris was a wonderful, fun, encouraging mentor. Taking primate behavioral ecology from Adriene Zihlman was one of the best moves I ever made. Bob Trivers' course on social evolution blew my mind and changed my life. My very good friend Kyle Summers, inspired by my report on Trivers' class, ended up taking a parallel track to Michigan and a career in animal behavior.

Thanks to Elizabeth Gawain for telling us about the tremendous potential of Monkey Mia.

In graduate school at the University of Michigan, Gary Fowler and Brian Hazlett were helpful thesis committee members. Barb Smuts, of course, shared in the "best day ever" on our project (August 19, 1987), helped improve my data collection methods tremendously, and was a superb thesis editor.

Richard D. Alexander, my PhD co-supervisor, was always ready to go out for a piece of pie and a discussion on some important topic in evolutionary biology. Richard Wrangham helped in innumerable ways on the project, from fund-raising to advice on data collection methods to fascinating discussions on behavioral ecology. His visit to Shark Bay with Irven DeVore in 1987 was a highlight of my career.

Many people have helped in many ways over the 35 years. In the early 1980s, Daryl Kitcher and the Western Australian Museum were very helpful with logistical support. Ron and Dawn Blakers were fun, gracious hosts in Perth for several years in the 1980s.

Richard Holst and Jo Heyman deserve special mention. I met Richard at Monkey Mia in 1986. He was a lecturer at the Human Anatomy Department at the University of Western Australia. Through Richard we established a relationship with the Human Anatomy Department, which provided logistical support for many years. Special thanks to Ron Swan and Jim Chisholm of the Anatomy Department for their help. While in Perth, I have stayed with Richard and his partner Jo Heyman since the late 1980s. They are treasured friends.

When we first started to work at Monkey Mia there were many retired couples who, having fled from the colder south, would spend a few of the winter months there camping and fishing. We became friends with some of these folks but Les and Dawn Cooper were especially friendly and helpful. Other favorites included Jeff and Ada Clarke, who kept me laughing for years, and in more recent years Jack Adams, who is a fount of Shark Bay history.

Fellow dolphin fans Nikki Fryer and Deb Glasgow were great friends and frequent dinner companions in the early days. Thanks to Bruce and John for saving us in 1982.

The "ranger station" at Monkey Mia has always been staffed by helpful folks. Unfortunately, there were too many to name them all here. I wish I could because the rangers work tirelessly to protect the dolphins and educate the public. But I have to send a special thanks to former head rangers Sharon Gosper and David Charles for all their help and friendship. Other folks affiliated with the Department of Conservation and Land Management (now the Dept. of Biodiversity, Conservation and Attractions) assisted in many ways.

Thanks to Barry Wilson, who was there with assistance and sage advice for many years.

A special thanks to Sam Ridgway who was always there to offer advice on various dolphin medical crises from the other side of the planet. I am so glad I was able to take you out to see a sponger on that choppy day!

In the 1980s, I didn't always see eye-to-eye with Wilf and Hazel

Mason, the first proprietors of Monkey Mia, but I owe them a debt of gratitude and we did become friends toward the end of their stay and afterward. It is nice to have their daughter Sally and son-in-law Keith back in Denham.

A very special thanks to Graeme Robertson, principal owner of The Monkey Mia Resort during the 1990s and the first decade of this century. He was extremely supportive of the research, providing free campsites for the first time and helping in numerous other ways. Also thanks to Bruno Camarri and Geoff Prendergast, co-investors in the resort.

One of Graeme's best moves was hiring a young manager, Dean Massie, who continued to support our research after Aspen Parks and more recently the RAC purchased the resort. Dean understood the importance of having researchers onsite for both the protection of the dolphins and public education. I thank Aspen Parks and the RAC for their support. In recent years park manager Martin Grenside has helped us in innumerable ways.

Another great move Graeme made was luring Harvey Raven and his magnificent catamaran Shotover, from Queensland, to Monkey Mia to escort tourists out into the bay to view wildlife. I have known Harvey and his lovely wife Fran for over two decades now; they are good friends. Harvey has helped us in too many ways to count: with equipment, work on our catamaran Nortrek, advice, a chat, occasionally a wonderful meal, and coming to our rescue, figuratively and literally! Harvey's "Mr. Fixit" Geoff Brooks is one of the most helpful and kindest people I have ever met. Thanks for all your help Harvey and Geoff!

I have had fantastic colleagues on The Dolphin Alliance Project over the years. Rachel Smolker and Andrew Richards worked with me on the males in the "early days." In the 1990s Mike Heithaus and Lynne Barre were assistants on the Wow Crowd study who returned for 2-3 years, and so became colleagues who joined me on publications. Thank you Lynne for allowing me to include as an appendix here, your humorous and accurate, "A day in the life." Mike continued to be a valued colleague as he launched the The Shark Bay Ecosystem Research Project with Larry Dill, bringing in lots of fun and interesting students and assistants. I finally had an overlapping field season with Amy Samuels, who worked on the juveniles, something that I will always cherish. We lost Amy in

2008. In the 2000s it was fun to work alongside Lars Bejder as he studied dolphin-boat interactions.

Special thanks to Michael Krützen, now at the University of Zurich, who began working on the genetics of the Shark Bay dolphins in the mid-1990s under Bill Sherwin at UNSW. We have a great working relationship in the field (where assistants describe us as interacting like "an old couple") and in "the office" working on grants and papers. I have greatly enjoyed my stays in Zurich with his lovely family, wife Anna and daughters Maria and Linnea. Thank you Bill, for bringing on Michael and all of your contributions. Whitney Friedman has been a great colleague in recent years as has Simon Allen, who with Michael established a second field site on the other side of the bay. Our most recent addition, Stephanie King, has been a pleasure to work with.

Over the years the Dolphin Alliance Project has had the great fortune to attract many truly wonderful assistants. They are listed below, with all team members, through 2012, the last field season described in this book. Each year I have enjoyed watching their knowledge and expertise grow, and getting to know them personally. Each field site develops a culture based on the personalities and practices of team leaders, but each season the assistants contribute to and tweak that culture in wonderful and refreshing ways.

Research doesn't happen without funding and we have been fortunate to receive funding from a variety of sources. Perhaps the most consistent source of funds during all four decades has been The National Geographic Society Committee for Research and Exploration. Beginning with that first critical grant to Bernd Würsig and Rachel Smolker (many in our field don't know the key role Bernd played in getting us started--thanks Bernd!) and most recently grants to support the research of Whitney Friedman and Stephanie King. The National Science Foundation and National Institutes of Health provided key grants during my doctoral and post-doctoral years, respectively. I am very grateful for major funding from The Ann and Gordon Getty foundation in the late 1980s through the 1990s. These funds were used, for example, to launch Per Berggren's study in 1991. The Francis V.R. Seebie Charitable Trust also provided significant help; thanks to Ken Musgrave and his daughter Ruth! The Australian Research Council, through Bill Sherwin's lab at UNSW, provided major funding for the work examining behavior, relatedness and paternity. Additional foundations helped with key grants including the Eppley Foundation for Research, the W.V. Scott Foundation, A.H. Schultz Stiftung; and the Seaworld Research and Rescue Foundation (Australia). Financial support was also provided by the University of Michigan and the University of Zurich.

Angelo Angelocci, Kris Bruner, Bill Carpenter, William Cioffi, Priscilla Demers, Whitney Friedman, Stephanie King, Virginia Morell, Nancy O'Connor, Brad Robinson and Paul Sidello read the manuscript in various stages and made very helpful comments and editorial suggestions. Thanks to Ann Hedrick for the final copy-edit, and to Pat Kellogg for book formatting.

The Dolphin Alliance Project Team

by decade*

1980s

Scott (James) Crane, Irven Devore, Eric Doran, Brenda McCowan, Ruth Musgrave, Denise Myers, Andrew Richards, Leslie Sharkey, Rachel Smolker, Barb Smuts, Kelly Waples, Richard Wrangham, Tracey & Liz.

1990s

Jenna Barbour, Lynne Barre, Per Berggren, Paul Bordeau, Bec Donaldson, Sharlene Fedorowicz, Nick Gales, Mike Heithaus, Michael Krützen, Karrisa Schecter, Bill Sherwin, Jennifer Skelly, Jeff Skelton, Rachel Smolker, Stephanie Whitmire & Andrea.

2000s

Maggie Allen, Simon Allen, Ina Ansmann, Rochelle Constantine, Felicity Donaldson, Maja Greminger, Gitangalie Katrak, Rebecca Hamner, Doro Heimeier, Ewa Krzyszczyk, Michael Krützen, Laura McCue, Ana Pinela, Ruth Pratt, Srdan Randic, Anna Sellas, Shelley Smart, Bill Sherwin, Brooke Ray Smith, Holly Smith, Dipani Sutaria, Nicole Volmer, Jana Watson-Capps, David Wrangham, Ian Wrangham, Ross Wrangham

2009-12

Simon Allen, Kathrin Bacher, Isabelle 'Izzy' Baker, Alex Brown, Whitney Friedman, Celene Frere, Livia Gerber, Anna Kopps, Sina Kreiker, Michael Krützen, Laura McCue, Rebekah 'Becca' McLeod, Nina Morris, Kim New, Joshua Silberg, Bill Sherwin

* Apologies to those whose names or last names I simply cannot retrieve.

A DAY IN THE LIFE (1996)

by Lynne Barre[*]

Characters

Richard Connor: Patriarch of DAP (Dolphin Alliance Project) which is a collection of scientists working in the Shark Bay area concentrating on various aspects of dolphin life. A slightly weathered field researcher with a sweet tooth, a great sense of humor and over ten years of experience with the local dolphins. He has a PhD from the University of Michigan and recently accepted a teaching position at UMASS-Dartmouth.

Mike Heithaus: Recent graduate of Oberlin College and future PhD candidate at Simon Fraser University in Canada. This constitutes Mike's third season in Shark Bay so he has achieved a status well above assistant, but next year he will be master of his own project regarding fish abundance and distribution and the effect on the dolphin population. Mike is a highly motivated and energetic 21-year-old with athletic tendencies and good taste in music.

Karissa Schecter: A lowly research assistant with no experience in dolphin research, but she has worked with captive primates. She was recommended by one of her professors that Richard knows well. Karissa is from Tennessee and just graduated from Harvard. She is in the process of taking a year off to decide her future (i.e., what programs and schools and projects to pursue or whether to go to graduate school at all.)

Me: Another lowly research assistant.

The setting: Daybreak on Nortrek, 7:00am

As the sun rises outside my porthole, a gentle wind rocks the 32-foot catamaran and I can see the water bobbing in and out of my view. Promptly at 7:15 Mike's watch alarm goes off with the familiar beeping modulation that changes tone after several minutes and beeps even faster. I can hear the faint beeping through the wall that separates Mike's bunk from my bunk in the left hull of the catamaran. The wind is slight so after several minutes…

[*] *Lynn worked with us from 1996-1997 and kindly allowed me to include "A Day in the Life" here. In 1997 Lynn ran a boat, a level of participation that led to co-authorships on journal articles.*

Mike: Lynne?

Lynne: How's it look? Is it dying down yet?

Mike: Good morning. I think it has already died a bit. We might as well head in.

Lynne: OK

This is the typical morning conversation we have as we stick our heads out of the hatches above our bunks. This gives us the opportunity to evaluate the wind and see each other's bed heads. If the wind is clearly too strong, it's back to bed for another hour, but today it is time to row into shore and consult with the higher power. Richard is the master of the wind decisions. So far this season the weather has not been great and we have not had any success videotaping the particular group of males that is the focus of this year's research. This lack of success so far means Richard is willing to go out in less than ideal conditions. This is fine with me because it is better than sitting around on shore reading and writing letters and waiting around to see if the weather improves.

At breakfast in the caravan, pickings are slim. Our supply of muesli has run out and we don't get a Bi-low grocery delivery until Friday. I enjoy several pieces of toast with some spread that is similar to Nutella. It's called Milky Way and is made from ground hazelnuts and has chocolate and milk flavored swirls. Rather tasty. And of course there is fresh squeezed orange juice. At least that is how we refer to the orange flavored cordial (basically, a sugary concentrate) that we mix with water in the morning. Breakfast conversation centers on the cruel and unusual forms of torture that Richard has read about the night before in "Through a Distant Mirror," a book on 14th century France that he has been buried in of late.

Well, the decision is made. Richard is ready to go out as soon as we can get all the equipment ready. We clean up from breakfast, put on our various field clothes. Mine consist of shorts, a T-shirt and windbreaker, no shoes and contact lenses so I can use the binoculars and video camera easily. I collect the usual gear- a bottle of water, extra survey sheets, rolls of film, a couple of apples and Granita Biscuits (otherwise known as Granny Bickies) and walkie-talkies with newly charged batteries because one of the radios isn't working. It's a short walk to the office where the rest of the equipment lives. The binocs, cameras, GPS, video decks and various other assorted electronics are stored in eskies (that's Australian for cooler, you know like Eskimo coolers). There are two for Richard's boat, Bony Herring, which is where I have been relegated because I arrived early and so had more experience than Karissa when we started getting out on the water regularly.

Our boats are moored right off the beach of the Monkey Mia Resort, although I don't think "resort" is really the right word. We load up and then it is time for my favorite activity. I get to wade into the water, pushing the boat out and then give a big push and jump up over the bow rail onto the front of the boat. I have received critical acclaim for my gymnastics during this routine and was even captured by a German film crew doing a story for "Die Reporter," some kind of German 60 minutes show. Richard often hums the "Chariots of Fire" theme to inspire me, but I think he really does it to keep from laughing at my less than graceful acrobatics.

Well, we're off. Time to prepare for a day on the water.

Richard: Where's the nose goo?

Lynne: Here you go.

Richard: ….and the lip goo? Remind me to put the orange stuff on later, OK?

Lynne: Sure.

Richard: Check the gas level and make sure the motor is pissing.

I check all the vitals and yes, there is a steady stream of water coming out from the cooling system on the motor, so all systems are go. We are now heading through Red Cliff Bay, past Nortrek, past the first mark, past a dugong and talking to Long Tom, the other boat. Mike is master of Long Tom and poor Karissa is stuck with driving duty most of the time. It is not a large boat and she has a tendency to get soaked in any conditions that aren't perfect. Today doesn't seem too bad, so they might stay dry for a little while.

The searching begins. We start to head toward a few areas where the target group has been found in the past. We're looking for the "Wow Crowd," named after Wow, one of the 14 members of the group. I didn't quite catch this name at first and was convinced Richard was saying "Wild Crowd." Wow's buddies are Myrtle, Roleypole, Anvil, Pik, Krill, Latch, Hobo, Gripe, Horton, Ajax, Veetop, Vax and Wannabe. The prime location for the Wowsers is directly offshore of a landmark called the Grooves north of Monkey Mia in Whale Bight. As I mentioned, our luck in finding these guys has not been great, but there are plenty of other dolphins around for us to survey.

Lynne: There are two dolphins over there.

Richard: Over where? How far off?

Lynne: Two o'clock. About 30 meters.

Richard: You saw two? Was it a mother and a calf?

Lynne: I'm not sure, they were heading north. I haven't seen them again.

Richard: OK, keep scanning and let me know if you see them again.

Lynne: There they are.

Richard: Great. Lights, camera, action.

This is my cue to get out Richard's camera and start filling in the survey sheet while he drives over to get a closer look. I fill in the location, GPS coordinates, depth, date, time and then wait for Richard to identify the animals. I'm still in the process of trying to learn some of the fins. Most of the dolphins can be identified on sight by the pattern of their dorsal fins. Some of them are very distinctive and easy to recognize, but there are a lot of them to learn.

Richard: Hello, who are you? (and then Richard greets the dolphins by letting out a squeal that he likes to think of as his "signature whistle," a bit shocking at first, but you get used to it.) OK, this female looks familiar. We've seen her up here lots of times and she's got an older calf with her. I don't remember her name, but she's real familiar.

Lynne: What would you say their activity is?

Richard: Well, I'd say they're traveling north, northwest. Tight group. There's a PD (a peduncle dive, where most of the tail comes out of the water, but not the flukes), looks like a resting pattern. I've got good shots of the female, but I still need to get the calf. I'm going to need another roll of film in a minute.

Lynne: I've got one right here.

We finish up with the pair, taking pictures, finishing the survey form and stowing the camera. The whole encounter lasts only five minutes and we move on. After a few hours of searching, we've done four surveys, seen five sea turtles, tons of birds and investigated some splashing at the surface which was just tuna feeding. It is important to recognize all the distracting marine creatures for what they are and not mistakenly point them out as dolphins because you could get demerits. Richard has a system whereby you accumulate demerits and when you reach fifty, you have to buy him an Icky-sticky pudding at the restaurant (although this "rule" was never really enforced and turned out to be yet another joke). As we search, we check in with the other boat about every 15 minutes.

Mike: Bony Herring, this is Long Tom. Do you read? (Mike likes to say the boat names in a way that suggests they refer to something other than a few kinds of fish in the Bay.)

Lynne: Go ahead.

Mike: Well, we've been taking the inshore route for a while. We are just coming up on North Saddle and we haven't seen anyone. What about you?

Lynne: No luck here.

Mike: Too bad.

Richard: Tell him to stay inshore and head up to Guich. We'll keep the offshore route.

Lynne: We're off Big Sand Beach and we're going to stay offshore and head to Guich, so you guys keep the inshore track and we'll talk to you in fifteen.

Mike: OK, sounds like a plan.

Lynne: Over and out.

The searching continues. We've looked in all the old familiar places and have now started to branch out into new territory. Richard and I head farther north than usual and go up around Guichenault Point and into Herald Bight, just in case the Wow Crowd might be there. On this excursion Richard decides he doesn't want to do any surveys unless we see the Wow Crowd. When we do see dolphins, however, one looks familiar and has a very cool bent over fin. Richard thinks it might be Flop, a dolphin they saw a lot in the eighties. We follow the dolphins into the shallows and end up doing a survey anyway, because Richard wants pictures. There are four dolphins fishing in the shallows and they seem to be a bit elusive as we try to get close enough to photograph them all. When we leave the group, we realize that we are in very shallow water indeed. We need to get over the shallows and into deeper water without running aground. It is a bit dicey as I watch the depth sounder read 4 feet, then 3 feet, then 2 feet. The water is clear and I can see every detail of the bottom, which seems very close. Richard weaves in and out a bit and manages to bring us through to a deeper area. Phew. The Wow Crowd tends to be deep-water animals, so we tool around for a while, staying along the 26-foot contour (which is deep for Shark Bay). They are nowhere to be found, so we head back south toward the main study area.

1 pm, lunch time

We enjoy our pleasant repast of apples and Granny Bickies, which are basically round graham crackers. After lunch the afternoon wears on and Shark Bay has become a "dolphin desert." Endless searching and scanning and as the sun begins to sink, the glare on the water makes things even more difficult. Luckily the wind has died completely and the water is glassy calm. While I'm scanning out to the horizon different songs and thoughts go through my mind. For a while I can't shake "Say, Say, Say" by Michael Jackson and Paul McCartney. A very random song to be stuck in my head and it is hard not to start singing out loud. I think I see a dolphin, but it's not and I start to think about the dolphins I have seen and about all the things I hope to see. The worst is when I think about my midgie bites and then they start to itch, of course. This makes me think of all the nasty critters in Australia and the next thing I know I have "Poor Little Critter in the Road" going through my mind. Richard played this song for us a few nights ago and the chorus is "Poor little critter in the road/where were you trying to go?/ Life's got a bucketful of woes for the poor little critter in the road." In such wide open spaces I can follow the convoluted patterns my thoughts take and sometimes there are no patterns and I think about home or how nice it would be to get an e-mail from Jay, the cute doctor I met in Seattle. Strange associations all strung together while searching for dorsal fins.

It's almost five o'clock, I mean 17:00. I really hate military time, but that is what we use for our data and I have my watch on the 24-hour setting. Off in the distance I see a couple of fins, which I point out to Richard. I'm actually getting pretty good at spotting dolphins, even at a distance. As we approach the group things get interesting, because at long last we've found the Wow Crowd.

Richard: Who is that, let's see…it's Pik and I think the other one is Wannabe. Yup, it's definitely them. We've still got enough light to do a follow of about 45 minutes, so start setting up. You've got 10 minutes and I hope you remember how to do everything.

Lynne: No problem.

I begin to set up the video equipment. The camera on the tripod, the cord from the power inverter goes into the camera, video deck power cable, plug in the headphones. Richard puts the hydrophone in the water and I connect it to one of the audio channels on the deck. While I'm setting up Richard has called Mike over so that they can help keep an eye on the dolphins while we get set up. I think that is everything. Power on.

Lynne: Here's your headset.

Richard: Is the inverter on? Remember to do that last. I've got the GPS hooked up. Get the time codes turned on.

Lynne: OK, do I need to hit the select switch?

Richard: Don't worry about that, I'll do it. You go ahead and start recording.

Lynne: Can you hear the hydrophone and your microphone.

Richard: Test, test, yes I can hear, but that beeping means we've got servo lock and something's not working. Check the camera.

Lynne: The camera is on and has power, but no picture.

Richard: Is the servo light on?

Lynne: Yes, I'll check the connections.

Richard: OK you got it, it's off. What did you do?

Lynne: Nothing, it just started working. I've got a picture.

Richard: OK, here we go. Now where are the dolphins?

Richard starts dictating information into the headset- date, time, location, who the focal animals are. We're trying to find them again and I point out a turtle. Oh no, demerits. Richard was very gracious, however, and erased all my demerits because I had spotted the Wowsers. The sun was going down, but we continued to follow the dolphins. Two juveniles joined the group and rode the bow for a bit. Richard laid down a track of constant information about synchronized surfacings, the vocalizations he heard on the hydrophone, and any behavior he saw. There wasn't any spectacular behavior going on, but it was great to stay with a group of dolphins for more than 10 minutes, especially after it took us nine hours to find them. It was a good opportunity to practice using the camera and the follow went well. I had to steal a few minutes to look away from the viewfinder. The sky was beautiful at sunset and there was a pink glow on the water and all around the horizon. Eventually we had to call it quits and pack up the equipment. It was going to be very dark by the time we got back to shore. Long Tom doesn't have running lights and it's pretty slow, so we cruised back at a leisurely speed to keep them in view. If it hadn't been getting dark, I'm sure Richard would have blasted right by, laughing.

Richard saw a shark, but I missed it. He estimated its length at 4 feet based on the distance from the dorsal fin to the tail at the surface. One of these days, I will have to see a shark. It is Shark Bay for Christ's sake.

The night sky slowly began to show itself as we headed for Monkey Mia. We saw a strange light on the horizon to the east. It looked like some kind of boat, but as the glow climbed into the sky we realized it must be a planet or a star. The moon was already out and was bright even at half. At one point we lost sight of Long Tom back behind us and signaled them by driving our boat in a circle so they could see our lights. They signaled back with a flashlight and we continued home. We spotted the first pole with its blinking red light and eased our way into the beach. A smooth landing as the sky grew dark.

The water was still glassy and there was no wind, but we had heard that a front was moving in to the area soon. We hauled the eskies back to the office and Richard took advantage of one of our few technological wonders of the outback- a weather fax. Things didn't look very good. I still didn't quite understand how to read the isobars to determine wind, but I did understand that the storm warning meant we may have to take the boats out of the water.

After such a long day, I barely cared that my hot shower was salty bore water. Shark Bay is hypersaline and all of the well water is about 10% salt. The shower felt great even if I didn't feel totally clean. I wondered if my hair would ever feel the same again. I was also starving at this point and Richard volunteered to make his infamous peanut sauce because a long day on the water gave him a fat craving that had to be filled with either peanut sauce or large amounts of cheese. We munched on cheese and crackers with sweet chili sauce to tide us over as the veggies and pasta cooked and Richard concocted the peanut sauce. I'm not sure what (if any) ingredients there were besides peanut butter, but it was good. Dinner usually ends with pleasant conversation and a package of bickies, but since we got back after the store closed we didn't have a chance to pick up any TimTams or Mint Slice.

I was glad we had a big meal to revitalize us because Richard decided we were taking the boats out of the water tonight before the strong winds started. Although we were all a bit weary, the time had come to prepare for the storm. We were resigned to getting it done, especially because it meant we could definitely sleep in the next morning. In fact Mike and I were forbidden from showing our faces on dry land before 9 am. The water was still calm and it didn't take long to load Bony Herring on the trailer and park it behind the reception area. We then pitched in to haul Long Tom up onto the beach. After a hearty meal full of peanutty protein, the task was actually easier than I expected.

It was finally time to say goodnight to Richard and Karissa and row out to Nortrek once again. I let Mike row so I could sit back and watch the stars that still seemed so different than the ones at home. I enjoyed the calm before the storm. Mike made quick work of the trip on the glassy water and we sat on deck for a few minutes before turning in. I was actually quite awake after hauling the boat up the beach and I stayed up to read the last pages of the novel I was reading. I felt like a kid again, reading a scary book by flashlight under the covers. Eventually I doused the light and thought about the full day behind me and all the things I'd seen. I could see the moon through the crack in my hatch and wondered what I would dream about.

SELECTED SCIENTIFIC PUBLICATIONS
(For full list visit http://www.sharkbaydolphins.org)

Connor, R.C. & R.A. Smolker. 1985. Habituated dolphins (*Tursiops* sp.) in Western Australia. *Journal of Mammalogy* 36: 304-305.

Connor, R.C., Smolker, R.A., & A.F. Richards. 1992a. Two levels of alliance formation among male bottlenose dolphins (*Tursiops* sp.). *Proceedings of the National Academy of Sciences* 89: 987-990.

Connor, R.C., Smolker, R.A., & A.F. Richards. 1992b. Dolphin alliances and coalitions. In: *Coalitions and Alliances in Animals and Humans,* (eds, A.H. Harcourt and F.B.M. de Waal) Oxford University Press, Oxford, U.K.

Smolker, R.A., Richards, A.F., R.C. Connor, & J. Pepper. 1992. Association patterns among bottlenose dolphins in Shark Bay, Western Australia. *Behaviour* 123: 38-69.

Connor, R.C. & R.A. Smolker. 1995. Seasonal changes in the stability of male-male bonds in Indian Ocean bottlenose dolphins (*Tursiops* sp.). *Aquatic Mammals* 21:213-216.

Connor, R.C. & M. R. Heithaus. 1996. Approach by great white shark elicits flight response in bottlenose dolphins. *Marine Mammal Science* 12: 602-606.

Connor, R.C. & R.A. Smolker. 1996. "Pop" goes the dolphin: a vocalization male bottlenose dolphins produce during consortships. *Behaviour* 133: 643-662.

Connor, R.C., Richards, A.F., Smolker, R.A. & J. Mann. 1996. Patterns of female attractiveness in Indian Ocean bottlenose dolphins. *Behaviour* 133: 37-69.

Connor, R.C.; Heithaus, R.M. and Barre, L.M. 1999. Super-alliance of bottlenose dolphins. *Nature* 371: 571-572.

Connor, R.C., Heithaus, M.R. & Barre, L.M. 2001. Complex social structure, alliance stability and mating access in a bottlenose dolphin 'super-alliance.' *Proceedings of the Royal Society of London, Biological Sciences* 268: 263-267.

Connor, R.C & M. Krützen. 2003. Levels and patterns in dolphin alliance formation. In: *Animal Social Complexity Intelligence, Culture, and Individualized Societies* (eds, Frans B. M. de Waal and Peter L. Tyack), Harvard University Press.

Krützen, M; W. B. Sherwin, R. C. Connor, L.M. Barré, T. Van de Casteele, J. Mann, R. Brooks. 2003. Contrasting relatedness patterns in bottlenose dolphins (*Tursiops* sp.) with different alliance strategies. *Proceedings of the Royal Society of London, Biological Sciences* 270: 497-502.

Krützen, M., Barre, L.M., Connor, R.C., Mann, J. & W.B. Sherwin. 2004. O father: where art thou? Paternity assessment in an open fission-fusion societyof wild bottlenose dolphins (*Tursiops* sp.) in Shark Bay, Western Australia. *Molecular Ecology* 13 (7): 1975-1990.

Connor, R.C., Mann, J., & J. Watson-Capps. 2006. A sex-specific affiliative contact behavior in Indian Ocean bottlenose dolphins, (*Tursiops* sp.) *Ethology* 112: 631-638.

Connor, R.C., Smolker, R.A. & L.Bejder. 2006. Synchrony, social behavior and alliance affiliations in Indian Ocean bottlenose dolphins (*Tursiops aduncus*). *Animal Behavior* 72:1371-1378.

Connor, R.C. 2007. Complex alliance relationships in bottlenose dolphins and a consideration of selective environments for extreme brain size evolution in mammals. *Philosophical Transactions of the Royal Society: Biological Sciences* 362: 587-602.

Connor, R.C. & Vollmer, N. 2009. Sexual coercion in dolphin consortships: a comparison with chimpanzees. *Sexual Coercion in Primates: An Evolutionary Perspective on Male Aggression Against Females* (eds. M. N. Muller and R.W. Wrangham). Cambridge: Harvard University Press.

Connor, R.C. 2010. Cooperation beyond the dyad: from simple models to a complex society. *Philosophical Transactions of the Royal Society: Biological Sciences* 365: 2687-2697.

Connor, R.C., J.J. Watson-Capps, W.B. Sherwin & M. Krützen. 2011. New levels of complexity in the male alliance networks of Indian Ocean bottlenose dolphins (*Tursiops* sp.). *Biology Letters* 7, 623-626.

Randić, S, Connor, RC, Sherwin, WS & Krutzen, M. 2012. A novel mammalian social structure in Indo-Pacific bottlenose dolphins (Tursiops sp.): complex male alliances in an open social network. *Proceedings of the Royal Society of London, Biological Sciences* 279: 3083-3090.

Vollmer, N.L., Hayek, L.A.C., & Heithaus, M.R. & R.C. Connor. 2015. Further evidence of a context-specific agonistic signal in bottlenose dolphins: the influence of consortships and group size on the pop vocalization. *Behavior* 152: 1979-2000

Connor, R.C. & Krützen, M. 2015. Male dolphin alliances in Shark Bay: changing perspectives in a thirty-year study. *Animal Behavior* 103:223-235

Connor, R.C., Cioffi, W.R., Randić, S., Allen, S.J., Watson-Capps, J., Krützen, M. 2017. Male alliance behavior and mating access varies with habitat in a dolphin social network. *Scientific Reports* https://www.nature.com/articles/srep46354